THE
INVESTMENT
TRUSTS
HANDBOOK

2022

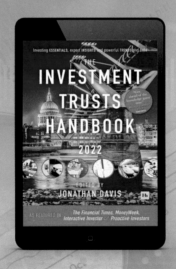

THE
INVESTMENT
TRUSTS
HANDBOOK

2022

*Investing essentials, expert insights
and powerful trends and data*

EDITED BY
JONATHAN DAVIS

Harriman House

www.ITHB.co.uk

HARRIMAN HOUSE LTD
3 Viceroy Court
Bedford Road
Petersfield
Hampshire
GU32 3LJ
GREAT BRITAIN
Tel: +44 (0)1730 233870

Email: enquiries@harriman-house.com
Website: harriman.house

First published in 2021.
Copyright © Harriman House Ltd.

The right of the authors to be identified as the Authors has been asserted in accordance with the
Copyright, Design and Patents Act 1988.

Hardback ISBN: 978-0-85719-966-9
eBook ISBN: 978-0-85719-967-6

British Library Cataloguing in Publication Data
A CIP catalogue record for this book can be obtained from the British Library.

Harriman House

www.ITHB.co.uk

CONTENTS

INTRODUCTION

A year of steady recovery

AFTER THE EXCITEMENT and drama of 2020, which gave us the pandemic and an unprecedented market and economic crisis, it was inevitable that the next 12 months would follow a rather different narrative. And so it has proved. This latest edition of *The Investment Trusts Handbook*, now in its fifth year, chronicles, among other developments:

- a continued period of equity market recovery;

- record issuance of new shares by investment trusts;

- some marked rotation in investment styles;

- a series of manager and mandate changes; and

- the arrival of some interesting newcomers (in such diverse areas as space, digital infrastructure and energy efficiency).

As we have noted in previous editions, one of the great strengths of the investment trust sector is its ability to adapt to a changing environment, so the way that it has over the past year is entirely in keeping. You can be sure that there will still be plenty of new topics to write about next year. This sector is never dull!

More high-quality content

The Investment Trusts Handbook 2022 follows a now familiar pattern:

- a detailed review of the last 12 months by our resident experts;

- a look ahead to the future and what it may bring;

- Q&As and conversations with a selection of analysts and fund managers;

- my own thoughts on the year just gone and the one that lies ahead;

- reviews of the models I monitor for readers; and

- a detailed how to/data section at the end of the book.

1

This year's *Handbook* includes articles by many of our regular contributors, including Max King, Sandy Cross, James Carthew, Alex Davies and Simon Elliott, plus three newcomers, Sir John Kay, William Heathcoat Amory and Stuart Watson. The forum features six of the best-known professionals who analyse or invest directly in investment trusts. As always the data and analysis sections have been completely revised and updated.

I am happy to report that many of the readers of the *Handbook* now also listen to the free Money Makers weekly investment podcast that I record every Friday with Simon Elliott, the impressively knowledgeable and articulate head of investment trust research at Winterflood Securities. He and I started the podcast at the height of the great market sell-off in April 2020, with the idea of helping listeners navigate their way through a traumatic phase in the markets.

The hour we spend each week going through the latest news from the investment trust sector seems to have struck a chord with many private and professional investors, and so we have turned it into a permanent offering with over a thousand listeners a week. Some of you also now subscribe to the Money Makers circle, a membership club which for a modest monthly or annual fee gives you access to a range of content relevant to an investment trust investor.

These include:

- regular Q&As with investment trust experts;
- a weekly series of in-depth profiles of individual trusts;
- a comprehensive weekly list of recent news announcements; and
- my current thoughts on the markets and individual trusts.

The connoisseur's choice

The Investment Trusts Handbook is where I pull together all the most important developments of the past 12 months into a single, handy reference volume, which I like to think might one day become recognised as the *Wisden* of the investment trust world. It has already been bought or downloaded more than 35,000 times and the publishers and I remain grateful for your continued support.

For reasons that have been well rehearsed here and elsewhere, investment trusts remain the connoisseur's choice when it comes to selecting investment funds. There are good ones and bad ones, just as in any field of activity, and while there are always challenges facing the sector, in my judgement a careful selection of the best in their field will continue to serve you well whatever the future brings, through both good times and bad.

JONATHAN DAVIS

JONATHAN DAVIS *MA, MSC, MCSI is one of the UK's leading stock market authors and commentators. A qualified professional investor and member of the Chartered Institute for Securities and Investment, he is a senior external adviser at Saunderson House. His books include* Money Makers, Investing with Anthony Bolton *and* Templeton's Way with Money. *After writing columns for* The Independent *and* Financial Times *for many years, he now writes a private circulation newsletter. Find out more from the Money Makers website:* www.money-makers.co.

Cut through with conviction

FIDELITY INVESTMENT TRUSTS

Truly global and award-winning, the range is supported by expert portfolio managers, regional research teams and on-the-ground professionals with local connections.

With 369 investment professionals across the globe, we believe this gives us stronger insights across the markets in which we invest. This is key in helping each trust identify local trends and invest with the conviction needed to generate long-term outperformance.

Fidelity's range of investment trusts:

- Fidelity Asian Values PLC
- Fidelity China Special Situations PLC
- Fidelity European Trust PLC
- Fidelity Japan Trust PLC
- Fidelity Special Values PLC

Past performance is not a reliable indicator of future returns. The value of investments can go down as well as up and you may not get back the amount you invested. Overseas investments are subject to currency fluctuations. The shares in the investment trusts are listed on the London Stock Exchange and their price is affected by supply and demand.

The investment trusts can gain additional exposure to the market, known as gearing, potentially increasing volatility. Some of the trusts invest more heavily than others in smaller companies, which can carry a higher risk because their share prices may be more volatile than those of larger companies and their securities are often less liquid.

To find out more, go to fidelity.co.uk/its or speak to your adviser.

Open the camera app on your smartphone device and hover over the QR code to find out more.

ACKNOWLEDGEMENTS

Producing *The Investment Trusts Handbook 2022* is, as it has been for the last five years, an intensive and collective effort. Thanks to all of those who have helped to bring it to fruition, whether as contributors or handmaidens to the production process.

At Harriman House: Myles Hunt, Sally Tickner, Christopher Parker, Kate Ahira, Chris Wild, Lucy Scott and Tracy Bundey.

At the publishing partners: Louise Bouverat (abrdn), Alex Denny (Fidelity), Lisa Ferris (J.P. Morgan), Vik Heerah (Polar Capital), Oliver Lago (Allianz Global), Vicky Toshney (Baillie Gifford).

Contributors: James Carthew, Sandy Cross, Richard Curling, Piers Currie, Alex Davies, Simon Elliott, Nick Greenwood, Peter Hewitt, Max King, William Heathcoat Amory, Alastair Laing and Stuart Watson.

Research: Ewan Lovett-Turner and Colette Ord (Numis), Simon Elliott, Kieran Drake and Emma Bird (Winterflood Securities), Christopher Brown (J.P. Morgan Cazenove), Alan Brierley (Investec), Annabel Brodie-Smith (the AIC), Richard Pavry (Devon Equity Management), William Heathcoat Amory (Kepler Intelligence), Ed Marten and James Carthew (QuotedData).

Statistics: big thanks again this year to David Michael and Sophie Driscoll at the AIC for all their help in providing the performance statistics and a lot of other data.

Transcripts: Ben Gamblin.

Actual investors think in decades.

Not quarters.

TRUST BASICS

For first-time investors in trusts, here is an overview of investment trusts – what they are and how they invest – from editor JONATHAN DAVIS.

What is an investment trust?

INVESTMENT TRUSTS, ALSO known as investment companies, are a type of collective investment fund. All types of fund pool the money of a large number of different investors and delegate the investment of their pooled assets, typically to a professional fund manager. The idea is that this enables shareholders in the trust to spread their risks and benefit from the professional skills and economies of scale available to an investment management firm. Funds are able to buy and sell investments without paying tax on realised gains.

Collective funds have been a simple and popular way for individual investors to invest their savings for many years, and investment trusts have shared in that success. Today more than £250bn of savers' assets are invested in investment trusts. The first investment trust was launched as long ago as 1868, so they have a long history. Sales of open-ended funds (unit trusts, OEICs and UCITs funds) have grown faster, but investment trust performance has generally been superior.

How do they differ from unit trusts and open-ended funds?

There are several differences. The most important ones are that shares in investment companies are traded on a stock exchange and are overseen by an independent board of directors, like any other listed company. Shareholders have the right to vote at annual general meetings (AGMs) on a range of things, including the election of directors, changes in investment policy and share issuance. Trusts can also, unlike most open-ended funds, borrow money in order to enhance returns. Whereas the number of units in a unit trust rises and falls from day to day in response to supply and demand, an investment trust is able to deploy permanent capital.

What are discounts?

Because shares in investment trusts are traded on a stock exchange, the share price will fluctuate from day to day in response to supply and demand. Sometimes the shares will change hands for less than the net asset value (NAV) per share of the company. At other times they will change hands for more than the NAV per share. The difference between the share price and the NAV per share is calculated as a percentage of the NAV and is called a discount if the share price is below the equivalent NAV and a premium if it is above the NAV.

What is gearing?

In investment, gearing refers to the ability of an investor to borrow money in an attempt to enhance the returns that flow from his or her investment decisions. If investments rise more rapidly than the cost of the borrowing, this has the effect of producing higher returns. The reverse is also true, meaning that gains and losses are magnified. Investment trusts typically borrow around 5–10% of their assets, although this figure varies widely from one trust to another.

What are the main advantages of investing in an investment trust?

Because the capital is largely fixed, the managers of an investment trust can buy and sell the trust's investments whenever they need, rather than having to buy and sell simply because money is flowing in or out of the fund, as unit trust managers are required to do. The ability to gear, or use borrowed money, can also potentially produce better returns. The fact that the board of an investment trust is directly accountable to the shareholders is important. So too is the ability of boards to smooth the payment of dividend income by putting aside surplus revenue as reserves.

Because their capital base is permanent, investment companies are free to invest in a much wider range of investments than other types of fund. In fact, they can invest in almost anything. Although many of the largest trusts invest in listed stocks and bonds, the biggest growth in recent years has been in a range of more specialist areas, such as renewable energy, infrastructure, debt securities, music royalties and private equity. Investment trusts offer fund investors a broader choice and greater scope for diversification, in other words.

And what are the disadvantages?

The two main disadvantages are share price volatility and potential loss of liquidity. Because investment trusts can trade at a discount to the value of their assets, an investor who sells at the wrong moment may not receive the full asset value for their shares at that point. The day-to-day value of the investment will also fluctuate more than an equivalent open-ended fund. In the case of more specialist trusts, it may not always be possible to buy or sell shares in a trust at a good price because of a lack of liquidity in the market. Investors need to make sure they understand these features before investing.

Polar Capital
Global Healthcare Trust plc

A global investment trust focused on leading healthcare companies

Healthcare developments are a positive and a constant in these ever-changing times, with innovation and disruptive technology rapidly transforming the sector.

Discover the healthcare investment opportunities at
polarcapitalglobalhealthcaretrust.com

London Stock Exchange Ticker **PCGH**

POLAR CAPITAL

How many trusts are there?

According to the industry trade body, the Association of Investment Companies, there were just under 390 investment trusts with more than £260bn in assets (as at the end of October 2021). They are split between a number of different sectors, reflecting the regions or type of investments in which they invest. Scottish Mortgage, the largest trust, has approximately £19bn in assets.

What are alternative assets?

While investment trusts have traditionally invested primarily in publicly listed stocks and shares, whose values are known every day, the last decade has seen significant growth in so-called alternative assets. These are trusts which invest in longer term assets which are mostly not traded daily and therefore can be valued only at less frequent intervals. Examples include commercial property, renewable energy, infrastructure and private equity. Many of these alternative trusts are popular because of their ability to pay higher levels of income.

How are they regulated?

All investment companies are regulated by the Financial Conduct Authority. So too are the managers the board appoints to manage the trust's investments. Investment trusts are also subject to the Listing Rules of the stock exchange on which they are listed. The board of directors is accountable to shareholders and regulators for the performance of the trust and the appointment of the manager and are legally bound by the requirements of successive Companies Acts.

How do I invest in an investment trust?

There are a number of different ways. You can buy them directly through a stockbroker, or via an online platform. A few larger investment trusts also have monthly savings schemes where you can transfer a fixed sum every month to the company, which then invests it into its shares on your behalf. If you have a financial adviser, or a portfolio manager, they can arrange the investment for you.

What do investment trusts cost?

As with any share, investors in investment trusts will need to pay brokerage commission when buying or selling shares in an investment trust, and also stamp duty on purchases. The managers appointed by the trust's directors to make its investments charge an annual management fee which is paid automatically, together with dealing and administration costs, out of the trust's assets. These management fees typically range from as little as 0.3% to 2.0% or more of the trust's assets.

What are tax wrappers?

Tax wrappers are schemes which allow individual investors, if they comply with the rules set by the government, to avoid tax on part or all of their investments. The two most important tax wrappers are the Individual Savings Account (or ISA) and the Self-Invested Personal Pension (SIPP). The majority of investment trusts can be held in an ISA or SIPP. There are annual limits on the amounts that can be invested each year (currently £20,000 for an ISA). Venture Capital Trusts (VCTs) are a specialist type of investment trust which also have a number of tax advantages, reflecting their higher risk. VCTs invest in start up and early stage businesses.

Who owns investment trusts?

Twenty-five years ago life insurance companies were the biggest investors in investment trusts, which they used to manage their client funds and pensions. These days such institutional investors mostly manage their own investments directly. Other than some specialist types of trust, the largest investors in trusts today are wealth management firms (formerly stockbroking firms), other types of intermediary and, increasingly, private investors. The growing number of individual investors reflects the growing influence of online platforms, which give individual investors the ability to choose their own investments for ISAs, SIPPs and taxable share/fund accounts.

Are they as difficult to understand as some people say?

Investment trusts are a little more complex than a simple open-ended fund, but no more difficult to understand than most types of listed company. It is important to understand the concept of discounts and premiums before you start to invest, but buying, selling and following the fortunes of your investment could not be easier. If you like the idea of making the connoisseur's choice when investing, you will find the effort of understanding investment trusts worthwhile.

Key terms explained

Investment trusts (aka investment companies) pool the money of individual and professional investors and invest it for them in order to generate capital gains, dividend income, or both. These are the most important factors that determine how good an investment they are:

SHARE PRICE
The price (typically in pence) you will be asked to pay to buy or sell shares in any investment company. Your interest is to see it go up, not down.

SPREAD

The difference between the price per share to pay if you want to buy and that you will be offered if you wish to sell – can be anything from 0% (good) to 5% or more (bad). The bigger the trust, the tighter the spread should be.

MARKET CAPITALISATION

The aggregate current value of all the shares a trust has issued – in essence, therefore, what the market in its wisdom thinks the investment company is worth today. (The market is not always wise and would be a duller and less interesting place if it were.)

NET ASSET VALUE (NAV)

The value of the company's investments less running costs at the most recent valuation point – typically (and ideally) that will be yesterday's quoted market price, but for some types of investment trust, whose assets are not traded on a daily basis, it might be one or more months ago.

NET ASSET VALUE PER SHARE

This is calculated, not surprisingly, by dividing the NAV (see above) by the number of shares in issue. You can compare it directly with the share price to find the discount or premium.

DISCOUNT/PREMIUM

When the share price is below the investment company's net asset value per share it is said to be trading 'at a discount'; if it trades above the NAV per share, then the trust is selling 'at a premium'.

DIVIDEND YIELD

How much a trust pays out as income each year to its shareholders, expressed as a percentage of its share price. The usual figure quoted is based on the dividends a company has paid in the previous 12 months. Over time you hope to see the dividend increasing at least in line with inflation.

DIVIDEND HERO

A catchy term invented by the industry trade body to describe trusts which have increased their dividend every year for more than 20 consecutive years (see the data section for a full list).

THE FUND MANAGER

The person (or team) responsible for choosing and managing the investment trust's capital. Will typically be professionally qualified and highly paid. How much value he or she really adds is a lively source of debate.

abrdn

Invest in good company

abrdn
Investment Trusts

We believe there's no substitute for getting to know your investments first hand. That's why we look to analyse and speak to companies intensively before we invest in their shares and while we hold them.

Focusing on first-hand company research requires a lot of time and resources. But it's just one of the ways we aim to seek out the best investment opportunities on your behalf.

Please remember, the value of shares and the income from them can go down as well as up and you may get back less than the amount invested.

Request a brochure: 0808 500 4000

invtrusts.co.uk

THE BOARD

Investment companies are listed companies, so they must comply with stock exchange rules and appoint a board of independent directors who are legally responsible for overseeing the company and protecting the interests of its shareholders, which ultimately means replacing the manager or closing down the trust if results are not good.

GEARING

A fancy word for borrowing money in order to try and boost the performance of a company's shares – a case of more risk for potentially more reward. A number of different types of borrowing (e.g. with fixed or variable interest rates) can be used.

FEES AND CHARGES

What it costs to own shares in an investment trust – a figure that (confusingly) can be calculated in several different ways. More important than it sounds on first hearing.

OCR

Short for Ongoing Charge Ratio, one of the most commonly used formulas used to measure the annual cost of owning a trust. Expressed as a percentage of the NAV.

SECTORS

Investment trusts come in many shapes and sizes, so for convenience are categorised into one of a number of different sectors, based on the kind of things that they invest in.

PERFORMANCE

A popular and over-used term which tells you how much money an investment trust has made for its shareholders over any given period of time – by definition, a backward-looking measurement. Does not guarantee future performance will be as good.

BENCHMARK

The outcome against which a trust and its shareholders have agreed to measure its performance. This is typically a stock market index relevant to the area or style in which the portfolio is being invested (e.g. the FTSE All-Share index for trusts investing in UK equity markets).

TOTAL RETURN

A way of combining the income a trust pays with the capital gains it also generates (you hope) over time, so as to allow fair comparisons with other trusts and funds. Shown either as a simple percentage gain over the period or as an annualised gain, the compound rate of return per annum.

RISK AND RETURN

Riskier investments tend to produce higher returns over time, typically at the cost of doing less well when market conditions are unfavourable and better when they are more helpful. Risk comes in many (dis)guises, however – some more visible than others.

BETA
This is a term used in financial economics to measure the extent to which the shares of a company rise or fall relative to the stock market as a whole. The stock market has a beta of 1.0, so if the market rises 10%, then a trust with a beta of 1.2 is expected to rise by 12% (=10 × 1.2). If it falls by 10%, the shares should fall by 12%.

ALPHA
A statistical measure of the additional returns that a trust has made after adjusting for the relative risk of its portfolio. It is often used (not entirely accurately) as shorthand for fund manager skill.

ACTIVE MANAGEMENT
What is going on when the investment manager of a trust makes a conscious decision not to include in its portfolio all the stocks or shares that make up its benchmark index. The latter can be easily and much more cheaply replicated by a computer – what is known as passive management. All investment trusts are actively managed.

INVESTMENT STYLE
An attempt to characterise the way in which the manager of a trust chooses to invest. One common distinction is between value and growth. The former style aims to find companies whose shares are cheap relative to their competitors or historic price. The latter concentrates on finding companies with above average sales and profit growth prospects.

IS THERE ANY DIFFERENCE BETWEEN AN INVESTMENT COMPANY AND INVESTMENT TRUST?

Basically no. Strictly speaking, investment trusts are investment companies but not all investment companies are investment trusts. Feel free to use either term interchangeably, without fear of embarrassment.

CLOSED-END FUNDS

Investment trusts are an example of what is called a 'closed-end fund', meaning that its capital base is intended to be fixed and permanent (unlike unit trusts, OEICs and horribly named UCITs 3 funds, which take in and return money to investors on a daily basis and are therefore called open-ended). The distinction is no longer quite as important as it was, as it has become somewhat easier for successful investment companies to raise new money through regular share issues.

UK | EUROPE | EMERGING MARKETS | FAR EAST | US | GLOBAL

We take
THE LONG VIEW

on
investment
trusts

J.P. MORGAN
INVESTMENT TRUSTS

At J.P. Morgan Asset Management, we're always focused on the long term.

When it comes to investing, taking the long view is vital. It's what's helped our investment trusts deliver sustainable income and attractive growth to investors for over 130 years. Make sure you're positioned for long-term success. Let our experience and insights guide your portfolio, whatever lies ahead.

The long view. Because we are invested for the long run.
jpmorgan.co.uk/long-view

LET'S SOLVE IT®

Past performance is not a reliable indicator of current and future results. Your capital may be at risk.

LV-JPM52898 | 09/21 | 0903c02a82b2ad1b

USEFUL SOURCES
OF INFORMATION

Industry information

The Association of Investment Companies | www.theaic.co.uk

Data, news and research

Money Makers | www.money-makers.co

Morningstar | www.morningstar.co.uk

Trustnet | www.trustnet.com

Citywire | www.citywire.co.uk

Platforms

Interactive Investor | www.iii.co.uk

Hargreaves Lansdown | www.hl.co.uk

A.J.Bell | www.ajbell.co.uk

Fidelity International | www.fidelity.co.uk

Research

Edison | www.edisoninvestmentresearch.com

QuotedData | www.quoteddata.com

Trust Intelligence (Kepler Partners) | www.trustintelligence.co.uk

Specialist publications

Investment Trusts Newsletter (McHattie Group) | www.tipsheets.co.uk

Investment Trust Insider (Citywire) | www.citywire.co.uk

Publications that regularly feature investment trusts

Financial Times | www.ft.com

Investors Chronicle | www.investorschronicle.co.uk

Money Makers newsletter | www.money-makers.co

MoneyWeek | www.moneyweek.com

The Telegraph | www.telegraph.co.uk

EDITOR'S NOTES

A remarkable recovery – JONATHAN DAVIS *reviews the year just gone.*

A s we plunged into the seeming catastrophe of a lethal global pandemic in February to March last year, sending financial markets into a deep dive, who would have thought that normality would have returned as quickly as it has? Looking back with the advantage of hindsight 18 months later, it is remarkable how well investors have come through the experience. A look at the chart below shows that the US, worldwide and emerging markets are all well above where they were in January 2020 before the coronavirus hit. The US market has been particularly impressive, delivering a return of more than 35% since January 2020.

Given that nearly all equity markets fell by 30% to 50% in little over a month not long after the start of this period, the scale of the comeback from the depths that the decline produced has been nothing less than extraordinary. Note too that returns from bonds have also been positive over the same period, albeit only producing small single-digit returns, but doing their diversification job by offering offsetting positive returns during the big equity market sell-off. As with the 1987 stock market crash, the more time passes the more likely it seems that the pandemic crisis will eventually appear as just a blip in the longer-term rear view mirror.

Stockmarket returns over 10 years

31/10/2011 - 29/10/2021 Performance Data from FE fundinfo

Key	Chart	Instrument	1m	3m	6m	1y	3y	5y	10y
D	✓	iShares Core S&P 500	3.6%	6.6%	12.0%	32.7%	71.6%	110.2%	410.2%
A	✓	FTSE World	2.4%	4.6%	8.8%	30.4%	58.2%	82.8%	262.6%
C	✓	FTSE All Share	1.5%	2.9%	5.6%	35.4%	19.4%	30.7%	101.2%
B	✓	UK Consumer Price Index + 5%	0.7%	2.2%	5.3%	8.2%	22.1%	41.9%	93.9%

Source: FE Trustnet October 30 2021

Equity market progress has been particularly noticeable in the year since the last edition of the *Handbook*. The announcement of an effective vaccine in November 2020 triggered a near universal surge in the value of shares, with renewed confidence morphing into optimism as an end to the wave of covid-related deaths, in most developed markets at least, started to come into view. Even a second lockdown and the emergence of the more transmissible delta variant failed to dent investors' belief that the world economy was heading for a stronger than first expected recovery. While 2020 was dominated by a narrow range of spectacular performers (with healthcare and new technology stocks well to the fore), 2021 has been a year of much broader improved performance.

Over the last 12 months even the UK stock market, having badly lagged its global peers after its feeble initial response to the crisis, but buoyed by the completion of Brexit, has been outperforming most of the rest, with the notable exception of the US market. The FTSE All-Share index is finally back above its pre-covid peak, though not by much. While unquestionably now looking cheap in comparison with most of its peers, the UK remains a laggard over the two-year period as a whole. As I write, it seems clear that investors have moved on from covid and Brexit to new preoccupations, notably the risk of rising interest rates and the potential for higher (and more permanent) inflation.

OUR INVESTMENT TRUSTS BRIDGE COUNTRIES, STYLES AND MARKETS. OUR EXPERIENCE SPANS CENTURIES.

Investment trust expertise since 1889

Allianz Global Investors and its predecessors have been managing investment trusts since 1889. Our trusts span investor needs – from income, to growth, to the specialist sector of technology – and offer a path to investment opportunities around the world. Whatever your investment goals, we believe that Allianz Global Investors' broad experience makes our investment trusts worth a closer look.

Please note: Investment trusts are listed companies, traded on the London Stock Exchange. Their share prices are determined by factors including demand, so shares may trade at a discount or premium to the net asset value. Past performance is not a reliable indicator of future performance. Some trusts seek to enhance returns through gearing (borrowing money to invest). This can boost a trust's returns when investments perform well, though losses can be magnified when investments lose value.

0800 389 4696   uk.allianzgi.com/investment-trusts

Performance of Investment Companies Sector since start of 2020

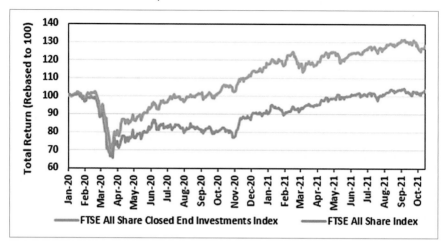

FTSE All Share Closed End Investments Index ━━ FTSE All Share Index

Investment trusts soldiering on

Against this backcloth it is pleasing to be able to report that investment trusts in aggregate have continued to deliver steady results. If you take the Equity Investment Instrument Index as a guide, in 2020 the investment trust sector outperformed the UK All-Share index by the best part of 27%, the highest margin of outperformance on that measure we have ever seen. While the return from the FTSE All-Share index was negative in 2020, down around 10% over the year, the investment trust index delivered a positive total return of nearly 18%.

That reflected the more global nature of the investment trust universe, as well as its bias towards growth companies, a style factor that until recently has performed particularly strongly. Scottish Mortgage went into 2020 as the biggest trust in the universe and finished it even further ahead of its nearest competitors, having produced a return of more than 100% in a single year – a phenomenal result for a fund of its size. China and technology trusts also delivered exceptional returns.

That margin of outperformance, by both the sector and its most dominant member trust, was never to going to last, given the exceptional characteristics of the pandemic year. As I write these notes, the investment trust index, now renamed the UK Closed End index, is up around 10% but is trailing the All-Share index by 5% and the still dominant US equity market by slightly more. Given the sector's traditional global bias, the strength of sterling in the first half of the year has worked against the sector to some extent, reversing the trend of the last few years. Scottish Mortgage for several months moved from trading at a premium to trading on a discount, in a change of sentiment that also affected the other big winners of 2020.

Just as significant perhaps is the fact that the composition of the investment trusts index, like the sector itself, has been changing. The popularity and continued rapid growth of alternative asset trusts, in property, private equity, infrastructure, renewable energy and other specialist areas, has increased their weighting in the index and in the trust universe. By their nature alternative asset vehicles are bought mainly for their secure income streams and single-digit total returns, not for their potential to produce startling capital gains, as Scottish Mortgage and some other conventional equity trusts have been able to do. In tough years those characteristics will stand shareholders in alternative asset trusts in good stead: in good years for equities, they will tend to lag.

What has been encouraging is how well overall discounts have held up since the market collapse 18 months ago. As chronicled in last year's *Handbook*, widening discounts magnified the fall in share prices across many sectors during the sell-off, but most have since recovered strongly. Discounts are now back, on average, to their pre-pandemic levels too, oscillating this past year in a range between 1% and 7%, but mostly below 5%. Many alternative asset trusts have continued to trade at premiums, reflecting the appeal of their solid and reliable dividends to income-starved investors in a period when yields on cash and bonds have remained at miserly levels. Once inflation is taken into account, yields on both cash and government bonds have remained decisively negative throughout the year, so the attraction of positive and sustainable real dividend yields has not been lost on investors.

Investment Trust Sector (ex 3i) average discount since start of 2020

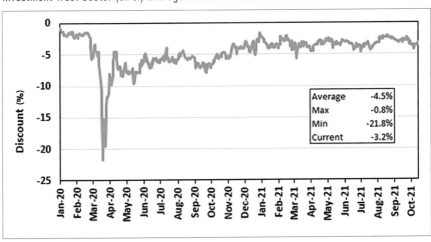

Plenty of style rotation

Any aggregated measure of investment trust performance inevitably disguises a smorgasbord of very different experiences as you look deeper into the picture. This year has seen a lot of volatility in the kind of investments that have found favour with the investment community. The first few weeks of 2021 saw the big winners of 2020 reach new peaks before falling out of favour, while the post-vaccine surge in value and cyclical stocks continued into the spring. (A special acknowledgement and note of thanks should be given to Kate Bingham, the head of the vaccine taskforce which engineered the UK's successful and world-beating vaccine campaign. She was made a dame for her extraordinarily effective contribution to fighting the virus, after ending her secondment and returning to her job as part of the management team at the International Biotechnology investment trust.)

After having been out of favour for years, value as an investment style continued its comeback over the course of the spring, with trusts such as Aberforth Partners, Temple Bar, Polar Capital Global Financials and Fidelity Special Values all performing strongly. During this period the biggest winners of 2020, including Scottish Mortgage, the two big technology trusts (Allianz and Polar Capital) and the sector's three all-China trusts, all sold off, moving from handsome premiums to discounts, as the growth style went out of favour. In the summer that trend largely reversed itself for a while, with growth to the fore again back in favour and value stocks falling back, before making a bit of a further comeback as we moved into the autumn – a real rollercoaster of a year from this perspective.

Investment professionals like to characterise this kind of behaviour as style rotation. Other style factors that move in and out of fashion include small versus large companies, quality versus deep value stocks (the latter a sub-set of the value bucket), high dividend yield versus low dividend yield and those with positive versus negative momentum. You can readily find investment trusts whose managers favour each of these different styles, some of which – notably growth, quality and smaller companies – have been dominant for the best part of a decade. Fund managers whose style happens to be in favour are not necessarily geniuses, any more than those whose approach does not fit the prevailing tides are incompetent – it's more about being in the right place at the right time.

The past 18 months have been, for a change, a period during which almost every kind of style has been able to boast of outperformance at some point. Whether these short-term changes in trend amount to an enduring range of direction remains to be seen. Suffice it to say that many professional investors are conscious of the importance of style, but in my experience the best ones to back are those who stick to a single approach, regardless of fashion. It is more productive to change the mix of styles among the trusts you own than it is to entrust your money to a fund manager whose job is to navigate from one style to another. That rarely seems to work well. The most important takeaway for investors, however, is the need to understand exactly what style of investment the manager of your trust is adopting and to allow for that when choosing whether it is right for you to own – or get rid of – that holding.

Consolidation is continuing

Style is one of the factors that has undoubtedly contributed to the wave of manager changes that has been another feature of the past 12 months in the investment trust sector. A timely and influential report from Numis Securities in mid-2020, highlighted in the *Handbook* a year ago, argued the case for continued consolidation across the trust universe. Its contention was that there are too many trusts that are either too sub-scale (too small to command attention) or insufficiently differentiated (by style, or objective, or performance) to justify their continued existence. Boards that are doing their job, it argued, should grasp the nettle and take action to remedy sustained periods of poor absolute or relative performance, either by changing the manager, changing the mandate, merging with another trust or, as a last resort, liquidating the trust and returning the cash to shareholders.

This call to arms was not entirely disinterested: Numis is one of the biggest and most active corporate brokers which stands to earn handsome fees from almost any kind of corporate activity. But nor was it misdirected, since one of the valid criticisms of trusts in days gone by was that boards of directors, even when nominally independent, were often slow to change or hold a failing manager to account (and certainly reluctant, on the turkeys-don't-vote-for-Christmas principle, to put themselves out of a job by liquidating the trust). Today's boards in general are made of more robust stuff and have become rather more active in taking decisive steps of this kind.

In 2020 we saw three sizeable trusts in the UK equity income, Perpetual Income and Growth, Temple Bar and Edinburgh, ditch their existing managers and switch to other firms after long periods of underperformance. This year the same process has claimed two notable scalps among trusts with global mandates. The mandate to manage Genesis Emerging Markets, with more than £1bn in assets under management, has been passed from Genesis Investment Management, the firm that launched the trust 32 years ago, to Fidelity, while the venerable Scottish Investment Trust, which dates its origins all the way back to 1887, is to be merged with J.P. Morgan Global Growth and Income. By a remarkable coincidence, the latter was founded (under a different name, the British Steamship Investment Trust) in the very same year.

A number of other, smaller trusts have also been wound up or merged, but what is striking about these two deals is that they involve well-established companies with hundreds of millions in assets. In the case of the Scottish Investment Trust, its deep value contrarian style has been completely out of sync with current market dynamics and has undoubtedly been a significant factor in the trust's poor track record of performance in recent years, so the change is not unexpected. The board will presumably be hoping, though, that they have not made the classic mistake of ditching the pilot just at the very moment that style and market conditions are about to change in its favour.

The Genesis/Fidelity change is a rather different story, as the outgoing managers evidently were shocked to discover that they were being replaced after more than 30 years at the helm of a trust they had founded and which has subsequently delivered a creditable near 12% annualised rate of return over the whole of that period. More recent performance has been less impressive, however, and the board appear to have concluded that, given a share register which is unusually still dominated by institutional investors, the Genesis team had become somewhat complacent and were less well suited to the task of marketing the trust in a period when private investors are an increasingly important target audience. As such this may be something of a wake-up call to the boards of other trusts that are struggling to remain relevant.

Record secondary fundraising

As detailed in the data and analysis section which makes up the back end of the *Handbook*, the performance of investment trusts has been less impressive this year than the ability of the sector to raise new money. The calendar year is not yet over, but already the amount raised through primary and secondary issuance is the best of any year since before the global financial crisis 15 years ago. Unlike 2006 and 2007, which witnessed the last great boom in fundraising, more than 80% of the money raised has come through secondary issuance by already listed investment companies. IPOs have been much rarer – only eight this year at the time of writing, compared with many times that number in those last two pre-crisis years. In other words, it has become harder and harder for new trusts to find a way to market but seemingly easier and easier for existing trusts to raise money once they have cleared that initial hurdle.

It is true that the bulk of the secondary fundraising has come from the most popular alternative asset sectors: renewable energy, infrastructure, private equity and niche property companies. Yields in the 4% to 6% range, based on secure and often index-linked income streams, are the primary attraction in these sectors. Many of these trusts are relative newcomers, but their ability to come back to scoop up more capital is remarkable by past standards. Trusts such as Tritax Big Box have raised more money in five years than the majority of conventional equity trusts will ever do. Even more remarkably, a trust that listed only at the start of this year, Digital 9 Infrastructure, has already raised almost as much from shareholders with two subsequent placings as Smithson, the smaller-company version of Terry Smith's popular Fundsmith fund, which holds the record for being the biggest investment trust launch we have seen on the London market. Nine trusts raised more than £300m through secondary issuance in the first nine months of the years.

The secondary fundraising phenomenon is a great boost for the investment trust business and an indication of the ability of the trust sector to adapt to change and provide popular new investment solutions in the low-growth, low-interest-rate world we have lived in since the global financial crisis. Even though they have been few in number, the IPOs that have succeeded in the last couple of years have brought an interesting range of new types of investment to the market, among them trusts that specialise in digital infrastructure (including the one just mentioned), energy storage and energy efficiency, space exploration, shipping and music royalties. Diversity, not the traditional old-fashioned me-too equity trust, is very much the flavour of the day.

This is all to the good, but it is only fair to add a mild warning. Periods when new money flows into popular sectors or asset classes in large quantities do not always work out well. As the internet bubble of 1999–2000 and the banking boom that preceded the global financial crisis in 2008 demonstrated, you can definitely have too much of a good thing. The City has always been very good at creating a new supply of whatever it is that investors think they want, but almost invariably it leads eventually to indigestion and subsequent disappointing performance from many of the new arrivals.

So, while many alternative trusts currently trade at big premiums, thanks to their temptingly juicy dividend yields while risk-free assets like cash and government bonds are paying next to nothing, you can be sure that at some point in the future those premiums will come under pressure and may even disappear. A trust that pays a dividend equivalent to 5% of today's share price, but later moves from a 10% premium to a 5% discount, can easily involve you giving back three years of past dividends. Don't get carried away, in other words. What goes around tends to come around, which suggests that after several years in which growth has taken the bulk of switched mandates there may well be good opportunities for trusts with a strong track record and a value approach to offer more choice in the sector in the years to come. Fidelity Special Values, Aberforth Smaller Companies and Temple Bar are obvious examples of those who could benefit.

There is theatre too

Money – and especially the stewardship of other people's money, which is the hallmark of the service that investment trusts provide – is a serious business, as it should be. That said, I hope that it won't be considered too flippant to observe that one of the pleasures of tracking the trust world this year has been the chance to enjoy some live corporate theatre, most of which has been concentrated in what remains of the hedge fund sector. Whatever you think of their performance history (and I have been a long-term sceptic about hedge funds), you could never call the managers of hedge funds blushing violets. As self-styled 'masters of the universe' they certainly don't like to be told what to do. This can lead to tensions when they are managing an investment trust, where boards – and, to a lesser extent, significant shareholders – traditionally expect their voices to be heard and respected.

In the past 18 months we have seen something of a power struggle at a number of trusts. Brevan Howard, the managers of BH Macro and BH Global, threatened to walk away as investment managers of both trusts unless their demands for higher fees were accepted. After a show of resistance, both boards eventually gave in to this rare show of defiance (the recent trend has been for managers to cut their fees under pressure from boards, rather than the other way round). Both boards also sensibly insisted by way of return that the two companies were merged into a single entity, allowing shareholders who were unhappy with the proposed increases to get out by means of a tender offer, which a minority did. Meanwhile another trust, Gabelli Value Plus+, which had a very poor track record of performance, was eventually liquidated after a shareholders vote this year, but only after a protracted and heated year-long standoff between the board and the management company. The latter had a 27% shareholding and was therefore able to veto any special resolution requiring a 75% vote in favour of change.

The bitterest war of words, however, has been reserved for the very public struggle between Dan Loeb, founder and leading light at Third Point Investors, and Asset Value Investors, an activist shareholder which has been leading a campaign on behalf of several investors for changes to help reduce the wide discount at which the trust has persistently traded. AVI's campaign was carried on through a series of open letters, rather than through a more usual behind-the-scenes approach to the board, which on this occasion – although announcing some plans of its own to reduce the discount – has so far mostly come down on the side of Loeb and his colleagues. While the discount has narrowed since these skirmishes began, for which both sides will doubtless claim the credit, it seems that this particular show has longer to run.

One of the problems in the Third Point case is the trust's dual share class, which gives some shareholders, including Loeb, more rights than others – always a potential source of tension and a deterrent to many sensible investors. Pershing Square Holdings, meanwhile, the biggest hedge fund investment trust, has also struggled to reduce the discount at which its shares trade. Given its exceptional performance in the last couple of years (it's not been so good over longer periods), this is another indication that there are persistent cultural and structural differences between managers and shareholders in the hedge fund space which make an investment trust a not entirely satisfactory vehicle for either party. While not quite such compulsive viewing as the TV series "Billions" or "Succession", these real-life cases of business confrontations still made for good spectator sport.

Change at the AIC

This year marked the retirement of Ian Sayers from the Association of Investment Companies, the industry's trade association, after 22 years – the first 11 as technical director and the last 11 as CEO. The Q&A with him we published in the 2020 *Handbook*, available on the Money Makers website, is probably the best potted history of the substantial changes that the investment trust business has experienced during his two-decade tenure. The journey that investment trusts have made from the depths of the split capital scandal to today's vibrant and successful industry is a tribute to Sayers' dedication and quiet but effective management style. His replacement, Richard Stone, who took over in September 2021 after a long stint as finance director and CEO of The Share Centre (itself recently taken over by a rival acquisitive platform, Interactive Investor), has a hard act to follow.

When I asked Stone what his immediate priorities were, he said updating the rules governing the need for prospectuses in secondary fundraising and making it easier for private investors to participate in them were top of his agenda. The arrival of the web-based platform Primary Bid, which enables private investors to participate in IPOs and secondary placings on virtually the same terms as wealth managers and other professional institutions, has been a welcome development this year. Its success in raising (admittedly small amounts of) money directly from private investors in more than a dozen issues has highlighted the disadvantage individual investors normally face when new primary or secondary share issues are announced. Stone's ambition to rectify the disadvantage is good to hear, and his experience running one of the bigger retail investor platforms for so long should effectively enable him to assist the moves many investment trusts are already making to improve their communication and interaction with individual shareholders.

At the moment participation by individuals in new and secondary issues is at the discretion of the issuing company and its brokers, while the amount of shares that Primary Bid, as a newcomer, is enabled to offer under existing rules is limited to a small percentage of any issue. The big platforms could – and should, in my view – be more active in promoting the more interesting fundraising opportunities. Because secondary issues are done at a premium to NAV but at a discount to the current share price, existing shareholders, although not diluted directly, can easily miss out on the opportunity to subscribe for more shares on the same attractive terms as the big boys – particularly when those shares immediately revert to trading at a bigger premium once the issue is completed.

The AIC has also called for the useless and much hated KIDs (key information documents) required by EU regulations to be scrapped now that Brexit is out of the way. Although a review of the regulations was promised after Brexit, the Financial Conduct Authority, the financial services regulator, has so far only announced that it is reviewing the regulations and will be proposing a new version in January 2022. As so often, the pace at which regulators move to resolve long-running issues is glacially slow. The problems with KIDs – which prompted the distinguished economist and academic Sir John Kay to offer the memorable advice "burn before reading" when they were first introduced – have been known for several years, and it grates that managers of open-ended funds have not been required to follow the burdensome and misleading requirements to the same extent.

Let the music play

My prize for the most entertaining and unusual piece of investment trust research this year has to go to Christopher Brown, the lead analyst at J.P. Morgan Cazenove, for his work on the two music royalty trusts, Hipgnosis Songs (ticker: SONG) and Roundhill Music Royalty Fund (ticker: RHM). By their nature, being trusts that invest in the earnings of publishers, composers and performers of the most well-known popular music of the last 70 years, these two trusts undoubtedly have a broader intrinsic appeal than many of their more mundane peers. The majority of individual investment trust shareholders come from a generation and demographic that will have grown up with popular music (of any genre) very much in their consciousness and very much part of their lives.

In an attempt to determine which of these two trusts had the better catalogue, Christopher decided to take a detailed look at a newly released list of the 500 greatest popular music tracks, as chosen and published by *Rolling Stone* magazine. This list was an updated version of a seminal earlier article originally published in the year 2000 and repeated in 2014. You don't have to agree with the decidedly idiosyncratic choices made by the panel of music experts who came up with the rankings in order to appreciate that this kind of exercise can produce enormous scope for argument and debate. (Bob Dylan has been knocked off the top spot by Aretha Franklin since the last review, while the highest-ranking Beatles song is only at number seven and the Rolling Stones don't even make the top ten.) Compare the streaming numbers of all the 500 tracks mentioned with the music rights acquired by the two trusts does, however, give the shareholders some basis on which to assess the likely earning potential that each enjoys.

All-time winners

Position	Song	Recording Artist	Year	Spotify Streams (m)	Top Twenty Position in 2004/10
1	Respect	Aretha Franklin	1967	363.9	5
2	Public Enemy	Fight the Power	1989	34.8	
3	A Change is Gonna Come	Sam Cooke	1964	115.4	12
4	Like a Rolling Stone	Bob Dylan	1965	239.9	1
5	Smells Like Teen Spirit	Nirvana	1991	1071.1	9
6	What's Going On	Marvin Gaye	1971	177.2	4
7	Strawberry Fields Forever	The Beatles	1967	123.1	
8	Get Ur Freak On	Missy Elliott	2001	190.6	
9	Dreams	Fleetwood Mac	1977	801.1	
10	Hey Ya!	Outkast	2003	761	
11	God Only Knows	The Beach Boys	1966	171.5	
12	Superstition	Stevie Wonder	1972	69.6	
13	Gimme Shelter	The Rolling Stones	1969	367.7	
14	Waterloo Sunset	The Kinks	1967	73.9	
15	I Want To Hold Your Hand	The Beatles	1963	260.8	16
16	Crazy In Love	Beyonce ft Jay-Z	2003	633.3	
17	Bohemian Rhapsody	Queen	1975	1598	
18	Purple Rain	Prince and The Revolution	1984	283.7	
19	Imagine	John Lennon	1971	383.2	3
20	Dancing on My Own	Robyn	2010	223.6	

J.P.Morgan CAZENOVE

Source: *Rolling Stone*, Spotify, J.P. Morgan

I cannot, unfortunately, share all the results of this exercise with readers, as wider circulation of the research is restricted by current regulations (so do write to your MP or the Financial Conduct Authority and demand some change if you think the current regime is misguided). Suffice it to say that the portfolios of the two trusts are clearly differentiated on a number of measures – RHM's catalogue has more 1960s and 1970s hits, including an interest in one of the famous Holland-Dozier-Holland combo of Motown hit writers, while Hipgnosis has a broader range of more recent music titans and more of the 500 tracks. You can find the *Rolling Stone* list online, and both trusts have filled their own websites with details of their key assets, so there is room to do your own happy hunting if popular music is your thing.

Reviewing the portfolio

Each year I provide a progress report on the model investment trust portfolio that I started for the first edition of the *Handbook* when it came out four years ago. The portfolio started life in January 2017 with ten investment trusts and £10,000 invested in each one. All of them were trusts that I either own or have owned myself at some stage. The majority were – and remain – run by longstanding managers with a significant personal stake in their trusts, a good track record over many years and, most importantly, a reputation for personal integrity and a willingness to put shareholders' interests above their own. That means (sorry) no hedge funds, because the fee structure they employ is too heavily weighted in the manager's favour. I would characterise the portfolio as being medium-risk and very much designed for long-term investors. It is not intended to constitute a list of recommended funds per se, but rather an illustration of the way that one reasonably knowledgeable observer thinks about investing his own money.

How the Handbook portfolio has grown

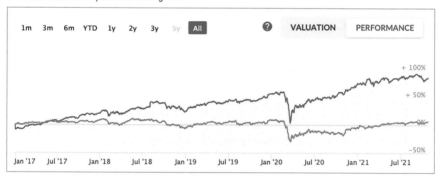

The initial £100,000 portfolio had performed satisfactorily when I reported on progress last year, increasing in value despite the intrusion of the pandemic from £148,000 to just under £160,000, including dividends reinvested, at the time of writing (which was just before the end of October 2020). Since then the value of the portfolio has increased again, to £187,000, an increase of approximately 13.5%. This, as it happens, is slightly above the annualised rate of return that the portfolio has achieved since it was initiated in January 2017. At one point early in 2021 the value of the portfolio touched £194,000, but it has since fallen back quite sharply, in part because of the style rotation factors I mentioned earlier. Poor relative performance by some key holdings, notably Fidelity China Special Situations, the largest and most successful holding coming into 2021, and Edinburgh Worldwide, also contributed.

My personal bias, on both temperamental and philosophical grounds, has always been towards managers who favour quality growth stocks and smaller companies over larger. I have also been reluctant to invest too much in the UK market while Brexit was still hanging over us. This year has prompted me to review those biases and make some slight adjustments. As a long-term buy and hold investor, the most important feature of the portfolio has always been my willingness to let the winners run, without annual rebalancing, and to keep portfolio changes to a minimum. Dividends are not automatically reinvested but used to make marginal adjustments to existing holdings or to add to new holdings that may also meet my criteria.

The number of holdings had crept up to 13 a year ago. This year, however, a combination of that style rotation, the evidence that the current equity market cycle is threatened by high valuations and the potential for rising bond yields, and the fact that the largest single holding had crept up to to more than 10% of the value has prompted me to review the balance of the portfolio and make some changes, most of which closely track the changes that I have made to my own real-life holdings.

The effect has been to increase the number of holdings to 14, cut back some of bigger positions and (ever so gingerly) commit a bit more money to the patently cheap UK market and (though it is not my preferred style) increase the amount awarded to managers with a value bias.

Turnover has therefore been unusually elevated. The increased number of names is intended to give a more balanced overall shape to what has become a bigger pool of money. New names added to the portfolio include Scottish Mortgage, bought when it was trading on a helpful discount, Fidelity Special Values and Temple Bar. Overall, however, given my caution about potential future returns, I remain reasonably pleased with the performance to date. Regular updates about this and other model portfolios I track can be found by subscribers on the Money Makers website, together with two other portfolios, including one for income investors, that I monitor on a regular basis.

Where next in 2022?

My crystal ball has always been clouded, and this year it is even more so than usual. There is much debate in professional circles about the risks of higher inflation and rising bond yields, both of which, if they materialise as more than transitory phenomena, will clearly have a significant impact on market returns. So too will many other specific corporate developments which remain by their nature unknown. The great beauty of investment trusts is that they give you plenty of scope to diversify your risk, while holding out – though never guaranteeing – the prospect of market-beating returns in individual sectors. The remarkable growth of alternative asset trusts in recent years has helpfully widened the universe of potential diversifying assets.

It is easier to note the most obvious cases of relative undervaluation than it is to predict the absolute level of returns that might be achieved over any future period. Mainstream UK equity trusts look cheap, as already noted, on most valuation measures, and it will be astonishing if the value style does not continue to do rather better over the next few years. Emerging markets, though not an area of great interest to me, have many professional advocates on current valuations. For those worried about inflation, defensive trusts such as Capital Gearing, Ruffer and Personal Assets will continue to look appealing. While wary of the big premiums on many alternative asset trusts, I have been adding holdings in some of the newer specialist property trusts to my personal portfolio.

We are moving into the second year of the US presidential cycle, which is historically not the greatest year for equity market performance. Discounts on investment trusts still remain on average narrow by historical standards, meaning there may be scope for sharper price falls if we get a significant market correction, or worse, in the next 12 months. So I believe caution continues to be called for, but there is no doubt that the investment trust sector remains in good health and the marked improvement in corporate governance and the range of available instruments gives me every confidence that the sector will continue to justify its billing as the connoisseur's choice.

YEAR IN
REVIEW

MONTH BY MONTH IN 2020/21

W E SUMMARISE HERE some of the main events of the past 12 months in the investment trust world.

OCTOBER 2020

Sector performance

Investment trusts outperformed the UK market for the 13th consecutive month in October 2020, with the FTSE Equity Investment Instruments Index up 1.0% compared with a fall of 3.8% for the FTSE All-Share Index. In the first ten months of 2020 the sector was ahead of the FTSE All-Share Index, with a rise of 2.4% compared with a fall of 23.0% for the index.

Corporate activity

Aberdeen Diversified Income & Growth announced changes to its investment team and a repayment of a substantial part of its long-term debt. The Board of Alternative Credit Investments agreed a cash offer of 870p per share from Waterfall. Glenstone Property launched a tender offer of 52.5p per share for up to 25% of the share capital of Alternative Income REIT. Baring Emerging Europe published proposals to diversify its investment policy to EMEA, while a discontinuation vote was triggered for Riverstone Energy. Key dividend announcements came from Scottish Oriental Smaller Companies, Amedeo Air Four Plus, Custodian REIT, GCP Student Living, Picton Property Income and British & American Investment Trust.

Share issuance

October 2020 was the strongest month for issuance in two years, with £1,735m raised across the sector, up 406% from £343m in September. The month saw the second and third IPOs of the year: Home REIT (£241m) and Triple Point Energy Efficiency Infrastructure (£100m). The largest fundraising was for Greencoat UK Wind (£400m), while other infrastructure funds raising additional capital included Aquila European Renewables Income (€128m) and SDCL Energy Efficiency Income (£105m). Specialist property funds also remained in demand, with Supermarket Income REIT (£200m), Urban Logistics REIT (£92m) and Triple Point Social Housing REIT (£55m) raising additional funds. In addition, Merian Chrysalis raised £95m through an oversubscribed placing.

NOVEMBER 2020

Sector performance

The UK market saw a spectacular rebound in November 2020, with the FTSE All-Share Index up 12.7%, its best monthly return in over 30 years. Investment trusts underperformed for the first time since September 2019, although the FTSE Equity Investment Instruments Index was up 8.6%. Despite this, the sector was ahead of the FTSE All-Share Index for the first 11 months of 2020, with a rise of 11.2% compared with a fall of 13.2% for the index.

Corporate activity

Three UK-focused investment trusts were in the spotlight following indifferent periods of performance. After an intensive review, the Board of Aberdeen Standard Equity Income decided not to make any changes to the fund's management arrangements, noting that its dividend would be jeopardised by doing so. Invesco Income Growth published proposals for a merger with the UK share class of Invesco Perpetual Select, with its board intent on finding a solution to its persistently wide discount. Meanwhile, its stablemate, Keystone Investment Trust, looked set on a move to Baillie Gifford and the adoption of a global positive change strategy, with its board questioning the longer-term prospects for UK equities.

Share issuance

November 2020 was another good month for issuance, with £865m raised across the sector. The sector saw IPOs for Round Hill Music Royalty Fund (US$282m) and Schroder British Opportunities Trust (£75m). The largest fundraising was by The Renewables Infrastructure Group (£200m). Demand remained strong for the asset class, with oversubscribed placings for Bluefield Solar Income Fund (£45m) and Gresham House Energy Storage Fund (£120m). Fundraising was also seen from BBGI Global Infrastructure (£55m), BlackRock Throgmorton Trust (£18m) and RTW Venture Fund (US$6m).

DECEMBER 2020

Sector performance

The UK market ended 2020 on a positive note, with the FTSE All-Share Index up 3.9% in December. The final month of the year usually sees a good return, and this was no exception. There have been only six occasions in the past 35 years when the market has fallen in December. With the gradual rollout of vaccines around the world, the prospects of economic recovery in 2021 galvanised markets in the last month of 2020, and in the UK a free trade agreement with the EU was eventually agreed on Christmas Eve. The investment trust sector outperformed in December, with the FTSE All-Share Equity Investment Instruments Index up 5.9%. The sector only underperformed in two of the previous 18 months and outperformed in the previous five quarters. This included a gain of 16.1% in the last quarter of 2020, compared with an increase of 12.6% for the FTSE All-Share. In 2020 the trust sector rose 17.8%, compared with a decline of 9.8% for the FTSE All-Share.

Corporate activity

Jupiter US Smaller Companies announced that it intended to appoint Brown Advisory as its investment manager. This followed the announcement in October 2020 of the forthcoming retirement of Robert Siddles, its manager since 2001.

Share issuance

December 2020 was a very strong month for issuance, with £1,191m raised across the sector. This was up 38% from November, when £865m was raised, and up 20% on the same month a year earlier. This included IPOs for Downing Renewables & Infrastructure Trust (£123m), Ecofin US Renewables Infrastructure (US$125m) and Schroder BSC Social Impact Trust (£75m). The largest fundraising in the month was by Greencoat Renewables (€125m), Gore Street Energy Storage (£60m) and Round Hill Music Royalty Fund (US$47m). Golden Prospect Precious Metals raised £13m from the exercise of subscription shares, while Premier Miton Global Renewables issued new ZDPs worth £14m following a rollover from existing ZDPs.

JANUARY 2021

Sector performance

The UK market delivered a negative return in January, with the FTSE All-Share Index down 0.8%. Investment trusts slightly underperformed the UK market, although the FTSE Equity Investment Instruments Index also fell 0.8%. However, over the 12 months to 31 January 2021 the sector was significantly ahead of the FTSE All-Share Index, with a rise of 18.9% compared with a fall of 7.5% for the index.

Corporate activity

Brevan Howard Capital, the investment manager of BH Global and BH Macro, threatened to resign if the funds' base fees were not reset to 2% of assets. Schroder UK Public Private announced that it had agreed to sell a basket of assets for £52m, with the proceeds to be used to reduce its gearing level.

Share issuance

The month saw £512m raised across the sector, the highest January level for 13 years. VH Global Sustainable Energy Opportunities started trading, having raised £243m through its IPO, and with more being marketed, including Cordiant Digital Infrastructure, Digital 9 Infrastructure and Next Energy Renewables. The sector continued to see healthy levels of regular share issuance at premium ratings to NAV. Some £493m was raised through smaller, secondary issuance in January, including Smithson IT (£73m), Pacific Horizon (£42m), Edinburgh Worldwide (£39m), Worldwide Healthcare (£38m), Monks (£27m), Baillie Gifford US Growth (£27m), JPM China Growth & Income (£27m), Impax Environmental Markets (£19m) and Personal Assets (£18m).

FEBRUARY 2021

Sector performance

The UK market delivered a positive return in February, with the FTSE All-Share Index up 2.0%. In contrast, the investment trust sector underperformed for a second consecutive month, with a decline of 0.9% for the FTSE Equity Investment Instruments Index. In the first two months of 2021 the sector lagged the FTSE All-Share Index, with a fall of 1.7% compared with a rise of 1.2% for the index.

Corporate activity

Invesco stablemates City Merchants High Yield and Invesco Enhanced Income announced plans to merge. Gabelli Value Plus+ said it would hold a continuation vote in July from which its largest shareholder, which had links to its manager, would abstain. A continuation vote was also announced for 30 March for Strategic Equity Capital after two of its shareholders, who owned 8% of its share capital, requisitioned a general meeting.

Share issuance

February was another strong month for fundraising, with £1,616m raised across the sector. The amount raised in the first two months of 2021 overall, £2,128m, was 125% higher than for the first two months of the previous year. February saw the second IPO of the year, with the launch of Cordiant Digital Infrastructure, which raised £370m. Demand for renewable energy infrastructure funds remained strong, with fundraising for Greencoat UK Wind (£198m) and SDCL Energy Efficiency Income (£160m). However, the IPO of NextEnergy Renewables was delayed. The month also saw successful fundraisings for Warehouse REIT (£46m) and AVI Japan

Opportunity Trust (£13m), while Hipgnosis Songs Fund raised £75m through its latest placing, and Sequoia Economic Infrastructure Income and Target Healthcare REIT raised £110m and £60m respectively through placings.

MARCH 2021

Sector performance

The UK market delivered a positive return in March, with the FTSE All-Share Index up 4.0%. The investment trust sector lagged, underperforming for a third consecutive month, with an increase of 2.2% for the FTSE Equity Investment Instruments Index. In the first three months of 2021 the sector trailed the FTSE All-Share Index, with a rise of just 0.4% compared with 5.2% for the index.

Corporate activity

Shareholders of BH Macro and BH Global approved increases to the funds' fees after being presented with an ultimatum by Brevan Howard. James Anderson, the co-manager of Scottish Mortgage, announced he would retire from Baillie Gifford in April 2022. Strategic Equity Capital passed a continuation vote that had been instigated by two shareholders, and the board said it was considering measures to address the discount level.

Share issuance

March was another strong month for fundraising, with £1,947m raised across the sector. This was up 20% from February and 202% higher than for the same month the previous year. In the first three months of 2021 overall £4,074m was raised, the strongest quarter in over 13 years, surpassing the £3,790m raised in the final quarter of 2020. March saw the third IPO of the year: Digital 9 Infrastructure, which raised £300m. Other large fundraisings included Chrysalis Investments (£300m), The Renewables Infrastructure Group (£240m), Tritax EuroBox (€230m), Supermarket Income REIT (£150m), LXi REIT (£125m), Sequoia Economic Infrastructure Income (£110m), Target Healthcare REIT (£60m) and Aberdeen Standard European Logistics Income (£19m). Meanwhile £415m was raised through regular issuance, including Smithson IT (£64m), HgCapital Trust (£37m), Polar Capital Global Financials (£37m), Worldwide Healthcare (£24m), City of London IT (£22m) and Ruffer Investment Company (£17m).

APRIL 2021

Sector performance

April saw the strongest monthly return for the UK market so far in 2021, with the FTSE All-Share Index up 4.3%. Investment trusts outperformed the UK market, with an increase of 5.2% for the FTSE Equity Investment Instruments Index. In the first four months of 2021 overall the sector lagged the FTSE All-Share Index, with a rise of 5.6% compared with 9.7% for the index.

Corporate activity

BH Macro and BH Global announced that discussions were under way over a possible combination following a request by a mutual shareholder. Dunedin Income Growth proposed the adoption of an enhanced ESG investment approach, while M&G Credit Income announced it intended to adopt a zero discount policy. Standard Life Aberdeen revealed plans to adopt 'abrdn' as its new branding.

Share issuance

April was another good month for fundraising, with £1,103m raised across the investment companies sector. In the first four months of 2021 overall £5,177m was raised, 191% higher than for the first four months of 2020. The sector saw the largest fundraising since October 2018, as The Schiehallion Fund raised US$700m (£504m) from a placing of C shares. Renewable energy infrastructure funds remained in demand, with Gore Street Energy Storage (£135m) and US Solar Fund (US$132m) raising new capital. Other issuance included Impact Healthcare REIT (£35m), UIL Limited's 2028 ZDPs issuance (£25m), Hipgnosis Songs Fund (£11m) and a convertible bond for CEIBA Investments (€25m). Meanwhile £417m was raised through regular issuance, including Smithson IT (£57m), City of London IT (£31m), Monks (£28m), Capital Gearing Trust (£25m), BB Healthcare (£21m), Worldwide Healthcare (£20m) and Personal Assets (£16m).

MAY 2021

Sector performance

May saw the UK market rise for a fourth consecutive month, with the FTSE All-Share Index up 1.1%. However, investment trusts underperformed the UK market in May for the third time in four months, with a fall of 0.9% for the FTSE All-Share Closed End Investments Index. In the first five months of 2021 the sector lagged the FTSE All-Share Index, with a rise of just 4.7% compared with 10.9% for the index.

Corporate activity

Acorn Income Fund proposed BMO Global Asset Management as its new investment manager and the adoption of a sustainable global equity income investment strategy. The Board of The Scottish Investment Trust announced a review of the fund's future investment management arrangements. Strategic Equity Capital proposed two contingent tender offers in order to address its discount. Asset Value Investors agitated for Third Point Investors to adopt a quarterly redemption offer capped at 25%.

Share issuance

May was a quieter month for issuance, with £667m raised across the sector, down 40% from April. However, in the first five months of 2021 overall £5,845m was raised, 158% higher than for the first five months of the previous year. May saw the fourth IPO of the year, with the launch of Taylor Maritime Investments, which raised US$254m. Demand for funds in the renewable energy infrastructure subsector remained strong, with fundraisings for JLEN Environmental Assets (£57m) and US Solar Fund (US$132m). May also saw a further placing for Impact Healthcare REIT (£35m), taking its market cap to £389m, while Hipgnosis Songs Fund raised £11m through its latest placing.

JUNE 2021

Sector performance

The UK market rose for a fifth consecutive month in June, with the FTSE All-Share Index up 0.2%. The investment trust sector outperformed the UK market for the second time in three months, with a rise of 2.1% for the FTSE All-Share Closed End Investments Index. However, in the first six months of 2021 the sector lagged the FTSE All-Share Index, with a rise of 6.9% compared with +11.1% for the index.

Corporate activity

BlackRock North American Income announced proposals to invest only in companies that showed a commitment to achieving sustainable business models. The board of Genesis Emerging Markets proposed the appointment of Fidelity as the fund's manager to pursue a long/short strategy within emerging market equities.

Share issuance

June was another good month for issuance across the sector, with £950m raised, up 42% from May. In the first six months of 2021 overall £6,795m was raised, 150% higher than the first half of 2020. June 2021 saw the fifth IPO of the year, with the launch of Aquila Energy Efficiency, which raised £100m. In addition, Literacy Capital began trading following its listing, although no new money was raised. Demand for infrastructure funds remained strong, with fundraising for Cordiant Digital Infrastructure (£185m) and Digital 9 Infrastructure (£175m). In terms of equity funds, the largest fundraising in June was for Polar Capital Global Financials (£122m), while other issuance included Hipgnosis Songs Fund (£156m), LXi REIT (£104m), Baillie Gifford China Growth (£11m), RTW Venture Fund (US$9m) and Ashoka India Equity (£5m).

JULY 2021

Sector performance

The UK market rose for a sixth consecutive month in July, with the FTSE All-Share Index up 0.5%. The investment trust sector underperformed the UK market for the fourth time in six months, with a rise of 0.3% for the FTSE All-Share Closed End Investments Index. In the first seven months of 2021 the sector lagged the FTSE All-Share Index, with a rise of 7.2% compared with +11.7% for the index.

Corporate activity

Aberdeen Emerging Markets and Aberdeen New Thai proposed a merger and the adoption of an all-China mandate. Custodian REIT approached Drum Income Plus REIT with an all-paper takeover offer. GCP Student Living received a cash bid from a consortium of investors. BH Global's merger with BH Macro moved closer to completion, while Pershing Square Holdings said it would invest directly in Universal Music after the US regulator effectively blocked plans for its SPAC to take a 10% stake.

Share issuance

July was the second strongest month so far in 2021 for issuance across the investment companies sector, with £1,629m raised. In the first seven months of 2021 overall £8,424m was raised, 140% higher than in the equivalent period the previous year. New IPOs were Seraphim Space Investment Trust and Hydrogen One Capital Growth, which raised £178m and £107m respectively. Demand for infrastructure remained strong, with oversubscribed placings in July for Octopus Renewables Infrastructure (£150m), International Public Partnerships (£135m), Bluefield Solar Income (£105m), Gresham House Energy Storage (£100m) and BBGI Global Infrastructure (£75m). July also saw fundraisings from Hipgnosis Songs Fund (£156m), Round Hill Music Royalty Fund (£63m), LXi REIT (£104m), Urban Logistics REIT (£108m), Augmentum Fintech (£55m), Taylor Maritime Investments (£55m) and Odyssean Investment Trust (£6m).

AUGUST 2021

Sector performance

The UK market rose for a seventh consecutive month in August, with the FTSE All-Share Index up 2.7%. The investment trust sector outperformed the UK market for the third time in five months, with a rise of 3.4% for the FTSE All-Share Closed End Investments Index. However, in the first eight months of 2021 the sector lagged the FTSE All-Share Index, with a rise of 10.9% compared with 14.7% for the index.

Corporate activity

The board of Acorn Income Fund had a volte-face after consulting shareholders on plans to adopt a sustainable global equity income strategy and appoint BMO as investment manager. The new proposals were for a voluntary liquidation, with a rollover option into Unicorn UK Income Fund or a cash exit. The battle between Asset Value Investors and the board of Third Point Investors showed no sign of resolution, with the latter rejecting the former's second attempt at a requisition.

Share issuance

August was the weakest month so far in 2021 for issuance across the investment companies sector, with £241m raised, most of which was from ongoing issuance programmes. Regular issuance totalled £3,541m in aggregate so far in 2021, including £232m in August. The leading issuers so far in 2021 included Smithson IT (£390m), Capital Gearing Trust (£171m), Personal Assets (£147m), Edinburgh Worldwide (£131m), Impax Environmental Markets (£127m), Worldwide Healthcare (£127m), Pacific Horizon (£112m), Ruffer Investment Company (£104m), BB Healthcare (£103m), Monks (£97m), City of London IT (£94m), Polar Capital Global Financials (£93m), BlackRock Throgmorton Trust (£86m), HgCapital Trust (£76m), Baillie Gifford US Growth (£74m), BlackRock Greater Europe (£70m), JPM China Growth & Income (£68m) and BlackRock World Mining (£63m).

SEPTEMBER 2021

Sector performance

The UK market fell for the first time in eight months in September, with the FTSE All-Share Index down 1.0%. The investment trust sector underperformed the UK market for the third time in five months, with a decline of 1.8% for the FTSE All-Share Closed End Investments Index. In the first nine months of 2021 the sector lagged the FTSE All-Share Index, with a rise of 8.8% compared with 13.6% for the index.

Corporate activity

The board of Gresham House Strategic appointed Harwood as its investment manager, following a strategic review. It said Richard Staveley, the fund's previous manager, would reassume responsibility for the portfolio from 1 December.

Share issuance

September was another strong month for issuance across the sector, with £1,611m raised. In the first nine months of 2021, overall £10,275m was raised, 155% higher than in the equivalent period the previous year and 64% up on the first nine months of 2019. Fundraising was dominated by funds in the property and infrastructure subsectors, with a number of oversubscribed placings. Examples of the former included Home REIT (£350m), Tritax Big Box REIT (£300m), Tritax EuroBox (€250m), Target Healthcare REIT (£125m), Aberdeen Standard European Logistics Income (£125m) and PRS REIT (£56m). In the infrastructure sector, successful placings came from Digital 9 Infrastructure (£275m), SDCL Energy Efficiency Income (£250m), The Renewables Infrastructure Group (£200m) and Aquila European Renewables Income Fund (€90m).

These month-by-month summaries are extracted from the excellent monthly investment trust reports prepared by the Winterflood investment trusts research team and are reproduced here with their kind permission.

The following charts are drawn from the invaluable monthly and quarterly round-ups of investment trust news produced by research firm QuotedData. In addition to these regular charts, the round-ups also provide news and commentary on recent trends in the investment sector and are free for private investors who sign up at www.quoteddata.com.

2020 TOTAL

Figure 1: Best performing funds in price terms in 2020

	%
Baillie Gifford US Growth	133.5
Pacific Horizon	128.6
Scottish Mortgage	110.5
J.P. Morgan China Growth & Income	95.6
Edinburgh Worldwide	87.7
Pershing Square	81.4
Allianz Technology	80.3
Geiger Counter	78.7
Golden Prospect Precious Metals	69.8
Fidelity China Special Situations	68.6

Figure 2: Best performing funds in NAV terms in 2020

	%
Baillie Gifford US Growth	118.3
Scottish Mortgage	106.7
Pacific Horizon	86.6
Edinburgh Worldwide	85.5
J.P. Morgan China Growth & Income	82.9
Allianz Technology	75.7
Geiger Counter	69.4
Weiss Korea Opportunity	66.9
Pershing Square	66.1
Golden Prospect Precious Metals	64.6

Source: Morningstar, Marten & Co. Note: Excludes trusts with market caps below £15m at 31/12/20.

Figure 3: Worst performing funds in price terms in 2020

	%
KKV Secured Loan	(78.1)
JZ Capital Partners	(73.9)
Amedeo Air Four Plus	(53.1)
Symphony International	(45.7)
Duke Royalty	(39.3)
Macau Property Opportunities	(37.9)
NB Distressed Debt Inv Extended Life	(36.7)
NB Distressed Debt New Glb	(34.7)
Aseana Properties	(32.6)
Temple Bar	(31.5)

Figure 4: Worst performing funds in NAV terms in 2020

	%
KKV Secured Loan Fund	(48.0)
JZ Capital Partners	(47.6)
Riverstone Energy	(39.4)
Symphony International Holding	(35.5)
NB Distressed Debt New Glb	(33.1)
Electra Private Equity	(31.7)
Temple Bar	(26.7)
Aberforth Split Level Income	(26.1)
FastForward Innovations Limited	(25.3)
Crystal Amber	(25.2)

Source: Morningstar, Marten & Co. Note: Excludes trusts with market caps below £15m at 31/12/20.

Figure 5: Money raised in 2020

	£m
Hipgnosis Songs	768.3
Smithson	460.2
Supermarket Income REIT	349.4
Worldwide Healthcare	328.1
Sequoia Economic Infrastructure Income	297.2
Impax Environmental	259.8
Edinburgh Worldwide	250.0
SDCL Energy Efficiency Income	219.1
Allianz Technology	205.6
Personal Assets	170.7

Figure 6: Money returned in 2020

	£m
Pershing Square	(363.0)
J.P. Morgan Indian	(186.3)
NB Global Monthly Income GBP	(151.9)
Witan	(148.1)
Fidelity China Special Situations	(127.1)
CVC Credit Partners Euro Opps. GBP	(124.5)
Scottish Mortgage	(120.2)
Polar Capital Global Financials	(112.0)
Amedeo Air Four Plus	(72.3)
SME Credit Realisation	(70.5)

Source: Morningstar, Marten & Co. Note: Excludes trusts with market caps below £15m at 31/12/20.

FIRST QUARTER 2021

Figure 7: Best performing sectors by total price return over Q1

	Median share price TR (%)	Median NAV TR (%)	Median discount 31/03/21 (%)	Median sector market cap 31/03/21 (£m)	No. of companies in the sector
Commodities and natural resources	10.2	6.4	(5.0)	263	6
North American smaller companies	8.8	3.4	(3.3)	217	2
Debt – structured finance	8.4	3.8	(8.5)	131	24
Property – UK logistics	8.1	2.9	(11.3)	335	3
UK smaller companies	6.7	2.4	(13.6)	281	5

Figure 8: Worst performing sectors by total price return over Q1

	Median share price TR (%)	Median NAV TR (%)	Median discount 31/03/21 (%)	Median sector market cap 31/03/21 (£m)	No. of companies in the sector
Japanese smaller companies	(10.9)	(4.7)	(4.8)	148	5
Latin America	(10.2)	(7.0)	(10.1)	88	2
China/Greater China	(9.6)	(0.6)	(1.1)	504	3
Technology and media	(4.8)	(0.6)	(4.6)	1,162	3
Infrastructure	(3.7)	0.0	2.1	1,146	9

Source: Morningstar, Marten & Co. Note: Inclusive of sectors with at least two companies.
Note: Many alternative asset sector funds release NAV performance on a quarterly basis.

Figure 9: Best performing funds in NAV terms over Q1

	%
Geiger Counter	36.6
Chelverton UK Dividend	23.8
Aberforth Split Level Income	23.0
Aberforth Smaller Companies	21.3
Miton UK Microcap	20.6
Marble Point Loan Financing	17.8
River and Mercantile UK Micro Cap	17.4
Oryx International Growth	16.3
Secured Income Fund	15.9
Temple Bar	15.3

Figure 10: Best performing funds in price terms over Q1

	%
Drum Income Plus REIT	69.4
KKV Secured Loan	43.9
Geiger Counter	38.3
Miton UK Microcap	37.1
Livermore Investments	35.1
Electra Private Equity	33.5
Chelverton UK Dividend	31.7
Riverstone Credit Opportunities Income	30.1
Schiehallion	26.9
LMS Capital	26.0

Source: Morningstar, Marten & Co. Note: Excludes trusts with market caps below £15m at 31/03/21.

Figure 11: Worst performing funds in NAV terms over Q1

	%
Golden Prospect Precious Metal	(20.1)
Keystone Positive Change	(12.7)
Atlantis Japan Growth	(10.3)
J.P. Morgan Japanese	(9.6)
Aberdeen Latin American Income	(7.8)
UIL	(6.7)
International Biotechnology	(6.4)
Biotech Growth	(5.9)
BlackRock Latin American	(5.5)
Aberdeen Japan	(5.1)

Figure 12: Worst performing funds in price terms over Q1

	%
Amedeo Air Four Plus	(25.6)
Globalworth Real Estate	(18.1)
Atlantis Japan Growth	(16.1)
Golden Prospect Precious Metal	(16.0)
J.P. Morgan Japan Small Cap G&I	(15.5)
Keystone Positive Change	(15.1)
Riverstone Energy	(13.1)
Life Settlement Assets A	(12.7)
Baillie Gifford China Growth	(12.5)
Aberdeen Latin American Income	(12.3)

Source: Morningstar, Marten & Co. Note: Excludes trusts with market caps below £15m at 31/03/21.

Figure 13: Money raised over Q1

	£m
Cordiant Digital Infrastructure	370.0
Digital 9 Infrastructure	300.0
Chrysalis Investments	300.0
VH Global Sustainable Energy Opportunities	246.6
Greencoat UK Wind	198.0
Tritax EuroBox	€230.0
Smithson*	186.1
SDCL Energy Efficiency Income	160.0
Supermarket Income REIT	153.0
LXI REIT*	126.5

Figure 14: Money returned over Q1

	£m
Scottish Mortgage*	(308.1)
Alliance Trust*	(44.7)
Gulf Investment Fund*	(42.7)
Witan*	(41.6)
Scottish Investment Trust*	(36.2)
TwentyFour Select Monthly Income*	(34.0)
CVC Credit Partners Euro Opps. GBP*	(27.3)
F&C*	(21.1)
UK Mortgages*	(19.6)
Polar Capital Technology*	(16.0)

Source: Morningstar, Marten & Co. Note: Excludes trusts with market caps below £15m at 31/03/21.
* based on the approximate value of shares at 31/03/21

SECOND QUARTER 2021

Figure 15: Best performing sectors by total price return over Q2

	Median share price total return (%)	Median NAV total return (%)	Median discount 30/06/21 (%)	Median sector market cap 30/06/21 (£m)	No. of companies in the sector
Country specialist	14.5	16.3	(14.4)	251	6
UK smaller companies	11.3	10.5	(8.4)	152	24
UK equity and bond income	10.9	9.9	(8.1)	140	2
China/Greater China	10.3	9.0	2.7	605	3
Latin America	10.2	11.9	(11.9)	97	2

Figure 16: Worst performing sectors by total price return over Q2

	Median share price total return (%)	Median NAV total return (%)	Median discount 30/06/21 (%)	Median sector market cap 30/06/21 (£m)	No. of companies in the sector
Property – rest of world	(1.7)	0.0	(45.9)	44	4
Japan	(1.6)	(0.0)	(7.9)	273	6
Biotechnology and healthcare	(1.4)	1.2	(0.2)	827	6
Renewable energy infrastructure	0.5	1.5	7.4	421	17
Japanese smaller companies	(2.6)	148	5	1.2	2.3

Source: Morningstar, Marten & Co. Note: Inclusive of sectors with at least two companies.
Note: Many alternative asset sector funds release NAV performance on a quarterly basis.

Figure 17: Best performing funds in NAV terms over Q2

	%
VietNam Holding	29.6
Vietnam Enterprise	26.2
Mobius Investment Trust	21.1
VinaCapital Vietnam Opportunity	20.9
Chelverton UK Dividend	16.0
EPE Special Opportunities	15.9
India Capital Growth	15.8
BlackRock Greater Europe	15.4
Scottish Mortgage	15.2
BlackRock Throgmorton	14.6

Figure 18: Best performing funds in price terms over Q2

	%
Electra Private Equity	65.9
Riverstone Energy	33.9
BMO Commercial Property	29.6
VietNam Holding	28.6
EPE Special Opportunities	26.8
Mobius Investment Trust	26.0
Chrysalis Investments	25.8
NB Distressed Debt Inv Extended Life	24.3
Schroder Real Estate	24.1
SME Credit Realisation	23.3

Source: Morningstar, Marten & Co. Note: Excludes trusts with market caps below £15m at 30/06/21.

Figure 19: Worst performing funds in NAV terms over Q2

	%
Gresham House Strategic	(36.8)
Aberdeen New Thai	(4.7)
TwentyFour Select Monthly Income	(3.6)
EJF Investments	(3.0)
Secured Income	(2.1)
JPEL Private Equity	(1.2)
BH Macro GBP	(1.1)
Hipgnosis Songs	(1.1)
Aberdeen Japan	(1.0)
CC Japan Income & Growth	(1.0)

Figure 20: Worst performing funds in price terms over Q2

	%
Secured Income	(19.6)
Ceiba Investments	(13.0)
Augmentum Fintech	(12.3)
Schroder UK Public Private	(9.6)
JLEN Environmental Assets Group	(9.3)
RTW Venture	(8.6)
Octopus Renewables Infrastructure	(7.2)
Symphony International	(7.0)
J.P. Morgan Global Core Real Assets	(6.5)
Jupiter Green	(6.1)

Source: Morningstar, Marten & Co. Note: Excludes trusts with market caps below £15m at 30/06/21.

Figure 21: Money raised over Q2

	£m
Digital 9 Infrastructure	227.6
Cordiant Digital Infrastructure C Share	187.3
Gore Street Energy Storage Fund	150.2
Smithson	133.1
Invesco Bond Income Plus	127.7
Polar Capital Global Financials C Share	122.1
Literacy Capital	114.0
Invesco Select UK Equity	108.8
US Solar Fund	97.0
Aquila Energy Efficiency	95.5

Figure 22: Money returned over Q2

	£m
Scottish Mortgage	(87.6)
River and Mercantile UK Micro Cap	(37.9)
Witan	(34.4)
Weiss Korea Opportunity	(32.0)
Fair Oaks Income 2021	(30.8)
Third Point Investors USD	(27.8)
Alliance Trust	(24.9)
SME Credit Realisation	(21.9)
UK Mortgages	(19.3)
European Opportunities	(16.7)

Source: Morningstar, Marten & Co. Note: Excludes trusts with market caps below £15m at 30/06/21.

THIRD QUARTER 2021

Figure 23: Best performing sectors by total price return over Q3

	Median share price total return (%)	Median NAV total return (%)	Median discount 30/09/21 (%)	Median sector market cap 30/09/21 (£m)	No. of companies in the sector
India	13.9	13.5	(10.2)	273.0	8
Infrastructure securities	12.5	11.3	(4.1)	116.7	2
Japanese smaller companies	10.9	7.2	(0.4)	164.1	5
Private equity	9.2	0.5	(21.8)	349.7	21
Japan	8.7	8.9	(7.6)	300.4	2

Figure 24: Worst performing sectors by total price return over Q3

	Median share price total return (%)	Median NAV total return (%)	Median discount 30/09/21 (%)	Median sector market cap 30/09/21 (£m)	No. of companies in the sector
China/Greater China	(25.7)	(19.5)	(9.0)	431.0	6
Commodities and natural resources	(11.9)	(2.8)	(7.1)	89.4	9
Latin America	(10.9)	(12.6)	(10.9)	82.8	2
Property – rest of world	(7.5)	0.0	(50.6)	40.4	4
Biotechnology and healthcare	(4.6)	(0.9)	(3.6)	788.4	6

Source: Morningstar, Marten & Co. Note: Inclusive of sectors with at least two companies.
Note: Many alternative asset sector funds release NAV performance on a quarterly basis.

Figure 25: Best performing funds in NAV terms over Q3

	%
Geiger Counter	21.5
Schiehallion	19.1
Ashoka India Equity	18.6
Premier Miton Global Renewables	16.9
Third Point Investors	15.7
Aberdeen New India	14.2
J.P. Morgan Russian Securities	13.7
J.P. Morgan Indian	12.8
Montanaro European Smaller	12.6
India Capital Growth	11.8

Figure 26: Best performing funds in price terms over Q3

	%
Literacy Capital	52.6
Riverstone Energy	39.5
Schiehallion	38.4
Symphony International Holding	31.7
GCP Student Living	31.4
Geiger Counter	28.5
Taylor Maritime	27.4
NB Distressed Debt	24.6
Dunedin Enterprise	23.3
Tufton Oceanic Assets	22.1

Source: Morningstar, Marten & Co. Note: Excludes trusts with market caps below £15m at 30/09/21.

Figure 27: Worst performing funds in NAV terms over Q3

	%
Fidelity China Special Situations	(19.7)
Baillie Gifford China Growth	(17.5)
EPE Special Opportunities	(16.1)
Golden Prospect Precious Metal	(15.2)
BlackRock Latin American	(13.7)
BlackRock World Mining	(12.0)
Aberdeen Latin American Income	(11.4)
Templeton Emerging Markets	(9.7)
UIL	(9.6)
Weiss Korea Opportunity	(9.6)

Figure 28: Worst performing funds in price terms over Q3

	%
J.P. Morgan China Growth & Income	(28.3)
Baillie Gifford China Growth	(25.7)
Fidelity China Special Situations	(24.0)
Secured Income	(23.8)
Civitas Social Housing	(23.2)
Golden Prospect Precious Metal	(19.7)
Syncona	(18.9)
Macau Property Opportunities	(16.3)
Gabelli Merger Plus+	(16.2)
J.P. Morgan Asia Growth & Income	(16.1)

Source: Morningstar, Marten & Co. Note: Excludes trusts with market caps below £15m at 30/09/21.

Figure 29: Money raised over Q3

	£m
Home REIT	348.4
SDCL Energy Efficiency Income	255.7
Tritax EuroBox	216.3
Renewables Infrastructure	200.5
Digital 9 Infrastructure	190.0
Cordiant Digital Infrastructure	187.0
Seraphim Space	178.4
Hipgnosis Songs	157.1
Octopus Renewables Infrastructure	155.9
Polar Capital Global Financials	134.0

Figure 30: Money returned over Q3

	£m
JPEL Private Equity	(48.7)
VietNam Holding	(38.0)
Witan	(29.7)
Alliance Trust	(28.9)
F&C Investment Trust	(18.6)
SME Credit Realisation	(17.5)
AVI Global	(16.7)
BMO Commercial Property	(15.4)
Highbridge Tactical Credit	(14.9)
J.P. Morgan American	(13.1)

Source: Morningstar, Marten & Co. Note: Excludes trusts with market caps below £15m at 30/09/21.

FROM CRISIS TO RECOVERY

Investment trust expert MAX KING *gives his personal take on the performance of equity investment trusts in 2021.*

AFTER THEIR EXTRAORDINARY performance in 2020, in which the FTSE Equity Investment Instruments index returned 17.8% compared with a decline of 9.8% for the FTSE All-Share Index, it looked likely that 2021 would be a much duller year. The 27.8% outperformance in 2020 was the largest for 30 years, but success was far from universal across the year. The giant Scottish Mortgage was one of three Baillie Gifford trusts that more than doubled in value while 11 others gained more than 50%, but the list of casualties was also long – some the result of pandemic-related problems, some due to the poor performance of 'value' relative to 'growth'.

You could argue that investment company performance should instead be compared with the MSCI All Countries World Index, which returned 12.7% in sterling in 2020, on which measure the outperformance in 2020 was less marked. The UK is still disproportionately important to investment companies, however – accounting for 24% of the equity component of the sector and more of the alternatives segment – so the dual comparison remains valid.

A slow start

The year 2021 did indeed start slowly, with the Equity Investment index lagging the All-Share. That was due partly to a return to favour of 'value' (most investment companies have a bias to growth), partly to trust discounts widening, and partly to better performance by the UK market. The gap was over 5% in late March, since when the trend has been for investment companies to slowly outperform. At the end of September, the gap was 4.8%.

At the start of the year, investment trusts accounted for 7% of the All-Share index, up from 3% ten years earlier. Despite good performance and strong equity issuance, that share was still 7% at 30 September. If you include 3i and other large alternatives trusts, which are excluded from the index, that would push the weighting higher. There are now three investment companies in the FTSE 100 index (3i, Scottish Mortgage and Pershing Square) but several close behind, notably Tritax and F&C.

The problem of trusts trading at a discount to net asset value has not disappeared, but the average sector discount started the year at 1.7% and ended September at 3.2%, having reached 3.9% at the halfway stage. Plenty of trusts still trade at significant discounts, but these now constitute an opportunity for investors or a problem for trust directors to address, not an endemic threat to the whole asset class.

Investment company performance was helped by growth funds returning to favour, with Scottish Mortgage Trust returning 18.8% in the first nine months and 17.6% in share price terms while Baillie Gifford US Growth returned 12.8% but -3% in share price terms. However, the most positive aspect for the sector in 2021 has been that many trusts which had lagged in 2020 did well.

Helped by their allocations to private equity, Caledonia returned 30.7% and RIT 24%, while Temple Bar (the disaster story of the pandemic meltdown) returned 17% under new management and Lowland reversed a disappointing few years with a 24.7% return. UK mid- and small-caps had an outstanding year, with the laggard of previous years, Aberforth, returning 44%. On average, the UK mid-cap specialists returned 30%, small-caps 44% and microcaps 37.4%, although share prices did not always keep up. All these numbers exclude dividends.

Increased confidence in the UK outlook was most clearly visible in the property sector, where valuations were barely changed – as they had been in 2020 – but discounts to net asset value fell sharply, even for hard-hit areas such as offices, student accommodation and leisure. Share prices also outpaced valuation uplifts in the private equity sector, on which investors had also been sceptical about the long-term prospects.

There were, though, areas of disappointment. Despite healthy prospects, rising profits and improving corporate governance, the Japanese market responded with negative returns in the first half. Japan, it seems, performs best when it is forgotten, not when its advocates are most confident. Why the announcement in September of Prime Minister Suga stepping down should have sparked a powerful rally remains a mystery, but the Japanese market is always a law unto itself.

Changing fashions

Emerging markets continued to be left behind by developed markets; the glowing economic, political and market outlook once set out by Goldman Sachs in 'the BRIC dream' continues to unravel, with China the latest casualty. India and Vietnam performed well, but most successful trusts owed their performance to stock-picking, not to a development tailwind.

Investors crowded into any fund carrying the buzzwords of the moment: 'ESG' (environmental, social and governance), 'social impact', 'sustainable' and 'renewable', all of which threaten a doing-good cloak for poor performance. Shrewd investors will tread warily, although Impax Environmental, up 18%, the pioneering trust that has been targeting innovative companies across a broad range of environmental areas for over 20 years, is surely an exception.

The new economy has benefited a very old economy sector, mining, through rising demand for metals. Blackrock World Mining returned 15% in the first half-year but lost it all in the third quarter. Polar Capital Global Financials, which survived a continuation vote by the skin of its teeth in 2020, had more enduring success, returning 21% in both net asset value and share price terms. This enabled it to raise new equity, showing that while investors continue to chase growth at almost any price, they are no longer turning their backs on the solid value offered by banks and insurance companies.

After three terrible years Riverstone Energy, which is reinvesting itself as an investor in renewable energy, enjoyed an abrupt reversal of fortunes, returning 62% in share price terms, though it still trades on a 30% discount to net asset value. No trust, it seems, can be safely written off while it still lives and breathes.

Record new issuance

The health of the investment trust sector is shown not just by steady, broadly based performance but also by continued issuance and good corporate governance. A record £11.5bn of new capital was raised in the first nine months while net capital raised was £8.4bn. More than £8bn of the total in the first nine months was for alternative assets, but not all of this was in the high-yield areas such as infrastructure, property and renewable energy; over £1.5bn was raised for private equity. Most of the money raised from equity funds was for those with minimal or no yield.

Some £1.4bn was raised for seven new issues in the first nine months, all in the alternatives space, but the failure of three flotations to get off the ground shows investors remain choosy about new offerings. The health of the sector is also marked by the readiness of directors to respond to poor performance or widening discounts. Some £3.3bn was returned to investors in the first nine months, including £640m from Waterfall's acquisition of Pollen Street Lending, £433m from BH Global, most of which was rolled over into BH Macro, and £170m from the wind-up of Gabelli Value Plus. Share buybacks totalled £1.5bn, of which £466m was from Scottish Mortgage, £105m from Witan and £95m from Alliance Trust. The remaining outflows came from tender offers and wind-down strategies.

Changes of management companies have worked well in recent years, so it is no surprise that, following a long period of poor performance, the board of the self-managed Scottish Investment Trust have invited proposals from other groups. The manager's enthusiasm for goldminers (the three largest holdings) cannot have inspired confidence in his 'value' strategy. More of a surprise was the decision of the board of Genesis Emerging Markets to move the management contract to Fidelity; performance has kept up with the benchmark index in recent years but not with its main competitors, managed by J.P. Morgan and Templeton. Over 20 years, it has multiplied investors' money twelvefold.

The boot was on the other foot when hedge fund manager Brevan Howard told the boards of its two trusts, Macro and Global, that it was doubling the fees it charged for access to its core funds to 2% per annum and adding a hefty performance fee. The two trusts had shrunk considerably over the years, thanks to dull performance, but their manager's bets paid off handsomely in the pandemic meltdown. The two trusts have now merged into one with combined net assets of around £1bn.

Brevan Howard's disdain for the little people of the investment world (you and me) is highly unusual. The little people, whether as direct investors or via IFAs and wealth managers, have turned the investment trust sector from a lame duck to the best-performing and fastest-growing investment vehicle in the market. As Ian Cowie pointed out in September, no fewer than 42 investment trusts have multiplied investors' money more than tenfold in the last 20 years, yet the FTSE 100 index is barely higher in capital terms than it was on the eve of the millennium.

At the same time investment trusts, whether in the equity or alternatives sectors, are providing investors with the income that deposit accounts, government bonds and even non-junk corporate bonds conspicuously no longer offer. Stock markets may look fully priced and uncertainties abound, but the managers I speak to and trust are full of enthusiasm about the long-term prospects. A setback is inevitable before long but this should be seen by investors as a long-term buying opportunity. The steady performance of 2021 after the breakthrough year of 2020 should tell investors that their money is in good hands.

MAX KING *was an investment manager and strategist at Finsbury Asset Management, J O Hambro and Investec Asset Management. He is now an independent writer, with a regular column in* MoneyWeek, *and an adviser with a special interest in investment companies. He is a non-executive director of two trusts.*

FROM STRENGTH TO STRENGTH

The alternatives sector has continued an upward trend in 2021 that looks set to continue next year, says MAX KING *in the second part of his review of the year.*

THE ALTERNATIVES SECTOR of investment companies weathered the storms of 2020 well. Issuance of £5.1bn was 30% down on 2019 and the lowest level since 2012, but still accounted for 60% of the investment company total in the most pandemic-afflicted year. Performance was mixed, with many funds producing negative returns in the debt, renewable energy and property sectors but, with the exception of the aircraft leasing funds, few were struggling to survive and most saw a steady improvement in the second half. As Winterflood Securities argued, there was clear light at the end of the tunnel.

So far, 2021 has seen continued progress by the funds that have either benefited from pandemic issues, been unaffected, or shaken them off. The private equity sector boomed, with some funds shooting the lights out. Many funds that had struggled but were recovering continued to come back strongly. Even the casualties of 2020 survived, giving hope that they too might bounce back. Equity issuance was strong, both from existing funds and new ones. By the end of September, concerns were growing about unsustainable private equity valuations and too much money chasing into fashionable areas, but the continued success of the sector is not in doubt.

This is despite continuing concerns about interest rates and bond yields. Most of the sector provides the majority of its return to investors through income rather than capital, so it is potentially sensitive to higher bond yields. These rose sharply early in the year amid expectations of a strong recovery and fears of inflation but subsequently tailed off. While inflation worries have been vindicated, it is still not clear whether this will prove to be a short-lived jump in prices or the start of a sustained upward move – or indeed both.

For the alternatives sector, this is not necessarily a negative. Returns are generally either economically sensitive or inflation linked, so returns should compare more closely with inflation-linked than with conventional bonds. Only the debt sector is vulnerable, but many of these funds have proven adept at generating positive returns without the help of falling bond yields. Valuations generally discount higher bond yields, and only if higher inflation pushes ten-year gilt yields above 3% should investors worry. That does not look likely.

Dominating issuance

Alternatives continued to dominate issuance in the first nine months of 2021. Most of the money raised was focused on yield, but more than £1.5bn was also raised for private equity. Alternatives also accounted for much of the £3.2bn returned to investors, largely due to Waterfall's £639m purchase of Pollen Street Secured. The surprise of the covid-19 era is that there have been so few casualties.

Numis calculates that alternatives now account for 44% of its universe of London-listed investment companies, which comprises 375 companies valued at £237bn. This is rising slowly as, although alternatives dominate net issuance, the capital performance of the 56% investing primarily in quoted equities is higher, despite the higher-performing private equity segment accounting for 31% of alternatives. Yet there were strong performers in other segments. Among the steadily shrinking hedge funds, Pershing Square, valued at £5.3bn and a FTSE 100 constituent, generated an investment return of 16.2% to the end of September, helped by its coup in acquiring a pre-listing stake in Universal Music. It is closer to being a long-only fund than a hedge fund in its traditional sense.

The property sector had seen many losers from the pandemic, as shopping moved online, leisure outlets were locked down and office workers stayed at home. Investors worried about the impact of lower long-term demand on office and retail rents, but this concern slowly abated in 2021, resulting in some strong performances. With share prices catching up with previously distrusted asset values, BMO Commercial Property returned 22.5%, TR Property (an investor in property equities) 15% and Secure Income 40%. GCP Student Living, which was bid for in July, returned 48%.

Recovery stocks, however, were not the only big winners. Tritax Big Box returned 28% – this £4bn REIT, close to being a FTSE 100 constituent, specialises in the big logistics warehouses that are key to online shopping and so had prospered in 2020. In the medical property sector, positive trading and net asset value progress were not reflected in share prices. PHP and Assura, owning GP surgeries, returned 0.5% and -5.3% respectively. Target and Impact Healthcare, owners of care homes whose operators protected their patients better than most in the pandemic, returned 0.9% and 3.3% although their business model shows considerable potential to improve social care.

Social impact investment has become a priority for many investors, and the residential property sector has provided a key opportunity. Five investment companies with £2.7bn of assets provide social housing, shared-ownership homes, supported living for the elderly and family homes for rent, while giving investors an attractive index-linked yield and modest capital returns. With the private sector providing the capital and housing associations the management, a solution to the shortage of affordable housing is starting to take shape.

Further growth in the property sector is promised by the continuing travails of open-ended funds. To meet potential redemptions, these need to hold significant liquidity, which drags on performance. "While investment companies appear to have moved onto the front foot," says Alan Brierley of Investec Securities, "structural flaws continue to be a dragging anchor for open-ended funds. Since these funds reopened, they have experienced a tsunami of redemptions."

Despite the absence of a tailwind from the bond market, the debt sector prospered. Funds that had struggled in 2020 recovered, helped by the strong performance of distressed and high-yield debt, while the rest squeezed out solid returns and continued to pay high yields. Few of these funds are exposed to the direction of bond yields, but rather make their returns from seeking under-valuations in credit markets. In a world in which ten-year gilts yield barely 1%, far less than the rate of inflation, and inflation-indexed bonds give a negative real yield, the solid returns are a godsend to multi-asset investors without the scale to have their own team of analysts.

Ups and downs in infrastructure

Conventional infrastructure funds were negatively affected by rising rates of corporation tax, despite positive trading. 3i Infrastructure announced the partial sale of its oil bunkering business, Oystercatcher, but still returned -1.6%. Bilfinger & Berger's return was just positive, but GCP Infrastructure – which invests only in debt – was affected by lower long-term price assumptions on its renewable energy projects. It returned -5.7%. The now long-established funds were joined by two new funds specialising in digital infrastructure, Cordiant and Digital 9. These funds raised £850m between them, are trading at significant premiums to net asset value, and are steadily investing the funds they raised.

The net asset value and share price performance of the renewable energy sector hardly reflected the enthusiasm of investors, who continued to shovel money into their frequent fundraisings. Initially held back by weak power prices, then by the absence of wind or sun in the summer, they failed to benefit from the surge in prices in September because of their long-term contracts. Diversification into Europe was no help, and the two North American funds have yet to gain traction. Returns were mostly negative. The two battery-storage companies and SDCL, the largest of the three energy-efficiency companies, performed much better, although prolific equity issuance creates the challenge of ensuring returns on the new projects are as good as on the old ones.

The hedge fund sector continued to disappear. After its strong performance in 2020, manager Brevan Howard decided to double its fees and add a hefty performance fee. The subsequent merger of the Global and Macro funds reduced assets to below £900m, but dull investment performance (+2.5%) suggests further shrinkage is possible. In contrast, Third Point, with £800m of assets, had an excellent year, returning 37% – which resulted in its discount falling to a still generous 16.5%. Pershing Square's shares still trade at a 30% discount, suggesting a lingering distrust of Bill Ackman and his team.

Private equity stars

Despite strong individual performances elsewhere, the stars of 2021 were undoubtedly in the private equity sector – where the good news just didn't stop coming. This has raised concerns about over-optimism and excessive valuations, but there is no evidence yet of disappointing underlying performance. Many of these trusts, especially the fund of funds, trade on ill-deserved discounts to net asset value, so it is hard to argue that euphoria has gripped investors.

The performance of some trusts was helped by discount-narrowing, but strong investment performance was far more important, and realisations at a significant premium to carrying values showed valuations to be conservative. Eleven funds returned above 25% in the first nine months of 2021; Electra, which is being wound up, led the pack at 114% but Schiehallion (+78%) and BMO Private Equity (+49%) were also notable. Chrysalis, now valued at £1.5bn, continued to perform strongly, returning 40%, as did Literacy Capital, which floated only in June, at 81%. Both funds are passive, late-stage investors in high-growth companies prior to flotation. Augmentum and Syncona, both early-stage investors in, respectively, financial technology and biotechnology start-ups, had contrasting performance, the former gaining 7.3% and the latter losing 35%. Both are classified as sector rather than private equity funds.

While the aircraft leasing funds appear to be on their last legs, as does reinsurance vehicle Catco, entrepreneurs and their sponsors continue to open up new areas for investment. Hipgnosis, now with £1.5bn of assets, introduced music royalties to investors in 2018; that was followed in late 2020 by Round Hill Music. Their returns to date in 2021 –1.5% and 2.7% respectively – have been disappointing. The flotation of Tufton Oceanic introduced ship ownership and chartering to the market in 2018; in May 2021 Taylor Maritime also floated. Strongly rising charter rates have resulted in returns of 43% and 31% to the end of September.

Innovation is likely to continue in the sector, but not all of it will survive the test of time. The number of alternative funds continues to rise (with seven new launches so far in 2021, raising £1.4bn), but much more important is the ability of existing funds to grow through secondary issuance (£6.5bn). This expansion is helped by the willingness of directors to return capital to investors where funds are not performing as expected and to agree to takeovers, whether supported by managers or not, where the offer to investors is compelling. Good corporate governance is proving critical to the success of the sector.

Despite the threat from higher inflation, interest rates and bond yields, alternative funds are likely to continue to offer attractive returns in nominal, real and relative terms, but not necessarily every year. The hunt for yield is eternal, and closed-end funds have been proven to be the ideal vehicles for investment in property, private equity and a growing number of niche sectors. Continued growth in 2022 looks assured.

Note: Since net asset values in the alternatives sectors are usually based on infrequent valuations, hopefully conservative and always disclosed in arrears, it is generally more useful to look at share price performance than investment performance.

Best and worst performers 2021 year to date

Share price total return

NAV total return

Year to date					Year to date			
Best Performers	**%**	**Worst Performers**	**%**		**Best Performers**	**%**	**Worst Performers**	**%**
Electra Private Equity	119.9	Global Resources IT	-52.0		Geiger Counter	82.3	Amedeo Air Four Plus	-37.8
KKV Secured Loan Fund	109.2	Syncona	-35.4		Chelverton Growth Trust	67.5	Secured Income Fund	-36.5
KKV Secured Loan Fd – C	92.1	Secured Income Fund	-32.0		Riverstone Energy	52.4	Golden Prospect	-28.9
Chelverton Growth Trust	89.3	Baillie Gifford China Growth	-28.3		Vietnam Holding	49.8	Syncona	-16.7
Drum Income Plus	86.5	Amedeo Air Four Plus	-27.1		Electra Private Equity	46.0	Biotech Growth Trust	-13.6
Geiger Counter	80.5	Golden Prospect	-24.8		Chelverton UK Dividend	41.3	JPM China Growth & Inc	-13.0
SME Credit Realisation Fd	66.5	Biotech Growth Trust	-23.5		Ashoka India Equity	40.8	Doric Nimrod Air Two	-12.7
Riverstone Energy	62.3	JPM China Growth & Inc	-22.6		Aberforth Split Level Inc	40.1	Baillie Gifford China Growth	-10.7
BMO Private Equity	59.1	Ceiba Investments	-20.7		Vietnam Enterprise	40.1	Doric Nimrod Air One	-10.3
Vietnam Holding	53.1	Edinburgh Worldwide	-16.9		India Capital Growth	38.3	Fidelity China Special Sits	-9.7
JZ Capital Partners	52.2	Fidelity China Special Sitns	-16.2		HarbourVest Glob PrEqu	37.0	Aberdeen Lat Am Income	-9.6
India Capital Growth	48.4	Civitas Social Housing	-13.4		R&M UK Micro Cap	35.7	Ceiba Investments	-8.8
GCP Student Living	48.2	Aberdeen Lat Am Income	-13.1		JPM Russian Securities	35.4	Edinburgh Worldwide	-8.7
NB Private Equity	44.0	NB Distressed Debt Global	-12.9		Aberforth Smaller Cos	35.4	BlackRock Latin American	-8.0
Chelverton UK Dividend	43.5	BlackRock Latin American	-10.8		KKV Secured Loan Fund	34.4	Urban Logistics REIT	-6.4
Chrysalis Investments	42.1	JPM Asia Growth & Income	-10.6		Gresham House Strategic	33.9	Aberdeen New Thai	-6.4
AEW UK	41.2	International Biotech	-8.3		NB Private Equity	33.5	Atlantis Japan Growth	-3.3
JPM Russian Securities	37.5	JPM Glob Core Real Assets	-8.1		SME Credit Realisation Fd	32.1	Genesis Emerging Markets	-3.1
Mobius Investment Trust	37.3	JPM Japan SmCos	-7.8		Mobius Investment Trust	31.8	Asia Dragon	-2.9
Ashoka India Equity	36.5	Baillie Gifford Japan	-7.4		Rights & Issues	31.0	Templeton Emerging Mkts	-2.8

Source: Winterflood Securities, data as at 1 October 2021

MAX KING *was an investment manager and strategist at Finsbury Asset Management, J O Hambro and Investec Asset Management. He is now an independent writer, with a regular column in* MoneyWeek, *and an adviser with a special interest in investment companies. He is a non-executive director of two trusts.*

"The hunt for yield is eternal, and closed-end funds have been proven to be the ideal vehicles for investment in property, private equity and a growing number of niche sectors. Continued growth in 2022 looks assured."

— MAX KING

A ROSE BY ANY OTHER NAME

SANDY CROSS *of Rossie House Investment Management offers his tips about investing in the alternative asset sector.*

I N AUGUST 2021 there were some 390 investment trusts and investment companies listed in the UK – with a cool £265bn under management. That was up from £90.4bn ten years ago. We often tend to think of investment trusts as ideal buy and hold private client equity investments, and in many respects they are, but we also should not forget another key thing about them: the sector has an extraordinary capacity to change and evolve. Over the past decade it has been doing exactly this – and the result is rather surprising: equities no longer account for the majority of assets under management.

Asset type breakdown for investment trusts

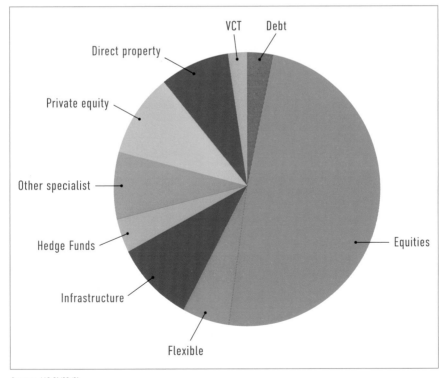

Source: AIC 31/08/21

How has this happened? Well, the answer is multilayered. The first part of it concerns the oft-discussed advantages of a closed-ended fund structure for an asset with limited, or at least slow or complex, liquidity. This means that alternative assets, which are not usually traded in liquid venues, are ideally suited to a listed fund structure. Throughout the financial crisis, property trusts continued to trade whilst OEICs and unit trusts had to close to redemptions or delay them.

You cannot just sell parts of a large office building on T+2 settlement with a low commission to fund a redemption request, but an investor can sell and buy investment trusts easily and cheaply. The downside? Well, there is no such thing as a free lunch – remember those property investment trusts? Sure, you could sell the shares, but only at a big discount to their NAV (or a reasonable estimate of the live NAV). The discount is the risk you take for the advantages of liquidity, although popular assets can also trade at a premium – which you need to be careful about when buying.

Discounts and premiums reflect a combination of other market participants' estimates of value, their assessment of the skill of a manager (in other words, the likely future returns) and simple supply and demand. And that was the problem for the vanilla equity trusts in the late 20th century. There was a lack of demand for funds without an appealing specialism (such as Latin American equities, or utility equities, which always fluctuate in popularity) or a red-hot track record.

Clients and private client investment managers, then emerging as the main buyers of investment trusts, were also questioning the benefits of equities as a long-term investment. This all had secondary consequences. Without a ready source of demand, equity trusts – even quite good ones – fell to a discount and so it became virtually impossible for them to issue new shares, which in turn made it very difficult for new equity trusts to be launched. It was a tough sell to suggest someone buy a new IPO in, say, a European equities trust, when many respectable existing options were on 10% discounts.

These two trends – the low popularity of equity trusts with high discounts, and the ideal nature of the listed structure for alternative assets with liquidity challenges – have meant growth has been very biased to alternative assets over the past 20 years. It is why alternatives now account for more than half the assets under management in the industry. It has, of course, done no harm to this trend that alternative assets typically command higher fees and so managers and sponsors find better money-making prospects among them.

Just how new?

But what is an alternative asset? It is a catch-all term, which at its broadest may even be said to encompass anything that is not an equity or a government bond. The range of such assets available globally is quite remarkable and at times even mystifying. I have mentioned property and office buildings already, but this is a fairly conventional area of alternatives in which the trend has been towards new specialisms (logistics warehouses, REITs letting buildings to supermarkets, care homes, doctors' surgeries, social housing, to name but a few) alongside the more generalist property trusts. Meanwhile we have seen a range of new kinds of alternative funds emerging: ones that invest in music royalties, timber, aircraft and ship leasing, and any number of sectors.

As investors, we have long periods of history in equity investing to which to refer and reams of academic research as well. We are naturally inclined to trust assets for which we can draw on experience and for which there are observable measurements of risk and return over long periods. However, one must remember that historically, land, gold and livestock were the principal stores of wealth for thousands of years, long before equities came into the picture. Equities are still new compared with those asset classes.

We need to bear in mind also that these other options which are now available can help us construct portfolios with better risk and return characteristics than a simple bond/equity/property construction. The alternatives listed space has grown up to fulfil that need. It is also worth considering that equities are often companies that may be trading in and owning many 'alternative' assets. An example would be the insurance assets held by listed insurance funds.

This is not a guarantee that familiarity will yield returns, but it means that 'novel' assets are sometimes not so novel as they appear, and there may be a good deal of information available on their likely behaviour (see my list of dos and don'ts, below). Examples might include **PRS REIT**, which provides affordable private rental housing to let, or even the ship leasing company Taylor Maritime Investments. Shipping has been a very longstanding asset class, albeit a highly cyclical one, which as a result requires specialist management. Assets that are genuine novelties (for example, cryptocurrencies) are the most difficult to analyse.

A golden key

In my view, the best way to think about alternative assets is to consider why you might want to own things other than equities or government bonds. The answer would typically involve diversification and a different kind of return, one with lower volatility or lower correlations to equities, or simply higher returns than equities. A listed structure is the golden key which frees assets that might be hampered by liquidity issues in an open-ended investment company or unit trust, which must provide a regular exit possibility for their underlying shareholders.

Managers have certainly used that key with enthusiasm. Private equity trusts such as Pantheon International were launched specifically to overcome the innate illiquidity of the typical LLP structure and provide access to smaller lot sizes and greater diversification. Hedge funds and funds of hedge funds were the most popular alternative asset closed-end funds of the mid-2000 years. The listed investment company structure overcame the liquidity problems associated with lengthy notice periods and esoteric investments that hedge funds normally face.

The funds of hedge funds have declined in popularity as returns disappointed and heavy fee structures took their toll, but they are still a lingering presence in the market. Venture capital trusts (VCTs) are a hardy perennial of the listed fund market, although the tax benefits of the investments have in many cases been accompanied by dull investment performance and, ironically, they are very illiquid.

Infrastructure is also a huge area for alternatives, with renewable energy and infrastructure funds such as The Renewables Infrastructure Group (TRIG) a large part of this. These are typically companies that own assets with either contracted or predictable revenues (think toll roads, or prisons) and specified, lengthy contract terms which enable them to offer an attractively predictable revenue stream and usually good dividends. Quite a number of listed debt funds have also been launched, taking advantage of the challenges of the banking sector in regulatory and capital terms following the debacle of the great financial crisis.

A bias to income

There is one thing that most alternative investment trusts have in common – and that is a bias to producing income. 'Demand creates its own supply' is one of the oldest economic laws. And the low-interest era we have lived through since the global financial crisis and before that the inflationary 1970s has fuelled a relentless demand for income. In their fan dance with investors, alternative asset trusts like to show a bit of liquidity and a lot of income.

Surely this is a pretty good thing? Well, yes, it is a good thing, but it can be a bit like designing an aeroplane starting with a focus on the first-class bar area – which can still make for an unsatisfactory aeroplane. Many of the assets that encompass alternatives do naturally produce a good income – take the case of commercial property rents – and so income is a natural bias. The problems tend to come when that unreliable partner, leverage, is introduced; it makes everything, including income and fees, so much bigger and better. It has also caused many of the problems in the sector.

Given the focus on income in the alternatives space, and also the use of leverage, it is vital therefore to consider the sensitivity of the investment to interest rate changes. While the majority of investments tend to have a negative correlation to interest rate rises, those with high income and leverage are likely to feel the greatest impact. At present, of course, interest rates have little scope to fall, but it would be no surprise to see them rise in due course.

It is true that many alternatives trusts have revenues that are inflation-linked in one form or another, as is the case with many infrastructure contracts, and this will mitigate the negative impact of interest rates. However, the devil is in the detail, as many contracts contain caps on the level of inflation that can be passed through. In the case of renewable infrastructure funds, companies have varying levels of subsidy-based revenue – and of the subsidy regimes, the exposure may be to either RPI or CPI (with the former generally tending to be higher). Whatever the details, while the concept of an alternative asset may be excellent, the execution is key. Listed timber vehicles, for example, have fallen foul of this very problem in the recent past.

An experienced and reputable management team is vital. Alternative assets at their best offer the possibility of outperforming inflation in diverse asset classes, such as shipping, forestry or infrastructure, which are not too highly correlated to equity markets and which typically produce a good income. That said, it behoves everyone to bear in mind the observation of David Swenson, the famed Yale Endowment investment manager, in the appendix of his book *Pioneering Portfolio Management:* "As a general rule, the more complexity that exists in a Wall Street creation, the faster and farther investors should run."

Dos and don'ts of alternative assets

This is my list of dos and don'ts when it comes to alternative assets.

Do:

- Do favour seasoned assets. They may not have been available in investment trusts before, but have people owned them for many years successfully in other structures? Property, private equity or shipping would pass this test.

- Do be wary of yields that seem too high.

- Do think carefully about leverage and how much is too much.

- Do check the fees and the salutary example of the funds of hedge funds that have charged high fees and performance fees on hedge funds which also in turn have charged high fees and performance fees.

- Do check out the managers. In a new asset class, you really are giving these guys the keys to your bank safe.

- Do remember that while investment trusts provide better liquidity, a small trust in an unusual asset may not always be very easy to trade.

Don't:

- Don't invest in things you do not really understand. The risk is too high.

- Don't believe the hype (to quote rappers Public Enemy). These fund launches are highly profitable for brokers and managers.

- Don't forget these assets may have cycles of their own, and 'buy and hold' may not be the best way to invest in them.

SANDY CROSS *is a partner in Rossie House Investment Management in Edinburgh. At the time of writing Rossie House had holdings in PRS REIT, Pantheon International, TRIG and Taylor Maritime Investments.*

Disclosure: At the time of writing Rossie House Investment Management has holdings in: PRS REIT, Pantheon International, TRIG and Taylor Maritime Investments.

Note: Since net asset values in the alternatives sectors are usually based on infrequent valuations, hopefully conservative and always disclosed in arrears, it is generally more useful to look at share price performance than investment performance.

VCTS: YEAR OF THE UNICORN?

ALEX DAVIES, *founder of Wealth Club, gives his annual review of developments in the venture capital trust sector.*

UNICORNS ARE ELUSIVE, mythical creatures, yet our herd of homegrown unicorns – UK private companies worth over $1bn – continues to expand at an accelerating pace. It took 24 years (from 1990 to 2014) to create the UK's first 20 unicorns. Today there are 105, with 20 joining in the first six months of 2021 alone.

Often, these companies are the sort of overnight success that only comes from years of hard slogging and significant equity investment (£100m on average). And whilst nine out of ten UK unicorns have received funding from international investors with deep pockets before achieving the coveted $1bn valuation, in some cases the early cheque that set the company on its growth trajectory has come from closer to home.

Six – soon to be seven – UK unicorns have received early backing from venture capital trusts (VCTs). The first VCT-backed unicorn was Zoopla: less than a year from launch, in January 2008, it received £2m from Octopus Ventures, manager of what is now the Octopus Titan VCT. Zoopla proceeded to raise a total of $25.6m and listed on the London Stock Exchange in June 2014 in a £919m ($1.56bn) IPO, eventually going private again in 2018, when US private equity firm Silver Lake acquired it for $3bn.

It then took six years – until June 2020 – for the second VCT-backed unicorn to emerge: that was online used-car marketplace Cazoo. Interestingly, Cazoo was founded by Zoopla co-founder Alex Chesterman and, like Zoopla, was backed by Octopus Ventures, which invested prior to launch. Cazoo was incorporated in October 2018, started trading in December 2019 and only six months later became the UK's fastest-ever unicorn. Cazoo listed on the New York Stock Exchange in August 2021, with a group valuation of $8bn.

At the time of writing, September 2021, there are six VCT-backed unicorns in total, with a seventh expected to join the list later in the autumn.

VCT-backed unicorns in the UK

COMPANY	YEAR FOUNDED	VCT BACKER	YEAR OF VCT INVESTMENT	DATE OF $1BN VALUATION
Zoopla	2008	Octopus Ventures	2009	June 2014
Cazoo	2018	Octopus Ventures	2018	June 2020
Gousto	2012	Hargreave Hale AIM VCT	2018	November 2020
Bought By Many	2011	Octopus Ventures	2017	June 2021
Depop	2012	Octopus Ventures	2018	June 2021
Matillion	2011	British Smaller Companies VCTs	2016	September 2021
Thought Machine*	2014	Draper Esprit VCT	2020	Autumn 2021 (expected)

*Thought Machine is reportedly expected to raise around £150m at a valuation of more than $1bn. A public announcement is expected in Autumn 2021.

BOUGHT BY MANY: ONE OF EUROPE'S LEADING 'INSURTECHS'

Co-founded by Stephen Mendel and Guy Farley in 2012, Bought By Many started as an insurance broker. It grouped people with similar insurance needs and negotiated better prices and a more tailored cover for them with insurance companies.

In 2017, after listening to its customers' needs, Bought By Many launched its own disruptive brand of pet insurance, which proceeded to win a number of awards, including Best Pet Insurance Provider of the Year at the 2020 Insurance Choice Awards. Today, the business insures over half a million pets globally, including in the US, where it launched in 2021.

Bought By Many experienced significant growth – it more than doubled gross written premiums annually to £220m in 2020. In June 2021, Swedish investor EQT led a $350m funding round which valued the business at $2bn. Octopus Ventures first invested into the business in October 2016 through Octopus Titan VCT, and to date has invested £10.0m. The holding is currently valued at £126.9m as at 30 June 2021.

Powering the UK's growth engine

Unicorns are (and remain, despite the accelerating trend) incredibly rare. However, beneath the headline-grabbing success stories, there is a wider – and much more striking – trend.

Until recently, most VCTs made fairly pedestrian, perhaps uninspiring investments, from private schools to pubs, wedding venues and renewable energy projects. In 2015, changes to VCT rules forced VCTs to shift their focus to younger companies seeking growth capital.

At the time, some were concerned the rule changes could have a lasting and damaging effect on VCTs. On the contrary, these rule changes have been the making of VCTs as a credible and hugely attractive asset class. Look at a VCT portfolio today and you will find some of the most interesting and exciting companies around, many of which are growing at a double- or triple-digit rate.

An example is data and analytics software company Quantexa. Its flagship product, a contextual decision intelligence (CDI) platform, gathers data across billions of external and internal systems to present a single view and help businesses make better decisions. Today, Quantexa's technology is used in more than 70 countries by blue-chip banks (including seven of the top ten banks in the UK and Australia), insurers and government organisations.

Quantexa reported revenues of £5m in its first full year, to March 2018; it more than trebled this to £17.5m in the year to March 2020. The Albion VCTs first invested in Quantexa just a year after it was founded, in 2017 at a valuation of £11.2m. In its most recent funding round, in July 2021, Quantexa reportedly raised $154m at a valuation of $800m-$900m.

Another example is Quit Genius, which has developed the world's first digital clinic delivering comprehensive medication-assisted treatment for addictions to tobacco, alcohol and opioids. Funded in 2017, the business grew revenues tenfold over the last 12 months and is now partnered with 55 employer and health plans covering 2.1 million lives.

Octopus Titan VCT invested £6.5m in Quit Genius in 2020, and Triple Point VCT 2011 invested at the same time. The company subsequently raised a $64m Series B funding round in July 2021. Whilst the valuation was not disclosed, it is estimated to be between €233m and €349m.

Of course, as impressive as these companies and their growth are, they are all very young and still have to prove themselves. Moreover, these are the standout examples. For every unicorn Quantexa and Quit Genius in a VCT portfolio, there will be many more companies that fail or languish. Risk capital is called risk capital for a good reason.

The few that do succeed, however, can deliver impressive returns. And VCTs are one of the few avenues for investors to participate in that. High-growth companies such as those mentioned tend to be woefully underrepresented in the UK main market, as measured by its 350 largest constituents by market capitalisation.

We recently looked at the growth rate of companies within ten of the top VCTs, and compared it with the growth rate of the 350 largest UK listed companies:

- 46% of the invested assets in these VCTs had grown by 25% year on year on average. By comparison, just 4.6% of the largest 350 companies achieved this;

- 22.5% of the invested assets in these VCTs had grown revenues by over 50%, compared with just 2% for the largest 350 companies.

The picture that emerges is clear: VCTs increasingly are the UK's high-growth asset class.

Record investor demand

The appeal of being able to back rising stars is one of the main factors behind investor soaring demand for VCTs. The total invested in VCTs has gone from £354m in 2010 to an impressive £685m in the 2020/21 tax year, even though we were in the depth of a pandemic.

Historic VCT fundraising

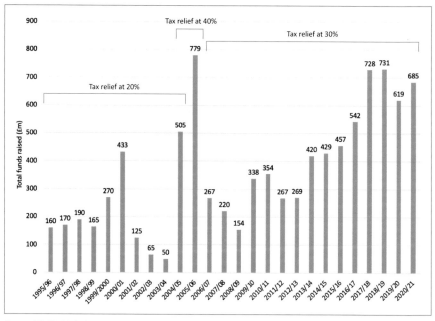

Source: AIC, Wealth Club.

The 2021/22 VCT season already looks promising, despite having only just started:

- Over £111.4m has been invested already – almost 4.7x the total raised at the same time last year (23 September 2021);

- Two VCT offers have already closed – Amati AIM VCT was fully subscribed in 4.5 working days, having raised £40m; so are the Octopus AIM VCTs, having also raised £40m in three weeks.

If this trend continues, funds raised this year could easily reach £800m, potentially making 2021/22 the biggest year in VCTs' history, even higher than the current record of £779m raised in 2005/06, when tax relief was temporarily raised from 30% to 40%.

Behind the appeal of VCTs

Tax increases – both those already announced and those expected – are likely to provide a further boost to the already buoyant demand for VCTs. If you are a high earner, options to invest tax efficiently are increasingly limited. Pensions have been restricted for years, and the recent freeze of the lifetime allowance will be the nail in the coffin for many wealthier investors.

The increase in dividend tax is also likely to mean more investors will turn to VCTs – the last remaining bastion of tax efficiency and an obvious next step once you have put money in your ISA and pension (those who still can). When investing in VCTs, not only do you get up to 30% income tax relief on a generous allowance of £200,000 a year, but also returns (which are paid through dividends) are tax free.

The fact that VCT dividends are tax free could be hugely valuable, even more so once the new rate of dividend tax becomes effective in April 2022. If a VCT pays a 5% dividend, you get 5p in your hand for every £1 invested. To match that outside of tax wrapper, you would need to get a dividend of 7.55% if you are a higher-rate taxpayer or 8.24% if you are a top-rate taxpayer.

In addition to delivering valuable tax savings, VCTs have also generated strong returns for investors. In the past ten years to June 2021, the ten largest VCT managers have on average more than doubled investor money on an NAV total return basis (NAV and cumulative dividends paid in the period).

Over the same period, AIM VCTs have more than trebled investor money on average, boosted by the fact that AIM has emerged as the real winner of the pandemic. The junior market had a strong 2020, outperforming the broader UK equity market by 31.6%, and its record this year has continued to be good. Of course, as any investor will know, past performance is not a guide to the future.

This probably goes some way to explain the increased popularity of AIM VCTs this year. The offers that have opened – from Amati, Octopus and Hargreave Hale – have all raised more money and more quickly than ever before. If you believe that AIM is going to continue to perform well, investing through a VCT makes sense, as – thanks to the tax relief – you are in effect buying companies at a 30% discount.

Ten-year performance: ten largest generalist VCT managers

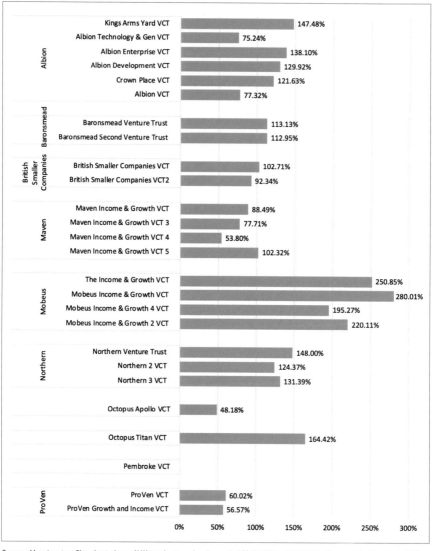

Source: Morningstar. The chart shows NAV total return for the period 30/06/2011 to 30/06/2021. Please note, Pembroke VCT launched in 2013 and therefore does not yet have a ten-year track record.

Ten-year performance: AIM VCT managers

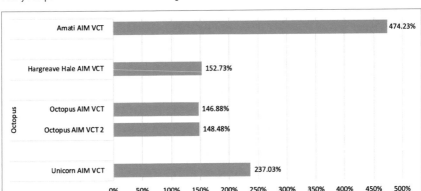

Source: Morningstar. The chart shows NAV total return for the period 30/09/2010 to 30/09/2020.

Who invests in VCTs?

Contrary to popular belief, there is no such a thing as a typical VCT investor. The average age of our clients who invest in VCTs is 59, while the youngest is 19 and the eldest 101; overall, 81% are male and 19% female. They invest £34,279 on average across a number of VCTs per tax year. The average amount invested in each VCT is £12,150.

We do not record occupation, but those we speak to who invest are typically professionals such as doctors, lawyers, higher earners in the City or business owners, but also head teachers and civil servants. They tend to have investments elsewhere (such as ISAs, pensions and property) to which VCTs add diversification, and they tend to have been affected by tax rises and pension restrictions.

For someone without sufficient assets or earnings or who lacks a clear understanding of the risks, VCTs are unlikely to be a suitable investment. Young, small companies are more likely to fail than older and larger ones. If something goes badly wrong for a small company, it is much harder for it to recover than it is for a large and well-established company. They are also a lot more illiquid, as are the VCTs themselves, meaning it may be difficult to buy and sell the shares.

However, if you have sufficient assets elsewhere, you have already used your pension and ISA allowances, and you have a certain level of financial sophistication, then VCTs may well be a worthwhile option for you to consider. As a general rule of thumb, VCTs should be no more than 10% of your total portfolio. Typically your money will be spread over 30 to 100 companies, which provides an important degree of underlying diversification.

Secondly, just as professional venture capital investors find it difficult to know in advance which start-up businesses are going to become their biggest successes, so investors in VCTs should consider spreading their capital across more than one trust. We always suggest you spread your annual investment over a number of VCTs, preferably with different investment strategies, to further diversify your risk. Don't forget you also have a 30% cushion in the form of tax relief should things go wrong.

A final thought

VCT season started early this year, and so far investor demand appears buoyant. Two offers have come and gone – around ten are open at the time of writing, and we expect around 25 to raise funds this tax year. But, of course, VCTs have a finite capacity. An offer launches with a specific amount to raise, and once that has been raised then the offer closes. And when a VCT is popular, it does fill quickly, even if it is raising significant amounts. This is a sign of the continued popularity of established VCTs, but also a reminder to investors that if they spot a VCT they like, they should act quickly whilst there is still capacity.

ALEX DAVIES *is the founder and CEO of Wealth Club, the largest broker of VCTs and tax-efficient investments for experienced investors.*

ALL CHANGE, PLEASE

JAMES CARTHEW *explores when and why boards choose to change their fund manager.*

I N MY OPINION, one of the greatest strengths of the investment companies industry is its system of governance. Boards of independent directors work for and on behalf of investors. Boards' ability to fire underperforming managers helps to keep these managers on their toes. The option of calling time on an outdated investment objective helps ensure that investors are not trapped in dead-end investments.

The process of evolution is more red in tooth and claw in the world of investment companies than it is in the open-ended fund industry, where the fund management companies call all the shots and have no great incentive to kill a poorly performing fund as long as the fees continue to roll in. It is, I believe, one reason why, on average, investment companies outperform their open-ended rivals.

The North American example

Take, for example, the large-cap North American sector, half of which has undergone some fundamental reshaping since launch. J.P. Morgan American (ticker: JAM) opted to switch managers internally within J.P. Morgan Asset Management. Jonathan Simon and Tim Parton replaced Garrett Fish (after 15 years) in 2019 as the trust switched to a higher-conviction approach in what, so far, has been a successful search for added value.

After 95 years, American Trust became Edinburgh US Tracker in 1997 when the mania for index-tracking funds was building. By 2012, the ETF industry had become so sophisticated and large that Edinburgh US Tracker looked like an anachronism. Many investors' focus had shifted to income, and North American Income Trust (ticker: NAIT) was born. More recently, BlackRock North American Income, launched in 2012, opted to become BlackRock Sustainable American Income (ticker: BRSA).

Triggers for a big decision

If you are a director of an underperforming trust, sacking the manager is a big decision. It is easier when it is clearly the manager's fault and the problem is demonstrably one of poor stock-picking. However, when the blame can be ascribed to the investment strategy or the investment objective, switching approach is fraught with timing issues.

A common trigger for management changes is the relative performance of value versus growth strategies. This was the subject of my article for last year's handbook. I cited a number of funds that had instituted manager changes in response to poor performance, usually as a consequence of the manager following a value approach. Among them were Baillie Gifford European Growth (ticker: BGEU – formerly European Investment Trust and, before that, F&C European) and Temple Bar (ticker: TMPL).

As we now know, the value style of investing had something of a renaissance from November 2020. The confirmation that various vaccines worked led to a swift rerating of cyclical sectors and companies that had been hit hard by lockdowns. Investors started to take profits on their growth funds.

For a couple of months, Baillie Gifford European Growth moved back to trade at a discount, while Temple Bar, whose board had chosen to stick with a value style, had a phenomenal run. However, concern about new variants of the virus then reversed the situation once again. Boards will be urging investors to look past these short-term gyrations and judge these funds over a much longer period. I would agree with them.

China the second time around

A good sign that something needs to be done is a persistent and wide discount, especially if this does not seem to be resolved by a programme of share buybacks. Shareholders are, clearly, already voting with their feet.

Aberdeen New Thai (ticker: ANW), which has been struggling to beat its benchmark for some time and has not traded anywhere near asset value since 2013, is a good example of this. As a stopgap, in May 2020, a frustrated board introduced a performance-triggered exit opportunity. If, over the three years ending 28 February 2023, the trust failed to beat its benchmark, shareholders would be offered a cash exit as part of a full review of the investment management arrangements.

Things did not get off to a good start. Over the first 12 months, the trust underperformed by 8.9%. By 30 June 2021, the gap had extended to 13.3%.

Aberdeen Standard (which has now rebranded itself as abrdn) was meanwhile also wondering what to do with Aberdeen Emerging Markets (ticker: AEMC). Despite posting reasonable performance – the fund ranks third in its sector over five years – the fund of funds approach it was using was seen as out of date by some investors (personally, I strongly disagree with this). The company was struggling to diversify the company's share register. This latter issue had become a real problem; the trust was in breach of the Listing Rules as its free float was less than 25% of its market capitalisation.

The boards of Aberdeen New Thai and Aberdeen Emerging Markets have now agreed to a proposal from abrdn to merge the funds and switch to a strategy of making direct investments in Chinese equities. Investors holding 73% of Aberdeen New Thai's shares were consulted before the announcement was made. Overall, investors holding almost 79% of Aberdeen Emerging Market's shares have now said that they are in favour of the proposals.

The idea of switching to a China mandate is probably a good one. It echoes the shift that Witan Pacific decided to make when it dropped its outdated pan-Asian strategy to become Baillie Gifford China. However, the proposal faces a hurdle in that sentiment has shifted dramatically against the Chinese market since the idea was mooted. Each of the three existing China-focused funds is now trading at a discount.

Those who are not keen on the idea have been offered 15% tender offers for each trust at a 2% discount to realisable value. In this case, limiting the size of the tender offers to 15% may run the risk that there will still be frustrated sellers once the tender offer has been implemented. Shareholders may also object to being forced to choose between a 2% haircut on NAV or a very different investment from the one they backed originally.

Is ESG still a differentiator?

ESG (environmental, social and governance) driven investing has become increasingly popular over the past year. Many boards and managers have seen this as an opportunity to rebrand existing funds or launch new ones. What was cutting-edge not so long ago has quickly become mainstream, however, and attempts to jump on this feelgood bandwagon have faltered.

Liontrust's decision to pull the IPO of the Liontrust ESG Trust, intended to complement its existing very successful range of open-ended ESG funds, was a good example of this. Despite attracting nearly £100m in demand, the response was deemed insufficient to warrant proceeding. Similarly, the decision by the board of Keystone (ticker: KPC) to adopt a Baillie Gifford managed positive-change approach was initially welcomed enthusiastically, but it was not long before the trust was back trading on a discount.

We also have the saga of Acorn Income Fund (ticker: AIF). As a split capital trust, with two distinct portfolios run by separate management houses and as a constituent of an AIC sector with just two members, Acorn Income Fund is hard for some investors to get their heads around. The year 2020 was a difficult one for the trust and, with the maturity of its zero dividend preference shares looming, the board opted to launch a strategic review.

The announcement of a strategic review or a beauty parade usually triggers a feeding frenzy, as managers see a chance to pick up a contract for minimal upfront expense. It took just three-and-a-half weeks for Acorn Income's board to decide to award the management contract to BMO Global Asset Management, with a proposal that the company become BMO Global Sustainable Equity Income Fund.

This looked like a done deal, but it turned out that shareholders were not in agreement. In August, the board reversed its decision, much to BMO's annoyance, and at the start of September it was announced that investors would get to choose between cash or a rollover into an open-ended fund run by the existing managers of Acorn's UK small-cap portfolio.

The need to talk

Boards can come up with great ideas, but if shareholders are not prepared to back them then these proposals can create worse problems than those they were designed to address. Canvassing opinion is important, therefore, as the board of Acorn Income will now know.

However, the danger in this kind of approach is that it is the largest shareholders who get to call the shots and their views may not necessarily tally with those of smaller investors. For example, a number of large investors have been pushing for the creation of ever-larger funds on liquidity grounds. However, provided that ongoing charges ratios are reasonable, small and nimble trusts can still offer attractive returns.

A succession of investors – institutional managers, pension funds and now large wealth managers – have insisted that funds need to be big to be relevant. However, there comes a point when the scale of an investing firm supports the creation of direct mandates. The institutional managers and pension funds have largely turned their backs on the sector since, and the largest wealth managers might not be far behind.

Some recent manager changes

TRUST	DATE EFFECTIVE	NEW MANAGER(S)	CURRENT/ PREVIOUS MANAGER(S)	REASON
Scottish Mortgage	April 2022	Tom Slater + Lawrence Burns	James Anderson + Tom Slater	James Anderson retiring April 2022
Scottish Investment Trust	To be decided	To be decided	Alasdair McKinnon	Merging into J.P. Morgan Global Growth and Income
Keystone	February 2021	Kate Fox + Lee Qian	James Goldstone	Baillie Gifford given the mandate
Invesco Perpetual Select	April 2021	Ciaran Mallon + James Goldstone	James Goldstone	Merger of two Invesco trusts
Troy Income and Growth	December 2021	Hugo Ure + Blake Hutchins	Francis Brooke	Francis Brooke steps back from fund management
Gresham House Strategic	May 2021	Richard Staveley	Tony Dalwood + Laurence Hulse	Mandate given to Harwood Capital
Pacific Horizon	June 2021	Roderick Snell	Ewan Markson Brown	Ewan Markson Brown leaves Baillie Gifford
Jupiter Green	January 2021	Jon Wallace	Charlie Thomas	Charlie Thomas has left Jupiter
International Biotechnology	March 2021	Ailsa Craid + Marek Poszepczynski	Carl Harald Jansen + team	Carl Harald Janson steps back from fund management
Fidelity Emerging Markets	October 2021	Nick Price + Chris Tennant	Andrew Elder	Mandate moved from Genesis to Fidelity
Schroder UK Public Private	September 2021	Tim Creed + Roger Doig	Tim Creed + Ben Wicks	Ben Wicks moves to other funds
UK Commercial Property	September 2021	Kerri Hunter	Will Fulton	Leave of absence on medical grounds
abrdn China Investment Company	January 2022	Nicholas Yeo + Elizabeth Kwik	Andrew Lister + team	Merger with Aberdeen New Thai

Source: Numis Securities, Q3 review

The problem of notice periods

One of the complicating factors in trying to change a manager can be excessive notice periods. It is right, given the considerable cost in time and money of setting up a new investment company, that initial notice periods on management contracts help protect them from the financial impact of being dismissed early in a fund's life. However, thereafter notice periods should only be as long as is necessary to give the board a chance to recruit a suitable replacement.

In April 2020 I was shocked to see the board of Target Healthcare REIT (ticker: THRL) hand its manager a minimum three-year term on their contract and a rolling two-year notice period after the end of the first year. The manager did not give up anything in return.

I don't have a problem with the way in which Target Healthcare REIT is managed or a desire to see the manager changed. However, if relations with any manager deteriorate to the point where a board decides they should be sacked, there is a good chance that such an excessive notice period will end up rewarding them for failure.

Boards don't always get it right

Sometimes boards find that shareholders are more loyal to investment managers than they had first thought. The dust-up in 2018 between the board of Invesco Perpetual Enhanced Income and its managers illustrates that. The board had felt that the management fees were too high. The managers quit, blaming a breakdown of their relationship with the board and concerns about governance.

The board went in search of alternatives, drawing up a shortlist of four. A small group of shareholders, including Invesco Perpetual, got together to try to oust the board and get the old managers reappointed. Paul Read and Paul Causer were reinstated as managers with Invesco Perpetual on a reduced fee structure. All well and good, perhaps, but just two years later the two managers stepped down, and a year after that the trust was absorbed by City Merchants High Yield, becoming Invesco Bond Income Plus (ticker: BIPS).

A failure to get the strategy or manager decision right can be costly. One sorry tale is that of British Assets, which became BlackRock Income Strategies in 2015 and Aberdeen Diversified Income & Growth (ticker: ADIG) in 2017. It tweaked its investment approach once again earlier this year. Despite a merger with Aberdeen UK Tracker, the fund has shrunk since its British Assets days. The trust has not fulfilled its various objectives for many years and is still trading on a wide discount.

More takeovers to come?

Sometimes directors find that change is forced upon them. Takeover bids for investment companies, especially successful ones, are very rare. The absorption of MedicX by Primary Healthcare Properties (ticker: PHP) in 2019 and the 2018 bid by a financial consortium for John Laing Infrastructure are examples of successful takeovers in the sector, but they are the exception rather than the rule.

However, such takeovers become more common as the proportion of the sector in alternative assets continues to rise. Unlike traditional equity trusts, which can be priced to market every day, infrequent NAVs, different views on valuation methodologies and more subjective valuations can create the scope for significant mispricing of alternatives. If the market fails to price the shares correctly, it opens the way for a predator.

One of 2021's surprises was a bid for GCP Student Living (ticker: DIGS). Scape Living, which was funded by APG, a pre-existing shareholder in GCP Student Living, and iQ, funded by Blackstone, made a joint bid for the company at 213p per share. This valued the company at £969m. The bid price was a 30.7% premium to the share price and a 19.1% premium to its end-of-March NAV of 179p. The bidders reasoned that the market was not correctly factoring in the post-covid recovery in demand for student accommodation.

Even as I write this, there are more manager changes under way. The board of Scottish Investment Trust (ticker: SCIN) lit the blue touchpaper on 2 June 2021 with an announcement that it was undertaking a review of its future investment management arrangements. It has appointed an external consultant, Stanhope Consulting, to assist it in the review. In October we learnt that it is to be merged into J.P. Morgan Global Growth and Income, ending its 135-year history as an independent company.

JAMES CARTHEW is a director at Marten & Co, which provides research and corporate advice for the investment trust sector and manages the QuotedData website (quoteddata.com).

BIG BEAST BATTLE

JONATHAN DAVIS *looks behind the scenes at the events that led the board of Genesis Emerging Markets to change its manager and give Fidelity the mandate to run one of the three big trusts in global emerging markets.*

C HANGE IS A constant theme in the investment trust world, but many observers were nevertheless surprised when it emerged this summer that the board of Genesis Emerging Markets (ticker: GSS) was going to change the manager of its £1.2bn trust. In September the board announced that the mandate would be transferred to Fidelity International, ending a longstanding association with Genesis Investment Management that dated all the way back to the trust's 1989 launch. The change was approved by shareholders and implemented in October 2021. The ticker of the trust has changed from GSS to FEML.

Although manager changes happen regularly, it is rare among the still somewhat exclusive club of trusts with more than £1bn in assets. Most trusts that ditch their manager do so after a sustained run of poor performance that puts question marks against the trust's viability and frequently involves the shares moving out to a hefty discount and the trust shrinking. What raised eyebrows in this case was that the performance of the trust, while lagging behind some of its larger peers in the last five years, was nothing like as obviously poor as is typically found when directors pull the trigger and move the management of a trust elsewhere.

As Genesis was quick to point out, over its 30-year tenure as manager of the trust shareholders enjoyed an annualised total return of just under 12% per annum, which is more or less in line with the return of the emerging markets index over that period. Over ten years it has actually outperformed Templeton Emerging Markets, one of its competitors in the £1bn assets pool – and was not that far behind the other big beast in the sector, J.P. Morgan Emerging Markets.

These three large trusts have been competing for shareholders' money and attention for more than three decades. Genesis launched its emerging markets trust in 1989, only a few weeks after Templeton had become the first fund management group to launch a generalist global emerging markets investment trust, run by the high-profile figure of Mark Mobius. J.P. Morgan came out with its own rival emerging markets trust two years later, in 1991.

Grievance or fair dos?

Over the past five years the share price performance of the Genesis trust has lagged behind the index by a larger margin than its two rivals. Given such a long association with the trust it had launched and given its name to, not to mention its track record and reputation as an established manager of emerging markets funds, Genesis might appear to have cause to be aggrieved at not being given more time to bring performance round. While the shares traded at a discount of around 10%, the rating was not blatantly out of line with the remainder of the sector.

Dig a little deeper, though, and it becomes easier to understand how it was that what on the surface seemed such a surprising development could come to pass. One clue lies in the unusually concentrated shareholder register, with two institutional shareholders, City of London Investment Management and the Strathclyde Pension Fund, holding 50% of the shares between them. Three other professional investment firms – Lazards (12%), Wells Capital Management (10%) and 1607 Capital (3%) – held a further 25%, meaning that 75% of the equity was in just five sets of hands.

While private investors are an increasing presence on the share registers of many equity investment trusts, they have not historically been a factor in this trust. Having a pension fund with such a large shareholding might have been common 20 years ago, but most pension funds have moved on from using investment trusts as building blocks in their portfolios. Strathclyde's holding certainly appears anomalous in today's market, not least because it has an equally large shareholding in an open-ended emerging markets fund that Genesis also runs.

Behind the scenes, and with the shares trading at a discount, it appears the board of the investment trust became aware that at least one of its larger shareholders, believed to be the pension fund, was keen to see greater liquidity in the market for the trust's shares, with the apparent intention of reducing its shareholding over time. This resulted in the board first authorising a tender offer for 10% of the shares in 2018, and then, after consultation with advisers and other shareholders, committing to make a tender offer in which shareholders could sell their holding for cash up to a limit of 25% of the issued share capital if performance did not improve. This second tender offer was scheduled for 2021.

The marketing miss

With that deadline already in its mind, the board came to the conclusion in 2019 that it needed to do more to broaden its share register, and in particular to make efforts, as many other trusts have done, to build up its following among wealth managers and private investors. With more than £1bn of assets, the trust was not one of those that could be considered too small to be viable. However, with its larger shareholders looking to reduce their holdings, there was a clear danger that it would start to shrink if continued lacklustre performance and its low profile led to repeated calls for tender offers or other liquidity initiatives.

The challenge that the board gave to Genesis was therefore both to reverse the relatively poor recent performance and to come up with a plan to increase demand for the company's shares through effective marketing to other types of investor. Some steps, such as improving the website and communication materials, and appointing a second corporate broker to assist in finding new shareholders, were taken during 2020, but performance – always the most important factor in driving fund flows – continued to disappoint. It was at this point, with the tender trigger of 30 June 2021 only months away, that the board lost patience with Genesis' efforts and decided to invite other fund management groups to pitch for the mandate.

Of more than 20 firms that expressed an interest, five were invited to make a final pitch to take on the trust, while Genesis, as is usual in such cases, was given the chance to make its case for retaining the business. The board, which is chaired by Helene Ploix, a former executive director at both the World Bank and the IMF, has said that Genesis was a genuine contender to keep running the trust it had first created 32 years earlier. The board was not in any way simply going through the motions by including Genesis on the final shortlist.

Be that as it may, once the final pitching process was complete, the board announced its decision to award the mandate to Fidelity, with shareholder approval for the change being voted through at an extraordinary general meeting on 1 October. The 25% tender offer will go ahead at a 2% discount to net asset value and is likely to be fully taken up. All five of the large existing shareholders voted in favour of the change, although one shareholder, believed to be Strathclyde Pension Fund, voted against one of the resolutions concerning the new investment policy proposed by Fidelity.

Genesis publicly expressed its disappointment at losing the business, and also pressed the shareholders unsuccessfully to vote for the tender offer to be made at NAV, rather than at a 2% discount. What is clear, however, given the weight of votes in the control of the five largest shareholders, is that whatever the case that Genesis might have made to retain the business, it was not enough to carry the day with either the board or the shareholders. Since monitoring the performance of the investment manager is one of the most important functions that the board of a trust is paid to carry out, it is rare for shareholders to reject a proposal for change that originates from the directors.

Benefits in the shorter term

It will not become clear for some years whether appointing a new manager for the trust was the right decision or not. For the shareholders, however, there are some tangible benefits already from the new arrangements. The annual management fee has been reduced from 0.9% to 0.6%, and a nine-month fee waiver should cover most of the costs of the transition process. Fidelity has agreed to the board making a tender in five years' time, offering the shareholders further opportunities to exit at close to NAV, if performance continues to underperform the benchmark on a total return basis.

As one of the largest fund management groups in the world, and one that already manages five other investment trusts, Fidelity was an obvious candidate to take on the running of the trust. It has one of the largest specialist emerging markets research teams and a strong performance record. The investment policy that it has proposed for the trust, which includes the use of derivatives that enable fund manager Nicholas Price to go both long and short in individual stocks, and also enables investment in a number of private companies, offers a useful point of differentiation from the other emerging markets investment trusts out there. While the firm manages an open-ended fund with a similar strategy to the one it is proposing for the Genesis trust, that is a SICAV fund and not open to the ordinary UK investor.

Just as importantly, Fidelity has the resources and experience to make a concerted attempt to reach out to new shareholders, including high-net-worth private investors and wealth managers, in a way that Genesis either could not or would not. For technical reasons, the trust will remain a Guernsey-domiciled company, and some of the nuts-and-bolts secretarial and administrative work will be outsourced there. It is the UK customer reach and marketing muscle of Fidelity, as well as its stronger track record, that was clearly an important factor in it winning the business. Because Fidelity Emerging Markets, as it will now be known, employs derivatives as part of its investment strategy – and could be viewed as a more complicated product, not suited to all retail investors – the initial focus will be on attracting more experienced and wealthier investors, as well as intermediaries.

Lessons for the sector

Ironically perhaps, until very recently Genesis has been extremely successful in growing its specialist emerging markets franchise in the highly competitive institutional market, to the extent that its assets under management at their peak, nearly $30bn in total, were some 20 times the size of the investment trust. It appears to have had no obvious incentive to invest in building a private investor and wealth manager following for what had become an increasingly less important part of its overall business. Did it take its eye off the ball as far as the investment trust was concerned? It is impossible for an outsider to know the answer to that one with any confidence, but it certainly looks probable, given the low profile that Genesis maintained for many years.

For Fidelity meanwhile, this win fulfils an ambition to expand further its investment trust range, which already includes UK, European, China, Japan and Asian funds. According to Alex Denny, the head of investment trusts at the firm, it has aspirations in due course to offer its client base an equity income trust and maybe a global dividend trust as well. The obvious gap in its range is a North American or US equity trust, but launching new trusts from scratch these days is not easy, so its focus is likely to be on pursuing more mandate wins from existing trusts that are facing issues like those that brought the board of Genesis Emerging Markets to its point of decision.

What general lessons might be learnt from this episode? One, obviously, is that boards do seem to be taking a more active approach to pursuing manager change, even in cases where loyalty to the founding or incumbent manager might once have carried more weight. A second factor is that it is becoming increasingly rare for institutional investors such as pension funds and insurance companies to remain on the share registers of general equity investment trusts, since they can now readily arrange their own investment solutions directly these days. Adapting to that change requires boards to take a more active role in marketing and promoting their trusts to new sources of demand.

For fund management groups, meanwhile, with new equity IPOs so difficult to launch, there is an obvious appeal in going out to look for existing mandates that are up for grabs. The challenge is to come up with an investment approach that is not just more of the same but ideally can be readily differentiated from other trusts already out there – and can also bring tangible benefits such as fee reductions and potential tender offers as an incentive for existing shareholders to support the change.

FAREWELL, OLD FRIEND

JONATHAN DAVIS *explains how and why the venerable Scottish Investment Trust will reach the end of the line after 135 years.*

T HERE IS NO doubt that the boards of investment trusts, which many once regarded as cosy clubs of old business chums, now generally behave in the disciplined and independent way that company law and good practice require. The hardest challenge that boards face, as I know from experience, is deciding when to call time on a management team that for whatever reason have not delivered the results that they were hoping or expecting to see. The last few years have seen several cases of directors instituting a 'strategic review' of the investment management arrangements of an underperforming trust.

The usual result is a beauty parade where rival management groups make a pitch to take on the business of managing a trust's investments. Almost invariably the result is the appointment of a new manager. As James Carthew describes elsewhere in the handbook, there have been several high-profile cases of such changes in the last two years, some of which have resulted in the trust adopting a wholly new investment approach, while others continue with the same approach but with a new set of hands at the wheel.

It was no surprise therefore to learn earlier this year that a strategic review was under way at the Scottish Investment Trust, another north-of-the-border investment company whose roots go back all the way to the 19th century. The trust, which has net assets of just under £600m,* was established in 1887 and is unusual in that it is one of only a handful of investment trusts that remain self-managed entities, meaning that both the investment management team and many of the administrative functions are carried out directly by the trust itself rather than by external appointees. Whereas most investment trusts have a board of directors but no employees, outsourcing the management of the portfolio, marketing and administration to third parties, the Scottish Investment Trust (ticker: SCIN) has an in-house team of nine employees (with functions supported by external providers).

---

* £590m as at 31 August 2021

Underwhelming recent performance

Unfortunately, the track record of the trust has been disappointing in recent years. The NAV total return over five and ten years has come in well below its peer group in the global investment trust sector. At the time of writing in late October 2021, the cumulative total return to shareholders was just 24% over five years and 141% over ten years. In the context of a global bull market, which has seen many trusts in the global peer group return between three and five times as much, the figures make for difficult reading. The shareholder returns might have been worse if the board had not intervened to buy back shares with the aim of keeping the discount below its 9% discount target.

To its credit, the trust has continued to pay out an increased dividend every year for the last 37 years. That and the discount control policy may have preserved the loyalty of many shareholders, but the board clearly felt that it had no choice but to review the incumbent team's performance when it announced the strategic review in June this year. In October the results were announced, with the board proposing to merge the trust with J.P. Morgan Global Growth and Income (ticker: JGGI). The transaction, if approved by shareholders, which it seems certain to be, will create a much bigger vehicle with more than £1bn in assets and lower management fees for both sets of shareholders.

Effectively this amounts to a takeover and marks the end of the line for the Scottish Investment Trust. By a strange conicidence the J.P. Morgan trust also dates its origins back to the same year, 1887. It was formed as the British Steamship Investment Company, with a mandate to invest in steamships, but amended its policy in the 1920s to become a generalist investment trust.

The intriguing thing about this particular case of potential corporate change is that there is no mystery about the reasons for the trust's relatively poor performance. Ever since his appointment as manager seven years ago, Alasdair McKinnon has stuck consistently to the contrarian deep-value style of investment that the board approved when he was promoted to the job in 2015. The problem for him and for the trust is that this style of investing has been persistently out of favour for the last ten years. It has been an era of low interest rates and loose monetary policy which has catapulted growth-oriented trusts, the polar opposite in style terms, to the top of the performance tables, and left deep-value investors of his ilk lagging way behind.

In the last interim report the trust published, covering the period to 30 June 2021, McKinnon struck a defiant tone: "Although it has been well documented that the way we invest has been unfashionable in recent years, we believe we are well positioned for a sustained change in market leadership which may already be under way. We have explicitly set out to invest in the unpopular areas of the market. Our view is that this is where we will find the best balance of risk and reward for our investments. Just as importantly, we aim to avoid the losses that accrue to investors who are late to join the party in the popular areas of the market."

Sticking to his guns

In other words, McKinnon and his team were determined to stick to their guns. While nobody will dispute the board's right to take action, given the trust's performance record, the reality is that styles in investment do come and go in cycles. Value investing did particularly well between 2000 and 2007, for example, while growth investors lagged behind. That trend reversed after the global financial crisis and the disparity between growth and value has reached exceptional and extreme levels. The challenge for the board is that history has many examples of managers with a contrarian approach being fired just as their style of investment was about to come back into favour. That could well be the case now, with many in the markets speculating that after a decade in the doghouse, and facing a period of higher interest rates, value investing may be on the verge of making a strong comeback.

There were signs of just that happening in the first few months of 2021, when Scottish Investment Trust put in a reasonable spurt of outperformance against the market, only for that to reverse over the course of the summer. While he acknowledged the risk of losing his job, McKinnon said he had no hesitation in holding to his last, because his contrarian approach is one that fits both with his professional experience and his personality and temperament. While he recognised the reality of the situation, he could no more change it than change his identity.

"I fully support the review that is going on," he told me when we spoke as the review rolled forward, emphasising that he had no idea what the outcome would be. "I am an employee of the company, and the most important thing is that the right thing for the company comes out of it. It is obviously a good idea to step back and look at where we are." As far as his own money is concerned, however, he has no intention of changing his investment philosophy.

He remained convinced that it would be possible for the trust to regain its lead over its peer group and the index by sticking with the contrarian approach. "I'm certain that relative lagging can be recouped. I can't say exactly the time frame over which that will happen. Quite frankly, every day something surprises me how bullish the market is about concepts that look flaky to me." The board's choice of future options boiled down in essence to a decision whether the poor performance of the trust was purely the result of the style or at least in part to the way that it has been implemented.

Markets can turn on a sixpence

In defence of his position, McKinnon argued, perfectly correctly, that it is striking how quickly markets can change direction. Things that seemed improbable ten years ago often turn out to happen, while what seemed certain back then singularly fails to take place. In 2007 investors were raving about the financial sector and the 'commodity supercycle'; those hopes soon turned to dust. Back in 2009 few if any predicted that the US stock market, led by just a handful of disruptive internet companies, would produce such staggering returns over the subsequent 12 years.

A look at the detail of the trust's portfolio on the eve of the announcement shows how distinctive its approach had become. The top ten largest holdings included three mining companies, two big banks, two big oil companies and BT, all of which have useful dividend yields but have been largely shunned by investors in recent years. North American stocks account for little more than half the trust's weighting in the world equity market index. The big tech stocks are nowhere to be seen.

McKinnon also makes the point that there are specific issues facing self-managed trusts that do not always arise in quite the same way for trusts managed by third-party investment managers. Having only one fund in the stable, if trusts like the Scottish are to make a mark in a sector with a number of very strong competitors they must work hard to develop and sustain a clear identity. As with any business, that often suggests the adoption of a niche and markedly differentiated strategy.

In the case of the Scottish, it pointed to emphasising and promoting the contrarian style that it has consistently adopted. According to McKinnon, the trust has effectively positioned itself that way, with investors noting and reacting positively to its "ugly ducklings" mantra, one of three simple phrases it uses in its marketing literature to describe its stock-picking style. "Our portfolio is unlike any benchmark or index, and we fully expect to have differentiated performance. Our approach will not always be in fashion, but we believe it delivers above-average performance over the long term, by which we mean at least five years."

It is unfortunate perhaps that the trust has had to face such a powerful competitor in the shape of Scottish Mortgage, which is the standout performer of the past decade not just in the global sector but in the whole of the investment trust world. Type "Scottish investment trust" into Google, says McKinnon, and the first name that used to appear would not be the eponymous company of that name but the Baillie Gifford trust. The marketing effort since has helped to redress that balance somewhat. Nonetheless, despite the prominent role that Scotland's banks played in the global financial crisis, he believes that having "Scottish" in the name still resonates with investors, drawing on the reputation and long tradition of investment expertise associated with Edinburgh and other centres.

Over its long history, Scottish has accumulated more than two-and-a-half years of reserves to draw on and, by its nature, the deep-value contrarian investing style that McKinnon employs is drawn to companies with higher-than-average dividends and would be expected to deliver above-average dividend growth over the course of the market cycle. Unfortunately the board's decision to authorise a step change increase in the dividend five years ago, after discussion with the managers, has failed to produce a material impact on the trust's rating, however.

Echoes from the past

The irony – and maybe bad fortune – for McKinnon is that he started his career in fund management in the 1990s, specialising in small-cap stocks for a small firm based in Liverpool, and witnessed first-hand the extraordinary boom and bust period of the TMT bubble in 1999–2000, during which he found himself officially working as the internet analyst.

It was a time, he recalls, when in the end "everyone lost their mind – and probably in the end I did too. I had been early into a lot of technology stocks and everyone started telling me what a brilliant job I was doing. I started thinking: I'm good at this and maybe there is a supercycle, or even a super, super, supercycle that is never going to end. But of course it didn't last. And then what I found really interesting was how people stopped listening and just sold everything anyway when the stocks started falling. Those were my formative years!"

That experience of the twin imposters, greed and fear, stood McKinnon in better stead a few years later when, having joined the Scottish Investment Trust in 2003, a time when the company had run into difficulties with some of its major shareholders, he was made head of strategy and was quicker than many to recognise, as the banks went on a massive lending spree, that they were all basically over-extended and about to go bust. That in turn helped to propel him to interim and then soon after permanent investment manager of the trust.

The philosophy of contrarianism in investment is based on the belief that what goes around will come around in the end. As things have turned out since then, McKinnon concedes, he would probably have done better to forget his formative year experiences and stick with the out-and-out growth style that briefly served him so well during the TMT bubble. The repeating cycle of boom and bust that characterises equity markets would normally by now have produced more favourable conditions for the Scottish trust's deep value approach.

Yet these have not been normal times: ultra-low interest rates, huge amounts of monetary stimulus and a wave of technological change have proved a fatal combination for value as a style. It means that when the transaction is completed in Q1 2022, the Scottish Investment Trust will have reached the end of the line after 135 years as an independent entity.

Towards a new future

From that point on, assuming the virtually certain shareholder approval, its assets will be managed by J.P. Morgan in line with the strategy of the enlarged Global Growth and Income trust. The annual management fee will reduce to 0.4% and be cut futher if and when it grows to more than £1.5bn in size. In the interim Scottish Investment Trusts' head office will be sold and its employees will depart, without their jobs but their pension benefits preserved.

JGGI has an enhanced dividend strategy, meaning that it commits to distribute 4% of its net assets every year as a dividend, whether or not the payout is covered by earnings. This policy, which is also adopted by a number of other J.P. Morgan trusts, has proved popular with shareholders and means that, with the brief exception of the pandemic sell-off in 2020, the shares in J.P. Morgan Global Growth & Income have consistently traded at a premium for the last five years. Existing shareholders have enjoyed a total return over the past ten years of 310%, well ahead of the Scottish's 141%.

The immediate market reaction to the announcement of the board's decision suggests that the outcome will be positive for both parties. The discount at which the Scottish Investment Trust has narrowed while the J.P. Morgan trust continues to trade around par. This could therefore turn out to be a rare example of a win-win outcome for both sets of shareholders.

Of course we do not know what the outcome would have been if McKinnon and his colleagues had been given more time to see their contrarian approach through to the end. The decision to switch from a value strategy to what is essentially a growth approach may prove to be a case of poor timing if there is an imminent switch around in market style. Boards have made exactly that mistake on occasions in the past.

The positive side of this story is the evidence that the directors have done their duty in keeping the management of a trust under careful scrutiny and being ready to make a change if circumstances demand. Nonetheless, given the cyclicality of markets, these kinds of decisions take years before they can be judged a success or failure, and the case of the Scottish Investment Trust is a useful reminder that there are human and reputational costs involved in the process too.

Comparative performance

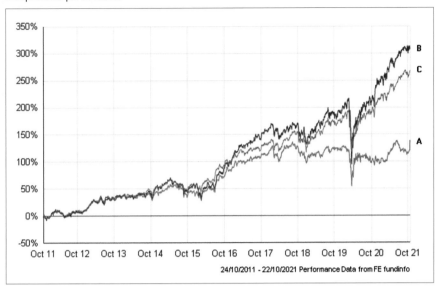

24/10/2011 - 22/10/2021 Performance Data from FE fundinfo

Share price total returns

Key	Chart	Instrument	1m	3m	6m	1y	3y	5y	10y
B	☑	JPMorgan Global Growth & Income plc	0.0%	1.9%	6.0%	30.9%	60.3%	108.3%	310.3%
C	☑	FTSE World	1.4%	3.1%	8.2%	25.5%	52.3%	80.4%	273.2%
A	☑	The Scottish Investment Trust PLC	9.5%	7.3%	6.3%	19.1%	9.2%	24.7%	141.0%

Annualised share price total returns

Key	Chart	Instrument	1y	3y	5y	10y	Start of Data
B	☑	JPMorgan Global Growth & Income plc	30.9%	17.0%	15.8%	15.2%	9.8%
C	☑	FTSE World	25.5%	15.0%	12.5%	14.1%	8.8%
A	☑	The Scottish Investment Trust PLC	19.1%	3.0%	4.5%	9.2%	7.5%

Source: FE Trustnet

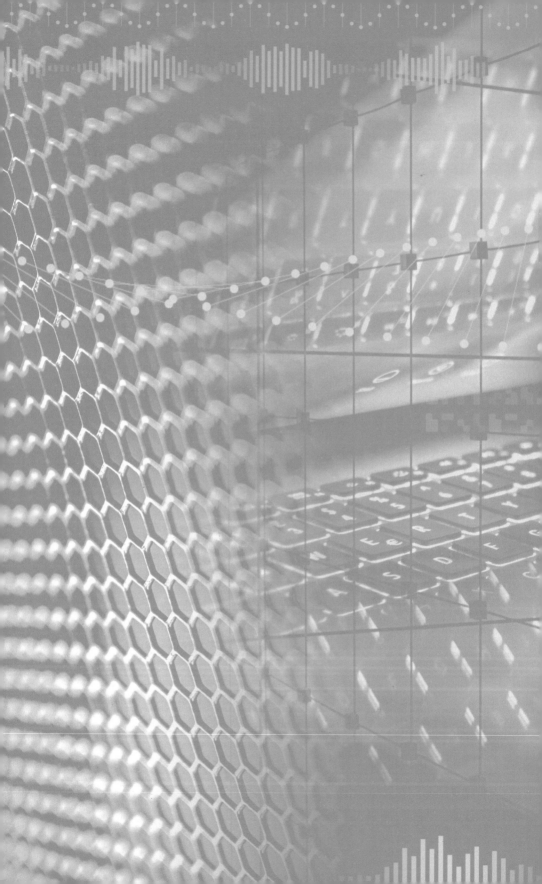

PROFESSIONAL
PERSPECTIVES

WHERE AND WHAT NEXT?

SIMON ELLIOTT, *head of investment trust research at Winterflood Securities, looks back on 2021 and ahead to 2022.*

How well has the trust sector responded to the pandemic in the last 12 months?

There was a moment last year when the investment trust sector stared into the abyss. With markets selling off and forced to close down, the sector saw discounts widen in March 2020 to levels last seen in the global financial crisis. In addition, a number of specialist investment companies were forced to cut or suspend their dividend. Fortunately, this did not last long and a V-shaped recovery was the story of 2020. Indeed, investment trusts ended up as one of the best-performing sectors in the UK equity market last year.

This year has been a different story. While discount levels have remained reasonably narrow by historical standards, the sector lagged the wider UK market in the first half of the year, as more cyclical companies and value investment strategies came to the fore. This provides some insight into the changing composition of the investment trust sector, with high exposure to overseas markets and a bias to growth, particularly amongst global equity funds. No longer can it be said that the trust sector is simply a geared play on the UK market. In general, though, demand for investment companies remains strong and the sector is set for a record year in terms of fundraising.

What has happened to discounts and where might they go from here?

This year has seen the sector average discount range between 2% and 6% so far, while averaging just over 3%. However, a small majority of sub-sectors were derated to a greater or lesser extent during the first nine months of 2021. According to data from Morningstar, of the 28 derated sub-sectors, the largest decline was for biotechnology and healthcare, followed by China/Greater China and insurance/reinsurance. Of the 21 sub-sectors that have been rerated, the largest move was for leasing, followed by property (UK logistics), growth capital and European property.

Discounts invariably reflect demand, and this year has been marked by the recovery of the various commercial property sub-sectors which struggled in 2020, while last year's winners, such as biotechnology and healthcare, global, and technology, have all struggled to varying degrees. This perhaps suggests that it helps to be contrarian when considering investment opportunities in the sector.

Despite the blip seen in 2020, the trend over the last ten years has been for discounts to narrow across the sector, and this can be expected to continue. The key driver for this trend is rising demand from mostly well-informed retail investors who are using platforms to access investment trusts, particularly the larger ones with strong performance records. In addition, trusts that can demonstrate an ability to maintain and grow their dividends are likely to remain in demand in a low-interest-rate environment. However, there is a well-documented correlation between market direction and discounts, in the sense that as markets rise so discounts narrow and vice versa. If we do see a pronounced sell-off in markets, we would expect discount levels to widen.

IPOs have come back – what has been the driving force behind that and what is the outlook?

The first nine months of 2021 saw eight successful IPOs, raising £1.6bn in aggregate. The demand for income remains a key investment theme, particularly from assets that are less correlated to markets overall. Unsurprisingly, a majority of this year's launches have high dividend targets when fully invested and provide exposure to specialist, less liquid asset classes.

Five can be broadly described as infrastructure plays, albeit they offer a fair amount of variation. The largest so far this year has been for Cordiant Digital Infrastructure, which raised £370m through its IPO. Another fund offering similar exposure, Digital 9 Infrastructure, raised £185m through its IPO and has already raised £450m in two further placings. The other three new infrastructure funds are energy plays: VH Global Sustainable Energy Opportunities (£243m), HydrogenOne Capital Growth (£107m) and Aquila Energy Efficiency Trust (£100m).

The year saw the launch of another specialist leasing investment company, Taylor Maritime Investments (£180m), which is invested in the shipping industry. While all six of the aforementioned funds have a substantial target yield when fully invested, the sector has also seen two launches that are not income plays: Seraphim Space Investment Trust (£178m), which provides growth capital to private companies in the space sector, and Literacy Capital (£96m), which was a securitisation of an existing fund that invests in private companies.

Why did the trusts that failed to get off the ground not succeed?

While eight IPOs have got away, a number of others failed to gain the sufficient support required to launch. This includes several high-profile funds such as The UK Residential REIT, Liontrust ESG Trust, Responsible Housing REIT and Blackfinch

Renewable European Income Trust. This underlines the difficulty in launching new investment companies and reflects the investment community's strong preference for supporting additional fundraising for existing funds that have proven track records.

Launching a new investment trust requires substantial support from a dwindling pool of institutional investors, including the larger wealth managers, who alone have the resources to ensure critical mass on day one. Even in benign market conditions, this seems unlikely to change and it would not be surprising to see the sector respond by looking to reposition the mandates of existing investment companies.

Will there be indigestion with all the primary and secondary fundraising that has taken place this year?

There are a number of dangers from over-issuance. In certain instances, the capital raised is not easily deployed, potentially causing cash drag, or is simply misallocated to lower-returning assets, thereby diminishing the returns. There have been examples in the past of investment managers apparently in a hurry to grow their assets under management rather than remain focused on the potential of investment returns.

In addition, we have seen a small number of investment companies flood the market with new paper (issuing new shares) when in favour, only to see demand dry up and discounts widen. It is possible that with the benefit of hindsight we will look back on the fundraising efforts of 2021 and recognise that some investment companies attempted to grow too quickly. In addition, it is guaranteed that not all the strategies will deliver on their target returns, although some will invariably over-deliver. Such is the world of investment.

However, my view is that this year's record levels of fundraising reflect the merits of the investment company structure and its ability to provide investors with exposure to a range of assets classes, including less liquid and specialist areas. The low-interest-rate environment of the last 12 years has led investors to broaden their investment horizons, and investment companies continue to play a huge role in that.

Which sectors have done well and which have disappointed in performance over the last 12 months?

This year is turning into a positive one for private equity funds in share price terms, reflecting the high levels of investment activity in that sub-sector. However, while some names consistently trade on premium ratings, such as HgCapital Trust and Chrysalis Investments, others continue to languish on wide discounts, including Pantheon International, HarbourVest Global Private Equity, Standard Life Private Equity* and ICG Enterprise.

It is also turning into a good year for property funds, both specialists investing in areas such as logistics, and generalists, the majority of which have seen their discounts narrow as valuations have recovered and dividend records been rebuilt. UK small-cap funds have also enjoyed a far better year as their underlying holdings have reported a strong rebound in earnings. In contrast, 2021 is turning into a difficult year for funds investing in biotechnology and healthcare, particularly names such as Syncona and Biotech Growth Trust*, while China has proven a disappointment too.

Manager changes have continued – why? And will they work? Do you expect consolidation to continue?

Manager changes have become an increasing feature of the investment trust sector in recent years. In my opinion, this reflects the willingness of independent boards to consider alternative investment houses or even strategies. In addition, it is partly a function of the headwinds facing value-orientated managers and their resultant underperformance.

This year has seen Jupiter US Smaller Companies* move to Brown Advisory, Genesis Emerging Markets move to Fidelity, and Gresham House Strategic move to Harwood. In addition, Acorn Income initially proposed a move to BMO and the adoption of a sustainable global equity income mandate, before shareholders indicated that they preferred a cash exit or a rollover into a Unicorn-managed open-ended fund. It is too early to state whether these moves will prove successful, although their discount levels have narrowed in each instance since the original announcement.

It seems a fair bet that the sector will continue to see more consolidation. The wealth management community has made it clear that investment trusts under £100m are too illiquid for them, and many of the larger groups have a preference for those with market caps of £400m or more. Unless there is a decent chance of material growth in a short time frame, smaller investment trusts have an increasingly hard job to justify their continuing existence.

What is the outlook for dividends now? Are some trusts overdistributing by calling on reserves for a second year running?

One of the key advantages of the investment trust structure was in evidence last year. The use of revenue reserves allowed many to preserve their dividend levels or even continue to grow them, despite a dramatic decline in their revenue. A number of mainstream equity income funds have managed to build up reserves equivalent to a full year's dividend, and this was put to good use in most, if not all, circumstances. There were obviously exceptions, and 2020 saw the fall of three AIC 'dividend heroes'.

The year has seen a rebound in dividend levels across global markets, including the UK. Indeed, the rebound in earnings in 2021 has led many corporates to resume

"UNLESS THERE IS A DECENT CHANCE OF MATERIAL GROWTH IN A SHORT TIME FRAME, SMALLER INVESTMENT TRUSTS HAVE AN INCREASINGLY HARD JOB TO JUSTIFY THEIR CONTINUING EXISTENCE."

or raise their dividends. This is clearly good news for investment trusts which are looking to harvest this income, and a number are making positive noises on the direction of travel.

For example, the annual results to 30 June 2021 of City of London Investment Trust showed a 9% increase in revenue per share year-on-year and an increase in the dividend cover from 83% to 90%, although its revenue reserve fell from 11.0p to 8.4p per share, equivalent to 44% of its annual dividend. The hope, no doubt, will be that a covered dividend is paid in the trust's current financial year and that it is able to replenish its revenue reserves in subsequent financial years.

How have enhanced dividend paying trusts performed – will we see more or less of that in the future?

The fortunes of investment trusts that have adopted enhanced dividend policies over recent years have varied in 2021. Some, such as J.P. Morgan Global Growth & Income*, have continued to command a premium rating, allowing them to issue new shares, while others, such as J.P. Morgan Asia Growth & Income and J.P. Morgan China Growth & Income*, have been derated as their asset class has moved out of favour. Despite these mixed fortunes and the ongoing debate surrounding the conversion of capital into income, I continue to believe that this is a legitimate use of the listed closed-ended fund structure as long as shareholders are aware of how their income is generated.

Have there been any significant developments on fees over the past 12 months?

The fees on investment trusts continue to be scrutinized, and the general direction of travel remains downward. Independent boards are clearly focused on securing highly competitive fee arrangements for their shareholders, particularly with an eye to the fee levels on any open-ended equivalent funds or immediate peers. However, one episode that did go against the grain in 2021 was when Brevan Howard tried to reintroduce a higher fee load on its (then) two investment companies: BH Global and BH Macro. This was ultimately successful, following a tussle with the respective boards which led to tender offers and a merger. The ongoing vehicle is BH Macro.

Which sectors look well placed to deliver good returns over the next three to five years?

Trying to gaze into a crystal ball is always a difficult business, and the events of the last few years have left most commentators looking more than a little foolish. I continue to believe that it pays to take a balanced approach to investing, in terms of both asset allocation and sector exposures. That said, I am susceptible to a contrarian viewpoint, and I find the value case for UK equities attractive. While I could have made the same comment (and probably did) at any stage over the last five years, I believe that UK mid- and small-caps are the likely beneficiaries of an economic rebound, with valuations supported by mergers and acquisitions activity.

The private equity sector also continues to offer substantial value opportunities, particularly compared with the wider investment trust sector. In addition, I suspect that this year's sell-off in Chinese equities will result in some attractive investment opportunities, albeit investors will have to be prepared for bouts of volatility. On a longer-term view, I still see the prospects for the healthcare and technology sectors as compelling, given their secular growth stories.

What have been the most positive and the most disappointing features of the past 12 months?

One of the most incredible features of the past 12 months, in my opinion, is how well the investment trust sector has operated despite the impact of lockdowns. The closed-ended structure of investment trusts has meant that managers have not had to worry about managing inflows or redemptions. Boards have continued to meet, albeit virtually, and demonstrate their independence in numerous ways, including changing managers or mandates and ensuring fee loads remain competitive. Investor relations have never been busier, with a cascade of Zoom calls allowing more frequent updates than were previously the case.

In addition, numerous funds have been launched despite professional investors never having met the management teams. This would have been unheard of before the pandemic. Technology has obviously been the enabler, as it has for society in general, but this is also evidence that the sector is prepared to adapt in order to thrive. That said, by far the most disappointing aspect of the last 12 months has been the difficulty or indeed impossibility of meeting people face to face. For an industry that is built on personal relationships, this has been a cruel blow.

How positive are you about the outlook for the sector going into 2022?

Like many, we at Winterflood started 2021 on a hopeful note, particularly given the unprecedented speed of the development and launch of the vaccination programme. Our first research report of the year focused on light at the end of the tunnel, and it certainly has been a year of recovery as well as a gradual return to normality. However, I am conscious that life rarely moves in a straight line and recent events have illustrated the difficulties involved in reopening the global economy from a standing start.

The three key investment considerations at present are: the likelihood that inflationary pressures are not transitory but rather will become ingrained; the investability of

China, given both regulatory and humanitarian headwinds; and the implications of investing in an ESG world. There are far more qualified commentators than me to answer these questions, but I would observe that, if history is a guide, the investment trust sector has consistently demonstrated its ability to meet an array of challenges. Whatever awaits us in 2022, I have no doubt the sector will continue to evolve and prosper as it addresses investors' needs.

Best and worst performers
12 months to 30 September 2021

Share Price					NAV				
Top 15									
Fund	Ticker	Now	Previous	Change	Fund	Ticker	Now	Previous	Change
Geiger Counter	GCL	60.50	16.40	268.9%	Geiger Counter	GCL	54.59	16.11	238.8%
Electra Private Equity	ELTA	606.00	181.00	234.8%	Georgia Capital	CGEO	1302.90	626.30	108.0%
KKV Secured Loan	KKVL	14.25	5.42	162.7%	Aberforth Split Level Income	ASIT	94.55	50.79	86.2%
KKV Secured Loan C	KKVX	22.00	10.36	112.3%	Chelverton UK Dividend	SDV	225.73	122.66	84.0%
Sherborne Investors (Guernsey) C	SIGC	62.00	29.90	107.4%	City Natural Resources Growth & Inco	CYN	202.73	112.35	80.4%
VietNam Holding	VNH	313.00	154.00	103.2%	Sherborne Investors (Guernsey) C	SIGC	79.20	45.43	74.3%
Schiehallion Fund	MNTN	2.46	1.32	87.1%	VietNam Holding	VNH	355.50	207.50	71.3%
India Capital Growth	IGC	128.50	69.70	84.4%	Aberforth Smaller Companies	ASL	1707.86	1007.85	69.5%
Aberforth Split Level Income	ASIT	80.20	43.60	83.9%	Riverstone Energy	RSE	703.95	419.76	67.7%
Chelverton UK Dividend	SDV	205.00	113.00	81.4%	Ashoka India Equity	AIE	194.80	119.04	63.6%
Gresham House Strategic	GHS	1780.00	985.00	80.7%	Schiehallion Fund	MNTN	1.82	1.15	58.8%
GCP Student Living	DIGS	212.50	118.20	79.8%	Vietnam Enterprise Investments	VEIL	864.32	544.24	58.8%
Riverstone Energy	RSE	489.00	272.00	79.8%	India Capital Growth	IGC	139.59	88.96	56.9%
City Natural Resources Growth & Inco	CYN	163.25	92.00	77.4%	Gresham House Strategic	GHS	1908.95	1227.10	55.6%
River & Mercantile UK Micro Cap	RMMC	283.00	162.00	74.7%	Chrysalis Investments	CHRY	226.62	145.83	55.4%
Bottom 15									
Fund	Ticker	Now	Previous	Change	Fund	Ticker	Now	Previous	Change
DP Aircraft	DPA	0.03	0.07	-61.5%	DP Aircraft	DPA	0.16	0.65	-75.0%
Myanmar Investments	MIL	0.35	0.74	-52.7%	KKV Secured Loan C	KKVX	27.20	91.51	-70.3%
Global Resources	GRIT	1.35	2.75	-50.9%	KKV Secured Loan	KKVL	22.90	61.00	-62.5%
Origo Partners	OPP	0.11	0.18	-40.0%	Secured Income Fund	SSIF	31.20	82.90	-62.4%
APQ Global	APQ	10.50	17.50	-40.0%	Origo Partners	OPP	0.35	0.89	-60.7%
Secured Income Fund	SSIF	25.00	41.61	-39.9%	JZ Capital Partners	JZCP	298.00	531.20	-43.9%
Syncona	SYNC	169.00	248.50	-32.0%	Global Resources	GRIT	0.81	1.44	-43.8%
Amedeo Air Four Plus	AA4	24.00	34.00	-29.4%	Amedeo Air Four Plus	AA4	74.90	117.96	-36.5%
Macau Property Opportunities	MPO	52.00	72.00	-27.8%	Golden Prospect Precious Metals	GPM	54.94	73.20	-24.9%
Golden Prospect Precious Metals	GPM	44.90	58.50	-23.2%	Doric Nimrod Air Three	DNA3	30.32	39.20	-22.7%
GRIT Real Estate Income	GR1T	38.50	48.50	-20.6%	Syncona	SYNC	165.45	205.67	-19.6%
Biotech Growth Trust	BIOG	1174.00	1468.00	-20.0%	Doric Nimrod Air Two	DNA2	102.86	123.16	-16.5%
Doric Nimrod Air One	DNA	32.00	40.00	-20.0%	GRIT Real Estate Income	GR1T	91.25	109.15	-16.4%
NB Distressed Debt - Global	NBDG	40.50	50.00	-19.0%	Macau Property Opportunities	MPO	150.00	179.00	-16.2%
Gabelli Merger Plus	GMP	6.05	7.40	-18.2%	Cambium Global Timberland	TREE	8.80	10.40	-15.4%

Source: Winterflood Securities

Denotes a corporate client of Winterflood Securities

SIMON ELLIOTT *has covered the investment trust sector since 2002 when he joined Winterflood Securities and has been head of investment trust research since 2008.*

KEEP UP TO DATE

Join Jonathan Davis and Simon Elliott for the free *Money Makers* weekly investment trust podcast, reviewing all the week's news, results and market movements in the investment trust sector. Every Saturday from *Money Makers* (www.money-makers.co).

60:40 AND OTHER DINOSAURS

One simple step can take your portfolio from the 1990s into the 2020s, says WILLIAM HEATHCOAT AMORY

O VER THE DECADES, investors' ideas about how to build the perfect investment portfolio have evolved. Large independent pension fund investors have typically led innovation, with consultants and smaller pension funds following, and then discretionary private client wealth managers followed by individual retail investors echoing trends as they trickle down.

Markowitz is identified as the architect of modern portfolio theory. Over time investors have been working with and adapting his theory. In the 1970s, perhaps as a function of the high interest rates available at the time, many institutional and pension investors still focused on fixed income. In the 1980s many of these investors started investing in domestic equities, and the 60:40 equity and bond split within portfolios became more common. The 1990s saw further diversification, and international equity investing became mainstream. In the new century, institutions started to further diversify portfolios, adding investments in alternative asset classes such as private equity, hedge funds, real estate, and other alternative or illiquid assets.

The history of the investment trust sector has in some ways echoed these developments. In the 1980s and 1990s new investment trusts were launched to capitalise on 'new markets' such as Europe, Asia and emerging markets, with institutions being enthusiastic supporters. Similarly, the booming listed hedge fund sector in the mid-2000s came on the back of the experience many institutional investors had of investing in Cayman-based hedge funds in the late 1990s and early 2000s. Trusts continue to launch, enabling investors to harness hard-to-access asset classes, often illiquid in nature, but offering the potential to diversify traditional equity and bond risks.

Lessons from Yale

The recent death of David Swenson, a pioneer in the evolution of institutional portfolios, gave us cause to examine what the future might hold for discretionary wealth manager or retail investor portfolios. David ran the Yale Endowment from 1985 until he died in May 2021 and delivered strong and consistent returns during his tenure. He revolutionised how and in what Yale invested by applying an extension of Markowitz's modern portfolio theory. Swenson identified eight asset classes, which we will come to later. Weightings are determined by risk-adjusted returns and correlations. Aside from setting a diversified strategic asset allocation to these eight asset classes and rebalancing regularly (which some researchers believe has contributed 40% of Yale's excess returns), the process also rests on a dedicated manager selection team.

So far, so not very different (in theory at least). In our view, the key lessons from Swenson and Yale are in attitudes to equity risk (with a high tolerance) and a willingness to embrace private markets and illiquidity. To some extent, Yale's ultra-long-term/perpetual investment mandate helps embrace risk and illiquidity. However, many private client, JISA or SIPP portfolios also have multi-decade investment horizons. As such, the differences between Yale's current portfolio and those of the various ARC Private Client Indices are stark. Below are shown the latest 'model' allocations from ARC, in which are notable the significant cash and fixed-income exposures – even for those with the highest risk.

ARC Private Client Indices Allocations

	EQUITY (%)	FIXED INCOME (%)	OTHER (%)	CASH (%)
Cautious	23	38	18	21
Balanced Asset	44	30	15	11
Steady Growth	63	22	11	4

Overall, Yale's exposure to equity may be seen as roughly similar to the 'equity risk' allocation of private client portfolios. However, the real difference is where Yale gets its equity exposure from. The chart below shows Yale's very high exposures to venture capital, absolute return and leveraged buyouts (together 60% of exposure), which represents perhaps ten times the exposure that private client or retail portfolios typically have to these asset classes.

Yale Endowment: Asset allocation

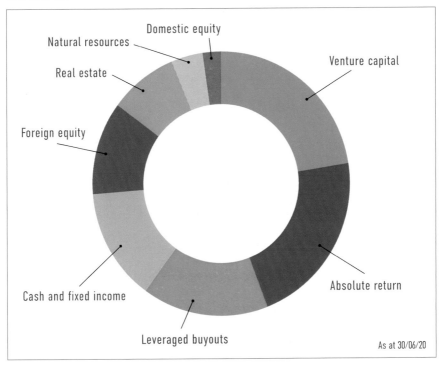

Source: Yale

Followers of fashion

Yale's success has prompted many smaller endowments to try to follow its example by adopting a similar asset allocation. Swenson and his colleagues have regularly warned against a blanket application of the Yale model, and the results of smaller endowments that have tried to adopt Yale's model have generally been mediocre. The reasons why Yale has been able to maintain its performance lead remain hard to pin down. However, most explanations centre around Yale having first-mover advantage (with many of its managers now closed to new investors) and the considerable resource and skill that its team bring to bear in manager selection, not to mention the practical difficulties of putting capital to work in these less liquid, private markets.

In our view, none of the reasons given for underperformance apply to a retail investor contemplating the investment trust universe. Investment trusts are by definition pretty much closed to new investment. The secondary market offers the entry point – which means, for small investors, all trusts are open for business during

LSE trading hours for subscriptions and redemptions. With regard to manager selection within the investment trust universe, this is clearly a significant barrier to achieving returns as strong as Yale's, but the investment trust universe represents something of a premier league for investment management talent.

Firstly, there are a limited number of trusts, and it requires demonstrable skill to be awarded a mandate by the independent board. Secondly, the board is there to continually monitor performance and to take action if performance is not maintained. Thirdly, the structural aspects to trusts give managers a higher chance of performing to the best of their ability, free to invest away from the pressures of inflows and redemptions and liquidity concerns of underlying stocks. Our contention is that the investment trust universe therefore provides a good source of talent to populate a long-term, Yale model allocation.

Using investment trusts to take the Yale road

The main takeaway from an analysis of the long-term returns from Yale's asset class buckets and those achieved by listed funds is that broadly similar returns are achievable. Therefore investors with long-term investment horizons, such as those with SIPPs or JISAs, could take a leaf out of Yale's book and adopt a more adventurous asset allocation framework, more akin to the endowment model. The biggest challenge is accepting the risk and illiquidity that comes with private market investments.

The change suggested by Yale for SIPP investors is certainly dramatic. But it is no more dramatic than the changes made by Yale itself in the 1990s. In 1990, 65% of the Yale endowment was targeted to US stocks and bonds. Today, target allocations call for 9.75% in US marketable securities and cash, while the diversifying assets of foreign equity, absolute return, real estate, natural resources, leveraged buyouts and venture capital dominate, representing 90% of the target portfolio.

Will investors follow – even just a little way – and take the plunge? The strong performance of the Yale endowment over the years would seem to justify it and, if history is anything to go by, many other investment portfolios will become less dominated by listed equities. We are already starting to see this trend towards private market investments, but Yale would suggest the trend has a long, long way to go.

In this regard, investment trust followers have an advantage, with a wide selection of strategies and managers available which give a relatively liquid way of gaining exposure to what Yale calls "non-traditional asset classes". Yale observes that the "endowment's long-time horizon is well suited to exploit illiquid, less efficient markets". Many SIPP investors have a multi-decade investment horizon, meaning they could adopt an 'endowment' model for their portfolio.

How, then, might one tackle filling each of Yale's buckets? Several buckets are relatively simple to populate from the open-ended or investment trust sectors, including domestic equities, foreign equities, cash and bonds, real estate and natural resources. Those who wish to find suitable absolute return funds might consider BH Macro, some of the constituents of the AIC flexible sector, or any of the plethora of absolute return UCITs funds.

Nothing ventured, nothing gained

Yale's real differentiator from traditional portfolios is its 35% target allocation to venture capital and leveraged buyouts. Unfortunately, there are relatively few directly comparable avenues for the venture capital allocation, which Yale targets at 23.5% of its portfolio. Yale's venture managers provide exposure to innovative start-up companies from an early stage. As in vogue as this area is, it is undeniably a high-risk strategy – Yale expects long-term real returns of 12.3% per annum but with risk of 37.8%. Over 20 years, Yale has achieved 11.2% per annum from its portfolio, which might be considered a little disappointing, given the risks involved.

The AIC's growth capital sector is the most obvious avenue to explore, but it is worth remembering that trusts in this area do have relatively short track records and that it takes time for managers to see the fruits of their investing labour harvested.

Other trusts that offer an exposure to venture include Third Point Investors (TPOU), the board of which has recently approved an increased allocation to venture and private equity up to 20% of NAV. Third Point is developing a strong track record in the venture space, with one of its investments recently achieving an IPO. SentinelOne's first day of trading valuation was more than 100 times the valuation at which Third Point first invested in 2015, illustrating the potentially explosive returns achievable from venture. This is the second high-profile IPO from Third Point's portfolio, with AI-driven lender Upstart having been listed since December 2020 and appreciating more than five times in value since.

As will be discussed below, venture is a differentiated strategy to private equity, but HarbourVest Global Private Equity (HVPE) has the highest allocation of the listed private equity trusts, with 35% of NAV represented by 'venture and growth equity' funds. Other trusts that might be considered as having exposure to venture capital include RIT Capital Partners (at least 8.9% of the portfolio represented by venture capital funds) and Scottish Mortgage.

Buyouts

Yale's leveraged buyout allocation represents a similar strategy to those employed by the listed private equity (LPE) sector, which offers a wide range of different approaches to access what Yale believes are "extremely attractive long-term risk-adjusted returns" from a strategy that "exploit[s] market inefficiencies". We believe that buyouts represent a lower-risk proposition than venture (a view shared by Yale). Private equity buyout investing is different from venture in that buyout managers control their companies, enabling them to set the strategy, drive value creation and – perhaps just as importantly – decide when to crystallise value by selling.

Yale's leveraged buyout portfolio is expected to generate real returns of 8.6% with risk of 21.1%, and over the past 20 years has delivered 11.2% a year. In many ways, the LPE sector offers a better access route than Yale, given that an investor today can buy into funds with established portfolios of investments, which in some cases are very mature. Most LPE trusts trade at material discounts to NAV.

First steps in a move towards Yale

As possible evidence of the acceptance of private equity's attractive attributes in a portfolio context, the venerable F&C Investment Trust has long had a commitment to investing in private equity as part of its global investment approach, which now sits near 10% of NAV. Those investors who wish to start to move towards an endowment model might consider being even bolder and allocating up to 20% of their portfolio into LPE trusts in place of equity exposure allocated elsewhere. This would mark a very significant divergence from traditional portfolios, which we understand might have between zero and 5% invested in LPE trusts.

The LPE sector offers a wide range of different approaches and slants, which means that investors wishing to make a meaningful allocation can easily diversify their exposure to managers, sectors and approaches. The table below splits the universe by how each trust makes its investments. Direct LPE trusts have a single management group making investments, and tend to have very concentrated portfolios, which in turn exposes investors to higher specific risk and potentially higher rewards. At the other end of the spectrum are the highly diversified fund of funds, which have underlying exposure to many thousands of private companies. Between these two poles, some LPE trusts have more concentrated portfolios but relatively little specific risk to individual companies. Investors can choose between these, depending on risk appetites, sector preferences and premiums/discounts to NAVs.

Listed Private Equity Trusts (not in wind-up, or returning capital)

DIRECT	CO-INVESTMENTS	CONCENTRATED FUND OF FUNDS/HYBRID	DIVERSIFIED FUND OF FUNDS
3i	NB Private Equity Partners	BMO Private Equity	HarbourVest Global Private Equity
Apax Global Alpha		ICG Enterprise	Pantheon International
HgCapital		Standard Life Private Equity	
Oakley Capital Investments			
Princess Private Equity			

Source: Kepler Partners

As highlighted above, the trusts within the LPE sector provide a wide range of different exposures. Whilst all operate in the same broad area of private equity investing, and are likely to be subject to the same broad market sentiment driving premiums and discounts, they have many complementary attributes in relation to each other, which enables investors to build a relatively diversified exposure to the space.

ICG Enterprise (ICGT) offers a hybrid approach to private equity investing – with around 52% of the portfolio through third-party funds and 48% within the 'high-conviction' portfolio where ICG has directly selected underlying companies through co-investments and through ICG funds. The strategy has delivered consistently strong value creation for shareholders, with ICGT on track to deliver its 13th consecutive financial year of double-digit portfolio growth.

NB Private Equity Partners (NBPE) offers a unique approach within the London listed private equity (LPE) sector, focusing on equity co-investments. These are equity investments made alongside third-party private equity sponsors and have generated strong returns for the fund. As such, NBPE has a wide spread of investments across sectors, companies and private equity managers – including 64 core investment positions (those greater than $5m) made alongside 38 different private equity sponsors (as at 31/03/2021). Making these investments directly means NBPE's investors pay only one layer of management and incentive fees. With the portfolio looking increasingly mature, the momentum behind realisation activity seen over recent months could continue.

BMO Private Equity (BPET) offers investors a distinctive approach to accessing private equity, investing with managers at a relatively early stage in their development.

BPET's manager believes this means being exposed to more motivated teams and to lower mid-market deals where BMO is more likely to be offered co-investment opportunities. We expect the level of co-investments to remain between a third and a half of NAV, reflecting a rise in the number of opportunities that BPET's managers have observed in this area over the years.

As part of a diversified portfolio, the higher returns generated by directly invested private equity trusts can be attractive, notwithstanding the greater volatility of returns. HgCapital has a well-established track record as a directly invested private equity trust. The managers specialise in software and business services in Europe. The trust has delivered strong long-term returns for shareholders, perhaps a reason behind the premium that the shares currently trade at.

Many of the same dynamics behind HgCapital trust's growth have benefited the underlying portfolio of Oakley Capital Investments (OCI), which focuses on investing in companies in the European technology, education and consumer sectors. Digital disruption and the opportunities it presents have long been a recurring theme in OCI's portfolio. This placed OCI well at the beginning of 2020, and portfolio companies have clearly been nimble in adapting to the digital opportunities presented to them during lockdown.

Entrepreneurial founders of businesses represent a key part of Oakley Capital's DNA, with a track record of being the first institutional investors in growing companies. The Oakley network is key in helping the team access compelling investments at attractive valuations at a time when competition is strong. OCI's strong balance sheet is also a differentiator, having gone into the market sell-off with net cash of 36% of estimated net assets. This put the trust in a strong position, and Oakley Capital has made a number of interesting investments since then. Cash now represents around 22% of estimated NAV.

WILLIAM HEATHCOAT AMORY *is a co-founding partner of Kepler Partners and leads the investment trust research business via Kepler Trust Intelligence. Prior to co-founding Kepler Partners in 2008, he was part of the Extel number 1 rated research team at J.P. Morgan Cazenove.*

INVESTOR FORUM

We asked some of the most experienced investment trust investors we know to give their answers to some topical questions.

Who's Who

Alan Brierley is the director of investment company research at Investec and has covered the sector since the early 1990s.

Richard Curling is an investment director at Jupiter Fund Management with wide experience of the investment trust sector, including managing the Jupiter Fund of Investment Trusts.

Nick Greenwood has been the manager of Miton Global Opportunities (MGO), a specialist trust that invests only in other investment trusts, since its launch in 2004.

Peter Hewitt is a director and fund manager in global equities at BMO Global Asset Management and is responsible for managing the BMO Managed Portfolio Trust, listed in 2008.

Alastair Laing is CEO of Capital Gearing Asset Management, where he has co-managed the funds since 2011.

Ewan Lovett-Turner is head of investment companies research at Numis Securities and has more than 15 years' experience in the sector.

The investment trust sector has recovered well from the virus – does that surprise you, and has it exceeded your expectations?

Alan Brierley: The resilience of the sector has not been a surprise, and we regard this a function of the underlying quality of the closed-end industry. That said, although a year ago we said that the main lesson was don't fight the Fed, the recovery of many parts of the global equity market, which have just enjoyed the fastest bull market ever, has far exceeded expectations.

Richard Curling: No surprise really – the sector has merely reflected general bullishness in markets.

Nick Greenwood: I don't think that the trust sector is alone in benefiting from the industrial amounts of stimulus ploughed into the financial system to fight off the challenges of the pandemic. We were positioned for rising markets but pleasantly surprised by the extent of the gains.

Peter Hewitt: Not really; the sector makeup of investment companies is weighted towards trusts that will have had a good or resilient pandemic. That said, the extent of the outperformance did surprise.

Alastair Laing: We were very surprised at how quickly all financial markets recovered after an unusually savage crisis. During spring 2020 our expectations were that equities would take at least 18 months to fully recover. It turned out that three months was all it took. Investment trusts were lifted, like all other assets, on a rising tide of central bank-created liquidity.

Ewan Lovett-Turner: The ability to take a long-term view in managing investment companies is useful during periods of volatility, and many funds proved resilient through the covid-19 crisis. Equity investment companies saw understandable volatility, but many funds were focused on growth trends that were beneficiaries of lockdown, whilst more value-orientated strategies have staged a recovery in 2021.

Alternative asset trusts proved their resilience through covid-19, with most, such as infrastructure, having been able to deliver a consistent return profile. In addition, private equity trusts have performed extremely strongly. This may have surprised many and reflects that portfolios are much less cyclical than investors perceived.

Are average discounts likely to widen or narrow from here, (a) in equity sectors and (b) in alternative assets?

Alan Brierley: The headline average discount returned to fair value relatively quickly after the onset of the pandemic and has remained there since.

Richard Curling: It is difficult to see average discounts tightening much more in equity sectors – so they are more likely to widen. The valuation of alternatives assets is less precise and so it is quite possible that discounts could narrow more (or premiums expand).

Nick Greenwood: Looking forward, there are a number of headwinds, such as disruption, tapering, China's new rules and declining protection against covid; uncertainty will cause discounts to widen across the piste.

Peter Hewitt: For equity sectors, they will either trade around where they are currently or widen a bit. Only a bear market would cause a significant widening. For alternatives, many are at large premiums and that could change if inflation picks up and the market believes it is no longer transitory.

Alastair Laing: In equity sectors – no strong view, although I would not be surprised to see a modest widening. In alternative assets – current premiums are unstainable, not least because issuance will continue until they no longer persist.

Ewan Lovett-Turner: Equity trusts are trading at average discounts of circa 5.5%. This has widened from all-time tights of circa 3% in early 2021, in part reflecting a derating of some growth-orientated funds from large premiums. Discounts remain relatively tight compared with the long-term history (7.5%), but I believe they remain supported by discount control mechanisms and consistent demand from retail investors.

Overall, alternative asset trusts are trading at an average premium of 7.5%. This masks significant variation, with infrastructure and specialist property trusts on premiums whilst most private equity and specialist debt investment trusts remain on discounts. The ability to deliver a consistent yield should support premiums for most funds, whilst there is scope for a rerating of private equity investment trusts.

Which trusts have you been most pleased with this year?

Alan Brierley: Merchants Trust. For many years, the company has been burdened with a truly horrific balance sheet, with very expensive, long-debt debt, a legacy of a bygone era. However, there has been an almost stealth-like transformation in the balance sheet in recent years, and a reversal of the value headwinds has contributed to some exceptional returns in the past year.

Richard Curling: Private equity (NBPE), India (AIE), Japan active (NAVF) and some of the specialist REITs (such as BBOX).

Nick Greenwood: River & Mercantile Micro Cap: the manager fully exploited the opportunity presented by the post-Woodford reaction to avoid anything deemed small or illiquid. The capital structure whereby excess AUM above £100m is returned to shareholders keeps the portfolio nimble enough to exploit opportunities in the micro-cap world and has meant that owning the shares has been a very profitable experience this year.

Peter Hewitt: Private equity trusts have performed very strongly in terms of asset growth. Share prices of many have also done well, with signs of discounts beginning to narrow.

Alastair Laing: Our largest investment trust holding, North Atlantic Smaller Companies: extremely strong share price returns, a portfolio of exciting companies, large cash balances due to recent disposals and a chunky discount that should narrow in time. What is not to like?

Ewan Lovett-Turner: Many funds have impressed this year in a range of strategies, including Schielhallion (+80% share price), Tufton Oceanic (+55%), NB Private

Equity (+44%). In addition, long-term consistent performers such as HgCapital Trust (+32%) and RIT Capital (+26%) have continued to perform very well.

And which trusts have most disappointed you?

Alan Brierley: Given significant shareholdings by the management team, Boussard & Gavaudan and Third Point Investors both featured in our latest *Skin in the Game* report. However, there has been a distinct mismatch between long-term performance records and egregious fees, while in both cases, 'shareholder value' masks have slipped.

Richard Curling: Japan and healthcare.

Nick Greenwood: Macau Property Opportunities. Whilst this trust has been competently managed, it has had a year to forget. The former Portuguese colony is the focus for the gambling industry in China, and covid-related travel restrictions have laid the local economy low. More recently the casino industry has found itself, like many other sectors, the target of new, hostile regulation.

Peter Hewitt: The dedicated China specialist trusts have had a hard time due to the actions of the Chinese government, which resulted in a sharp pull-back in Chinese equities generally and the technology, digital and internet companies specifically.

Alastair Laing: The large private equity fund of funds have enjoyed strong NAV uplifts but have left their discounts to widen into the mid-20s discounts. The boards should be instructing shares buy-back programmes to protect investor interests and to increase NAVs further.

Ewan Lovett-Turner: I think Syncona has a strong management team and an exciting portfolio of transformational life sciences companies. It therefore has lots of long-term potential. However, near-term performance has been weak, with recent IPOs of portfolio companies failing to excite. Upcoming clinical data in the next 18 months will be key to a recovery.

Value versus growth – is this a false dawn for value or the start of a new trend?

Alan Brierley: I can see a less hostile environment for value managers, particularly in an inflationary environment, but would still expect the leading growth managers to outperform over the longer term.

Richard Curling: I am firmly in the growth camp on anything other than short-term cycles.

Nick Greenwood: That distinction doesn't always exist at the sharp end. It would be difficult to define many of our holdings as one or the other. Looking at the mega-cap tech names, it does feel like they will suffer the same fate as many of the Nifty 50 which commanded very full valuations in the early 1970s, only not to see their share prices return to that level for a generation, despite most proving to be very successful businesses in the real world.

Peter Hewitt: Jury is still out, but on balance value is definitely past the worst and may well assume market leadership in 2022.

Alastair Laing: Value will have its time in the sun… I feel like I have been saying that for quite a long time, but it will happen!

Ewan Lovett-Turner: Expectations around tapering of QE and interest rates are likely to lead to some flip-flopping between growth and value. However, if companies can continue to compound high revenue and earnings growth, we expect them to continue to deliver.

Are we seeing transitory inflation or a new era of higher inflation?

Alan Brierley: Given the amount of debt in the system – government, corporate and personal – inflation seems to be the only way out. That said, achieving a Goldilocks level of inflation (not too hot, not too cold) will be incredibly challenging.

Richard Curling: I believe we will see a structurally higher level of inflation (say, 5%) in the future as it is the only realistic way to deal with debt, but I think it unlikely we will suffer hyperinflation.

Nick Greenwood: Cost push inflation is likely to be transitory as disruptions and logjams are resolved. Should the authorities need to launch further experimental fiscal and monetary policy initiatives, then there is the risk that currencies will break. If you double the amount of money in circulation, you have not created any wealth: simplistically, each unit of currency should only be worth half what it was.

Peter Hewitt: A new era of higher inflation will eventually take hold but may not be obvious until later next year.

Alastair Laing: The risks of persistently higher inflation are very materially underestimated in current equity and bond prices.

Ewan Lovett-Turner: We have already gone beyond the point of transitory impact in several areas. Supply chain disruption and labour market issues point to more entrenched inflation. In addition, an increased focus on ESG is likely to be inherently inflationary. For investors with concerns about inflation, many areas of the trust sector offer a degree of interest rate or inflation protection.

What was the most interesting or most promising IPO of the past 12 months?

Alan Brierley: Cordiant Digital Infrastructure – this company gives investors exposure to the core infrastructure of the digital economy, including data centres, telecom towers and fibre networks. The company seeks to generate a total return of at least 9%.

Richard Curling: D9 and Cordiant both made interesting additions to the infrastructure sector and introduced a new subsector (digital infrastructure). Seraphim Space demonstrated how an investment company can open up a very specialist area to investors.

Nick Greenwood: Seraphim Space. This may well be a situation where the market overestimates the effect of new technology over two years but underestimates it over ten years. Notwithstanding the current excitement surrounding the shares, holders may become bored in a couple of years' time just as investee companies are beginning to make real traction and exiting their cash flow negative phase.

Peter Hewitt: Digital 9 Infrastructure.

Alastair Laing: Digital 9 Infrastructure plc – a listed infrastructure investment company that owns sub-sea fibre optic cables and cutting-edge data centres, the plumbing of the global digital economy. We are more comfortable selling 'picks, shovels and lodging' to the technology sector than trying to assess which individual company is best placed to strike digital gold.

Ewan Lovett-Turner: Space-focused IPO Seraphim Space certainly raised some eyebrows. It is seeking to invest in private companies benefiting from the use of increased data access through space/satellite infrastructure. It will be an interesting one to watch.

In which sectors would you most like to see new IPOs?

Richard Curling: I would like to see further expansion amongst alternatives, particularly showing how using the investment company structure can give investors access to normally illiquid real assets and new sources of income.

Nick Greenwood: Forestry. We do have Foresight's fund on the launch site. It is a sector that is crying out for the closed-end structure, but perception has been blighted by the travails of Phaunos and Cambium launches during the last new-issue boom.

Peter Hewitt: Alternatives.

Alastair Laing: The investment trust market is poorly served for high-quality American conventional equity investment companies. We have little hope of seeing new IPOs in this space but would be delighted if there were some.

"I WOULD LIKE TO SEE FURTHER EXPANSION AMONGST ALTERNATIVES, PARTICULARLY SHOWING HOW USING THE INVESTMENT COMPANY STRUCTURE CAN GIVE INVESTORS ACCESS TO NORMALLY ILLIQUID REAL ASSETS AND NEW SOURCES OF INCOME."

– RICHARD CURLING

Ewan Lovett-Turner: I expect the focus to continue to be on less-liquid assets that are well-suited to the investment company structure. Alternative income strategies such as specialist property, renewables and energy transition are likely to remain popular, but we are seeing increasing demand for more capital-growth orientated returns such as private equity as well. Equity strategies will remain the exception but, as Smithson has proved, they can be successful.

Which trust or manager are you most sorry to see leave the field of play since last year?

Alan Brierley: April 2021 witnessed the retirement of not one but three leading managers. Alistair Whyte, one of the founding partners of Aberforth, retired after 31 years, during which time the company delivered long-term annualised outperformance of 1.9%. Tony Foster initially joined Baillie Gifford in the 1980s where he developed the first spreadsheet, and he went on to be a leading investor in closed-end funds. And finally, there was Charles Plowden, who played a key role in the reinvigoration of Monks. Since the board appointed Baillie Gifford's Global Alpha team in 2015, the market cap has more than trebled to £3.4bn.

Richard Curling: Charles Plowden.

Nick Greenwood: Alistair Munday, the former manager of Temple Bar, is still missed.

Peter Hewitt: Matthew Dobbs of Schroders, who has had a brilliant career.

Alastair Laing: This year the only answer could be James Anderson of Scottish Mortgage. It is impossible to have anything other than the greatest respect for his achievements in creating the poster child of the investment trust sector.

Ewan Lovett-Turner: The biggest news of the year around manager changes was the announcement that James Anderson will leave Baillie Gifford in April 2022. James was the architect of Scottish Mortgage's investment approach, using a high-conviction, unconstrained approach seeking exceptional growth companies around the world. He leaves the fund in safe hands, with the next generation of managers at Baillie Gifford well placed to continue the long-term approach.

Is there more consolidation on the way?

Alan Brierley: I hope so. There are still too many zombie companies – those that lack critical mass and have poor liquidity. We would welcome greater creativity/proactivity to address these.

Richard Curling: I hope so – there are still too many sub-scale, undifferentiated, expensive trusts.

Nick Greenwood: Most trusts have already decided either to merge, with the hope of becoming big enough to attract the mega-sized wealth management chains, or to focus on the burgeoning number of retail self-directed investors following the trust sector.

Peter Hewitt: Yes.

Alastair Laing: Yes, although at a pace that Samuel Beckett understood well when he wrote *Waiting for Godot*.

Ewan Lovett-Turner: Yes. Many investors are heavily focused on trading liquidity and favour trusts of a large size. As a result, small and underperforming trusts will remain under pressure to merge or reinvent themselves. In addition, if illiquid assets fall out of favour in listed investment trusts there is scope for specialist investors to bid for assets of funds.

What is the most vulnerable sector or specific trust?

Alan Brierley: Latin American trusts – after a lost decade, most investors seem to have given up.

Richard Curling: Any trust that trades on a high discount, with poor performance, and does not offer its shareholders a compelling investment proposition.

Nick Greenwood: Some renewable energy trusts. There is a lot of capital chasing this space and loads of paper in the trust market. Solar and wind cannot always be relied on and may end up becoming a slightly smaller part of utilities energy portfolios than currently expected.

Peter Hewitt: It could well be in alternatives.

Alastair Laing: The issues that have affected certain social housing property REITs look like they could have some way to run.

Ewan Lovett-Turner: Small trusts are under the most pressure and need to justify their existence, as many investors are increasingly focused on trading liquidity. Boards need to ensure that mandates are differentiated and small trusts have a strategy for growth and a supportive shareholder register.

What is top of your wish list for the investment trust sector? Do you have any advice for the new director general of the AIC?

Alan Brierley: Over the past decade, there has been a significant increase in interest from the retail investor, and we would like to see this trend gain further momentum.

Richard Curling: Liquidity remains an issue. The DG should strive to ensure a level playing field with unit trusts.

Nick Greenwood: I think the sector is doing just fine, but it would be good to sort the KID document debacle.

Peter Hewitt: Guide more clearly on what trusts should do regarding ESG (environmental, social and governance factors).

Alastair Laing: That investment trusts remain regulated under rules devised by the EU's Alternative Investment Fund Managers Directive is crazy. It was always an anomaly that investment trusts were captured by this regulation that was designed for hedge funds and private equity. The extensive compliance costs of this regulation are all borne by investors who receive almost no benefit in return.

Ewan Lovett-Turner: A level playing field on costs. Reporting of costs in the KID for investment companies is not consistent with open-ended funds, which do not currently include transaction costs in their KIIDs documents. In addition, investment companies include the cost of debt without consideration of its impact on returns. I am in favour of transparency and low costs, but this reporting distortion is causing investors to sell trusts needlessly.

What are your best tips for long-term outperformance (own trusts or clients excluded)?

Alan Brierley: Buy high-quality managers with a clear objective and process, ideally with low ongoing charges, and then do nothing.

Richard Curling: Healthcare.

Nick Greenwood: Georgia Capital – an investment trust which owns a small eastern European country (a slight exaggeration).

Peter Hewitt: Technology/biotech trusts, Baillie Gifford trusts.

Ewan Lovett-Turner: Invest for the long term in high-quality management teams that are experts in their field.

What are the best choices for investors seeking yield?

Alan Brierley: As we sail ever further into uncharted waters, it's never been more important to have a diversified portfolio of investment companies, both equities and alternatives, including infrastructure, real estate and debt funds.

Richard Curling: Look at the alternatives trusts – REITS and infrastructure.

Nick Greenwood: Real Estate Investors – a Birmingham property generalist that suffers from poor perception. Given the level that the shares languish at, new buyers should enjoy an 8% yield largely from cash flow.

Peter Hewitt: UK equity income trusts.

Alastair Laing: Secure Income REIT – if you are relying on yield, make sure it is inflation protected!

Ewan Lovett-Turner: Best-ideas portfolios from specialist credit managers are good options for investors seeking yield, such as NB Global Monthly Income (5.3% yield) or TwentyFour Select Monthly Income (6.3% yield). In addition, the infrastructure asset class also offers attractive income, with a high level of inflation protection, from funds such as International Public Partnerships (4.7% yield).

What have you been buying or recommending this year?

Richard Curling: Digital infrastructure and private equity trusts.

Nick Greenwood: Georgia Cap, Hansa, Strategic Equity Capital and Schroder Public and Private.

Peter Hewitt: Private equity trusts.

Ewan Lovett-Turner: Listed private equity funds have been amongst our top picks over the last year. They benefit from high-quality management teams, and portfolios are performing very strongly and have shown low cyclicality after being resilient through the covid-19 crisis.

What are the most striking anomalies in ratings (as at 30 September 2021)?

Alan Brierley: Generally speaking, the sector tends to be efficiently priced. However, there are always exceptions. We've always struggled to reconcile the seemingly embedded discounts of listed private equity. As global financial markets evolve, we believe that these companies will have an important role to play in giving investors exposure to an increasing number of companies with strong growth characteristics who are choosing to stay off-market for longer.

Richard Curling: Pershing Square Holdings, which is run by US hedge fund activist Bill Ackman, trades on a 30% discount to NAV – ironic!

Nick Greenwood: Private equity – high OCFs (annualised costs per share) under the new rules mean that advisers are selling just as the sector reaches the sweet spot in its cycle.

Peter Hewitt: North Atlantic Smaller Companies. Great record over the short and long term.

Ewan Lovett-Turner: Several listed private equity funds are trading at over 20% discounts despite strong NAV performance. This stands out as an exceptional value opportunity, in my view.

Are you long-term bullish or bearish about the renewable energy sector?

Alan Brierley: Bullish. Strong long-term fundamentals are deeply embedded, although we believe a compression of returns is a natural function of the evolution of this sector.

Richard Curling: Bullish. Renewables are integral to achieving net zero carbon and will require massive funding to expand. For this to happen, investor returns must be acceptable.

Nick Greenwood: See my earlier answer about the vulnerability of the renewables sector.

Peter Hewitt: Long-term bearish.

Alastair Laing: Returns from the sector will be modest, although these could still be better than the broader equity market, given how high valuations are today.

Ewan Lovett-Turner: We remain positive on the long-term dynamics in the sector, given the attractive dividend yields and the relatively high degree of inflation linkage of revenues. In addition, the environmental credentials are likely to support demand for the assets. Over time, we expect there to be increasing dispersion of performance based on the quality of portfolios.

Is the investment trust sector doing enough/doing the right thing about ESG?

Alan Brierley: It's now difficult to find a company that doesn't talk about its ESG credentials; a challenge for the industry is to be able to differentiate between those where ESG is deeply embedded in their DNA and those who are greenwashing.

Richard Curling: Yes. Many investment companies, especially in the alternatives area, are inherently ESG positive in what they do (for instance, social housing, renewables and energy efficiency). But I am sceptical about the lack of a proper framework to measure and report on ESG amongst many equity trusts.

Nick Greenwood: It's finding its way as best as it can, like we all are.

Peter Hewitt: Not yet. Starting a long journey on this one.

Alastair Laing: The thought police do not allow me to answer this question.

Ewan Lovett-Turner: In many ways the investment trust sector has been on the front foot in this area, with a wide range of options in the renewable energy and infrastructure sectors as well as recent launches focused on energy transition and energy efficiency.

GOLD IN THE UNDERGROWTH

IAIN MCCOMBIE, *co-manager of the Baillie Gifford UK Growth Trust, discusses the outlook for the UK market and the growth style of investment for which his firm is well known.*

The UK stock market has been a dull performer for many years, certainly compared with some of the more exciting global funds that your colleagues run. What is the appeal to you?

Well, I've probably done less travelling than some of my colleagues, but I disagree that the UK is a dull place to invest. Obviously, people say it's terribly dull and why on earth do you want to waste time on that? They will cite the fact that there are some very big companies in the UK market, and at the top of the market it is true that there are some very dull companies indeed. But we don't own them, and we don't need to own them.

When you come to work in the UK sector, stock-picking skills are really important. And the thing about stock-picking is that if you're prepared to get into the undergrowth, as it were, you can find some really good businesses. We've had a lot of experience running pension fund money for many years; we've always had a bit of a bias towards mid-sized and smaller companies, and if you look at the performance of those funds, they've actually done much better than the market.

I think that was why our track record was of interest to the board when they made the change (switching the mandate from Schroder UK Growth to Baillie Gifford in 2018). Having worked with smaller companies for many years, I still find the UK market fascinating. If you're just talking about the FTSE 100 you could be having a miserable time, but when you see the kind of companies that are coming through, there's a lot to be excited about. I could list 50 companies that one day could become FTSE 100 companies. Yes, of course there is a structural issue about the UK market, but as long as you're an active stock-picker you can always find things to own.

I think the other point is that if you look at the managers of the other trusts, quite a lot of them have spent time in the UK team. I have learnt a lot from working with the likes of Tom Slater and Douglas Brodie. Baillie Gifford is a partnership, and what's really good about that is that it creates links. You are not just looking at the UK market on your own. It is great to be able to compare your companies with other companies and ask them questions. The fact that you've got these people who have worked for the UK team and have pretty warm feelings about the UK makes it a pleasure speaking to them. These kinds of intangible links are part of the culture of Baillie Gifford, and I think that is really important.

The UK team at Baillie Gifford run £11bn for institutional clients. What difference does having a £400m investment trust really make?

What is unique about the trust is that it is a bespoke portfolio. Milena [Mileva, McCombie's co-manager] and I both run separate pension models. But the trust is almost the best of both. It is unique in that sense. There's no open-ended version of this. When we were pitching to the board in 2018, we thought that was one of the attractive things: that you can genuinely say you can't get this anywhere else. We're believers in investment trusts, and having something unique is important.

What is the difference, then, between the trust and your other portfolios? What makes it bespoke?

We said right at the start: we will have no tracking error. We want to be able to have a high active share, which will mean the portfolio will be volatile, but the closed-ended structure of investment is perfect for that, as it is for us holding private companies and deploying gearing. We wanted to run a best ideas fund – a just over 40-stock portfolio with low portfolio turnover – to enable us to just follow our enthusiasms. We have some very broad guidelines to make sure we don't go absolutely mad; not too much money in one area and so on. In terms of managing the volatility – which, as you know, a lot of pension funds are unfortunately still very keen on – we said, "Look, we just don't think this makes sense for a trust," and the board obviously agreed with that.

So, you have an All-Share benchmark but the portfolio looks very different?

Yes, and the difference is quite pronounced. We just don't think about whether a business is a large company or a mid-sized company; what we're asking is: are they a growth company or are they not? If a big company is a growth company, that's great; but if it's not, it's not. We are liberated by not having to worry about the benchmark or the volatility against the benchmark. If we don't want to come play, we don't. So, for example, we don't own any of the big banks or any of the oil majors – anything like that – because we just don't think they're attractive long-term growth businesses.

If you're worried about risk, this is not a trust for you, because it's not trying to mimic the All-Share. What we're trying to do is find individual companies which we think have attractive growth characteristics. That's very similar to what you will hear elsewhere at Baillie Gifford, but what we found when we researched the investment trust market was there were actually very few UK growth managers in it. People obviously thought: there's no growth here so let's go elsewhere. Actually, there are a lot of growth businesses out there, but they're just smaller. They're not as well known as the big companies, but who cares if you're trying to invest for the long term?

There are some good growth companies on AIM, and you are not restricted from investing there as well as in the main market?

Yes, there are, and we are not restricted. Given my background in smaller companies, I'd invested in AIM before, and yes, it is a bit of a caveat emptor market, but there are some really good companies there too. In the US you often see some companies that start off as a little bit raw – a little bit, dare I say, naive in some of their governance issues – but then they grow up, and some of them move on to the main market. Part of our job is to help UK companies do that too. One of the things we really pride ourselves on is building good relationships with the management teams of the companies that we own. We've always been very low-turnover – 10% a year is typical for our portfolio and sometimes it is 5% – and we genuinely try to maintain a relationship with all our companies for as long as we can.

How would you describe your stock selection process?

Well, we don't start with a blank piece of paper, as we have the companies that we already own. But as a team we get together every month and we have our prospects meeting, which is a review of the market, and we're also looking for ideas, either things we own, or things we don't own which we think are interesting at the moment and that we need to do more work on.

We're not trying to cover every part of the market. If it's not 'growthy', we don't bother looking at it. Let's say our universe is 500 or 600 companies: we're whittling that down to about 100 to 150, and then of that we're picking 40 names. I'd say it's a 'simple, not easy' kind of process. It's important too to keep abreast of things that are new and things that are coming into the market.

One of the perennial headaches of the UK is: how do we get these new growth businesses coming through? How do we incubate them? There was a problem in the venture capital kind of style, but things are starting to change. We own Draper Esprit, which is an investor in some of these early-stage companies. But also you're starting to see some overseas companies list in the UK. So it's not all doom and gloom when it comes to finding exciting growth businesses in the UK.

What we say is: we are trying to tilt the odds in your favour. We're not market-timers; we've been around long enough to know that that's a bit of a mug's game. It's not our strength – some people might be good at it, but we're not. What we think tilts the odds in your favour is if you've spent a lot of time trying to get to know a company and its prospects, and then the benefit is being able to hold it for as long as you can and not to be worried about drawdowns or volatility.

Everyone says they're long-term, but the numbers don't really back that up. The interesting question is why. From our perspective it's that people have to be seen to be doing something, whereas actually sometimes the most important thing is doing nothing. It's not being lazy or sneaking off to the cinema for an afternoon; it's just thinking and saying don't overreact to noise. Only react to things that are important – which is a really difficult thing in this day and age, with all the news and social media and the constant chatter about things.

How well have things gone since you took over the trust in 2018?

I think it is too early to tell. We always said judge us over five years, so let's try not to fall into that trap, but the tentative signs are encouraging in terms of performance. The other thing to say is that when we took over the trust, the previous manager's house savings scheme owned 22% of the shares, and value houses had another 18% to 20% of the business as well, and that's all gone now. It is not just the portfolio but the shareholder base that has changed a lot.

The board members will obviously speak for themselves, but we think that the board is pleased at how the shareholder base has changed, because obviously that was a big issue for them. The big in-house saving scheme holding could have been seen as a poison pill, but they were sold in the market without us having to buy back shares. To be honest, I'm pretty proud of that. Our brokers did a great job, but Milena and I were out meeting as many people as we could to tell the story as well. It was a lot of hard work.

Growth as a style has had a very good run and value has done very poorly for a decade or so. But even if those external factors change, you're not going to change what you do?

Absolutely not. What are we going to do about it, if that happened? Our answer is: well, nothing; we're not going to drift into buying things, because that really goes against exactly what we've done before. The reassurance we can give to shareholders is that, although we have only been running the trust since 2018, we've been running pension fund money since the late 1990s. And we've gone through periods in the past when growth is out of favour and people start to say, "It's great when it works, but it's not so clever when it's not working," but the thing for us is almost to say: "Well, it's not working but we aren't going to change it."

I'm not being arrogant or complacent: the fact is that the most important thing is not to drift or lose faith in what we do, because in the long run we think share prices follow fundamentals, so if you're buying stocks which have got above-average growth, the market will reward you for that. In a funny way I am most bullish about my portfolios when the stocks have performed relatively poorly, because that's the point where you're seeing the best of these growth stocks becoming fantastically attractive as the markets are not appreciating the growth in them. What's important is you have a board and an investment culture at the firm to support you.

How did the institutional funds perform between 2002 and 2007 when, unlike the past decade, value was doing very well as a style?

Not too badly, in the end. The funny thing, going into the financial crisis, was that we owned Northern Rock. That was not great but, ironically enough, because it was a canary in the mine, it made us suddenly very aware of the banking issue. So, although that was a big negative for us, when we did that analysis we actually did quite well relatively. We sold some of our other banks at that point because we could see that this was a disaster waiting to happen. And so, in a funny way, it has helped us because we preserved a lot of capital at that point, so our performance wasn't too bad. But, as you know, it comes and goes.

I remember after Brexit our performance was terrible for a while, because everybody panicked about the UK market and our growth style was out of favour, but it came back because people went back to look at the fundamentals. I don't want to be over-sanguine about these things but, having been through a lot of market cycles, the key is to make sure that you're still always looking for the growth businesses and can recognise what is a growth business and what is a growth industry. You have to keep looking – but the underlying philosophy doesn't change at all.

What other lessons did you draw from the financial crisis?

A number of colleagues had done big reports on the banking sector before the crisis, and liquidity was the one thing we didn't really look at. Yet in a way, when the crisis came, that turned out to be the most important thing of all. It was more about liquidity than solvency or bad debts. Because I was in the mid- and small-cap area, I had always looked at the insurance sector, and the thing that struck me about looking at really successful insurance companies was that they didn't try to manage the business to produce annual reports where the numbers go up all the time.

My theory on the banks is that they were trying to grow their earnings come what may, whether the conditions were attractive or not. The danger of that is that as you get closer to the top of the cycle, it's becoming more risky and therefore you have to take more risks to keep growing, whereas what some of the great insurance companies do is always say: "Well, when returns are attractive I'll write lots of business and when returns are not attractive I will shrink my business."

Now, to me that's what a bank ought to do, but they don't. And that's one reason why we have nothing really in banking, and we like insurance because they think about it differently. As a long-term holder I don't care about the short term, because I know that the good businesses will manage it on a five-year view, whereas if you only care about the short term – as a lot of people do – you hate that type of insurance, because the numbers can be up or down, depending on the conditions.

As an example: we own a company called Lancashire in the portfolio. Earlier this year, they disappointed short-term expectations because they were writing business in some new parts of the market. Because it's new parts of the market, they have to be very conservative and they're reserving a lot at the start. But the reason why they're insuring in those areas is that returns are very attractive because other people are retreating.

On a three- to five-year view, they've done a really smart thing. But if you care about the one- to two-year view, you don't like it – because the numbers have gone down. To me that's a fundamental misunderstanding of what the business is trying to do. We try and think about it as embracing volatility, and understanding it, rather than being worried about it. A lot of businesses have got into trouble trying to tell shareholders: "Oh, you can grow every year, come what may." There are very few business models that have got that resilience.

It is also about the quality of the management, not just the strategy itself?

Yes. We own a lot of companies not because we like them on a top-down view but because from a bottom-up basis we think the management teams are very good stewards of owners' capital. It's unfortunate that the UK has a pretty chequered history in that respect. Some of the business leadership has not always been great.

You have low turnover, but what kind of situations will prompt you to sell a shareholding?

Some are just mistakes: one we sold last year was Carnival, and that was really in reaction to the pandemic, because pre-pandemic we thought the business was doing pretty well. But then we started to think and we didn't know how long the lockdowns were going to last for, and what we were worried about was that the industry background had probably changed for the worse. Linked to that was the fact that they had a lot of debt on the balance sheet. One of the lessons we remembered from 2007-08 is that businesses with a lot of debt, where the industry backdrop is deteriorating, is not a place where there is usually a happy ending for shareholders. We weren't the first to sell, and we weren't too trigger-happy, but we could see a bad outcome for shareholders so we decided to sell.

One of the best questions I got asked once was: what is the downside of being a long-term investor? I think, from our perspective, the potential downside is that we can be overly patient, because we are trying not to react to things and to be thoughtful and not to be the equivalent of shouting "Fire!" in a theatre. In the case of Carnival we probably should have sold it earlier, but we do it our own way – and you can contrast that by saying there's plenty of other companies where we didn't react because we were patient and we didn't sell, which would have been at the worst possible point. So there will be examples when we get it wrong, but we still think the process is the right one.

It may be an idiotic question, but what is the best stock you have had over your career in the UK – and did you foresee it when you first bought it?

It's an easy question to answer, and the company is Ashtead. And no, I never had any idea it was going to be as good as it turned out to be. I think we bought it at under £2 and it fell to £1 quite quickly. So we bought more, but we didn't buy enough of it, because it was one of these things where you are thinking: does the market know something that we don't?. The thing that struck us was its competitive position as a business seemed to get stronger and stronger every year and the management team were smart enough to deploy the capital very wisely. The industry background was also very favourable, and the management was executing very well.

What is the main lesson you have learnt from the ones that have gone wrong?

Going back to the banking crisis, it was quite shocking how close we came to a complete financial meltdown. That was a very scary moment, because we were very close to running out of money in ATMs and yet I couldn't quite believe that this was happening. Logic told you that the banks were going to go bust, but your heart said it couldn't be true. We sold a lot of banks but we didn't sell everything – and we could have sold even more.

The UK market looks cheap, and we are seeing more takeovers. Do you think this is just a phase, just a cyclical phenomenon, or is it something more fundamental?

I don't spend too much time worrying about it, because I just think, "Well, I'm not the market, and there are smarter people who can worry about that." The UK has had a unique combination of issues, as we know. In terms of its mix of businesses, it's got quite a lot of old economy stocks. And then we've had Brexit on top of that, and for a lot of people it's been quite a toxic combination. I think the UK has been somewhat tarnished a little bit by that – we've been puzzled by that, because if you look at the fundamentals of a lot of businesses, there's no reason to. In the end, the markets will do the business for you. Another company will come in and say, "I'm going to pay a substantial premium to what the public markets are willing to do." That is the risk for something like Ultra Electronics. But I think these things will work themselves out. At some point the markets will look at the fundamentals again; despite the pandemic and Brexit and so on, actually a lot of our businesses are in pretty good shape.

IAIN MCCOMBIE *has been a partner of Baillie Gifford since 2005.*

VALUE MERCHANT

SIMON GERGEL, *manager of The Merchants Trust, tells*
JONATHAN DAVIS *about the challenges facing equity income
fund managers in a period when value has been out of style.*

INVESTMENT STYLES COME and go over the years, with value and growth competing for the honours from one year to the next, and small- and large-cap approaches doing likewise, often for several years at a stretch. Momentum is another powerful factor that can heavily influence whether a particular fund is doing well or not at any given point in the market cycle. And then there are the unexpected bolts from the blue, like the covid pandemic, which caused such trouble when it swept into the world's consciousness in the spring of 2020.

Simon Gergel had a first-hand insight into the vagaries of investment style during the early part of his career which he spent working for Phillips & Drew Fund Management, a firm well known for its commitment to value investing in its traditional sense. By that I mean having an intense focus on high dividend yields, low P/Es and other metrics such as price-to-book value, an approach favoured and popularised by the famous investment writer and high priest of value investing, Ben Graham.

PDFM, as it was known for short, was one of a handful of investment management firms that dominated the business of managing pension fund money in the run-up to the internet bubble of 1999-2000. During that bizarre period, however, when the share prices of almost every company even remotely involved in the key sectors of telecoms, media and technology soared to crazy levels, regardless of valuations, the head of PDFM, Tony Dye, became notorious for his refusal to contemplate investing in any of these high-flying stocks that so conspicuously failed to meet his valuation criteria.

As a result, the performance of PDFM's portfolios lagged almost everyone else in the business, the funds flowed out of the firm, and Dye was summarily fired in the spring of 2000. This was the point, almost to the day, when the TMT bubble burst and value investing came storming back into style, outperforming growth for the next seven years. That vindicated Dye's views but was not enough to save his job – a perfect example of how a refusal to follow the herd in investment can bring with it extreme career risk for fund managers.

Value with a twist or two

Simon Gergel is happy to call himself a value investor, a style that he imbued during his 14 years at PDFM, but is careful to explain that his approach is more nuanced than the rigid shackles adopted by value investors in years gone by. While acknowledging that the past few years have been tough for the value style, which once again has been lagging in a market dominated by big-tech stocks, he believes that the growth cycle appears to be peaking and there is plenty to play for.

"To some extent, value investing is a bit of misnomer," he points out. "What it really means to me is that you pay a lot of attention to the price you pay for an asset, whatever that asset is. Provided you do that, it doesn't matter whether you're buying high-growth companies or low-growth companies. Historically, there's a huge amount of evidence that value investing has generally worked over most time periods, although the last few years have certainly been pretty challenging.

"We don't interpret value investing to mean that everything you buy has to have a low P/E ratio. It's not as simple as that. It's about the right valuation for the company concerned. Some cheap companies you should steer clear of, and some highly rated companies are also good value." Gergel says cash flow is probably what he and his team look at most closely, but only as part of a wider approach that takes into account not just valuations, but a range of fundamental factors and a number of medium- and longer-term themes that can be expected to influence stock and sector performance.

So-called thematic investing is a key part of the investment process at Allianz Global Investors, where after a spell at HSBC Gergel has been employed as a specialist UK fund manager since 2006. In that year he took over the running of The Merchants Trust, a trust whose origins date back to the 1880s, and since then he has earned himself a reputation for reliable if volatile performance through some challenging times.

His investment approach has evolved, he says, through experience at the three firms he has worked at and now combines elements he acquired in each place: the fundamentals of a business (hat tip to PDFM), inflation and the business cycle (favoured by HSBC), and the broad global themes that are an integral part of the Allianz process. He says: "Of the three firms, PDFM was much the most focused on valuation. There's a lot of merit in that approach, but you've got to be really careful that you don't buy things just because they look cheap. They can be value traps."

Emotional resilience matters too

What he did learn at PDFM was how "to have an independent view and how to relish that feeling of uncertainty or discomfort when you're buying a share that's going down. It's a skill that I think you have to hone and work on, because we're all emotional beings. If I've got a share that's going down, I feel the pain as much as anyone else, but I've just learnt that that is not necessarily a sign that I should be selling it. It can be a signal to buy more. PDFM was a great grounding in managing that emotional response."

In terms of fundamentals, he says, "what we look at is how good a business it is, how attractive the industry is, how much debt it's got, what the balance sheet is like, the financial structure, how well managed it is, all of the environmental, social and governance risks and issues. You don't start with a pure valuation screen, because otherwise you'd be excluding a lot of things that might be of interest.

"When I worked at HSBC, we focused a lot on what they called business cycle investing, the principle being that you want to invest in cyclical companies in an up cycle and defensive companies in a down cycle. It sounds easy, but actually it's very hard to do. At Allianz we do a lot more with long-term structural themes or trends which can make a difference in the medium to long term – so, for example, how a business is affected by the internet, by demographic trends, and so on.

"Cycles – where we are in the economic cycle, where we are in the cycle for defence spending, for example, because that tends to be a long-term cycle – are also important. However, it is important to say that we're not starting with the theme and trying to find companies that fit in with that. We're starting with the companies and trying to work out which of the themes are affecting them."

Riding the pandemic cycle

We had a dramatic example of a new and unexpected cycle with the pandemic, I say; how did that play out for the trust? "Some cycles can be nothing like you've seen before," he replies, "but this one was really quite extraordinary. In a way you could have seen it coming, because clearly the problems were emerging in Asia, in China, before they hit Europe. But from the moment the virus hit Italy the reaction in the market was savage and very, very quick. There wasn't a huge amount of time to react initially.

"We'd started the year with a fairly optimistic and slightly pro-cyclical positioning because, if you remember, Boris Johnson had won an 80-seat majority, the economy looked to be picking up, Brexit seemed to be getting sorted, and so we were slightly positively positioned. We got hit by the pandemic early on, when companies were having to batten down the hatches, slash costs, suspend dividends, slash cash flow, and really preserve themselves because no one knew at that stage how bad it was going to be.

"We tried to make a few adjustments where we could sensibly, at sensible prices, to make the portfolio a bit more defensive and to build a bit more income into it. So, in the early days we were adding to some areas like telecoms, or some of the more defensive industries with good cash flow, and selling one or two cyclicals where the shares had held up, like Prudential, or a company called Sirius Real Estate where we could sell shares at sensible prices.

"But we didn't panic and sell things when they'd fallen 30%, 40% or 50%. We held on and reassessed. The big opportunity for us came over the summer, when we saw the start of this huge polarisation in the market, which has continued to this day. There were some really good companies trading on crazy low valuations, and equally some more defensive companies were trading at very full valuations.

"We did a lot of portfolio moves in the summer last year to pick up what turned out to be some great bargains – really good companies at silly prices. We bought businesses like Next, Close Brothers, the specialist investment bank, another housebuilder, Bellway, and RSA Insurance. We added some good companies that were really beaten up and out of favour, and we also topped up many existing positions in the fund.

"Towards the end of last year, once you had the vaccine bounce and the market had rotated towards value again, we were able to exit one or two companies which had performed well but where we had low conviction. For example, Senior Engineering, which is an aerospace company, was hit very hard by the pandemic and it's going to be a long time until they pay a dividend. We sold that in the second half of last year when the shares had recovered quite a lot. We switched much of that into Meggitt, which has since attracted a takeover bid.

"Towards the end of the year and into this one, we were adding some higher-quality businesses that had been derated a bit, like RELX, the financial information company. In the summer we also sold companies which had performed well but which looked fully valued: for example, Balfour Beatty the construction company, Pennon the utility company, which had sold their waste business for a very high price." The reason the trust has been able to manage through a tricky year is "touch wood, that we've had a good record of avoiding the value traps. Last year we still had a few – Hammerson, for example, was a very difficult situation – but we've generally avoided the most problematic companies. And even in the case of Hammerson, for example, we supported the rights issue last summer, the shares performed very well after that, and we exited at a much better price than we would have done if we'd panicked and sold early in the pandemic."

These moves have paid off. While the shares in Merchants fell by more than 40% at one point during the sell-off in Q1 2020, they have rebounded strongly since then and are now back trading only a short way below where they were before the pandemic struck. The scale of the recovery means that the three-, five- and ten-year share price returns are now ahead of the peer group average in the UK equity income sector, although the sector itself has inevitably lagged other sectors with more growth names in them.

So it was another valuable learning experience, I suggest. "Well, in the last five years we've had the Brexit referendum, we've had the potential of a relatively hard-left Labour government, and we've had the pandemic, all of which have been quite important events for the market and we've had to manage through. I'd like to have a period of quiet, but these events do throw up opportunities. The opportunities last summer were similar to what we saw in 1999/2000 in terms of the extreme polarisation of the stock market. It's still pretty polarised."

The chart he points to tells that story. "About 20% of the stock market is on a price-earnings ratio of over 24, and a big chunk of the stock market is on a price-earnings ratio of under 12 – there's not much in the middle. That's not what you would normally expect. High-growth companies or the perceived high-quality companies are on pretty high valuations by any stretch of the imagination, while many other companies are languishing."

Valuations in a polarised market

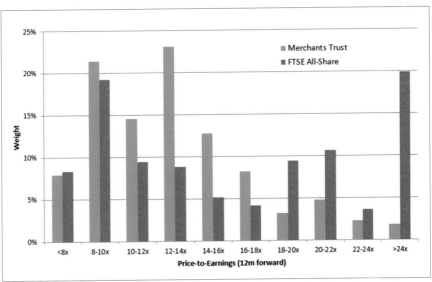

Source: Merchants Trust, September 2021.

What that also means is that the trust's portfolio is very different from the UK equity market in terms of its shape, something that helps to differentiate it from others in its peer group. Yet, Gergel says, "we're not buying low-quality companies. Many of them have proved their worth through the recession, or through the pandemic, and have come out stronger on the other end. You've got to be careful, though, because there are clearly lots of cheap shares that should be cheap."

Managing the debt

Two other features help to make Merchants stand out in the sector, as well as going some way towards explaining its distinctive pattern of performance. One is the relatively high level of gearing compared with many other trusts, which by accentuating gains and losses has clearly contributed to the volatility in the share price. For many years the trust was hindered by having inherited a significant amount of fixed-rate structural debt, a legacy from a period in the 1980s and 1990s when interest rates were much higher than they are now and nobody on the board anticipated quite how low the cost of debt might fall.

"When I started at Merchants in 2006, I inherited three long-term debentures taken out in the 1980s with an average cost of debt of 8.5%, so we didn't have a lot of choice really! It would have been incredibly expensive to buy that back in. It is not that we weren't comfortable with 20% gearing. The portfolio had a large-cap and UK bias, so although there's underlying currency exposure in the portfolio, most of the shares are UK listed and many of them have sterling reporting."

Since 2017 the board has taken a more active approach to tackling the cost of the debt, refinancing one long-term debenture when it matured, paying off another one early, taking the hit to NAV, and taking out a revolving credit facility. This has brought the average cost of debt down from over 8% to a more manageable 3.5%. The target remains to keep the gearing between 10% and 25%, and in mid-2021 it was around 15%. "We don't try to muck around with it too much," Gergel says. "The decision last year to pay back some of the debt was the first active decision we'd made on the debt since I've been around."

The commitment to maintaining a significant amount of gearing, while painful in a down market, is helpful in enabling the trust to offer a significantly higher dividend yield than its competitors. At the end of September 2021 the yield on the trust was a fraction over 5%, while the average in the UK equity income sector was around 3.8%. Having drawn on revenue reserves to sustain the dividend during the pandemic, the trust is likely to have to do so again in the current financial year, though not to the same extent.

Putting the yield in context

What is the thinking behind the strategy on the gearing and the yield? "Well, firstly, it's now quite cheap. The cost is 3.5%. We're getting a yield on the portfolio of 4.5%. So, provided we don't lose money, we don't need any capital growth from the portfolio for the gearing to make sense financially. The second point is that the gearing does give us more income to distribute. That's a bit smoke and mirrors, because we charge a third of the cost of debt to the income account and two-thirds to the capital account, which has the effect of boosting the income. That is obviously very helpful for a trust that's trying to pay out a high dividend.

"We are happy with that, because I think many shareholders at Merchants clearly want a high income. Many of them use it as a retirement vehicle, so they want and expect a high income, and gearing is one of the ways to get there. The combination of better total return and boosting the income is quite beneficial for shareholders. Obviously, it comes at the cost of higher volatility. In rising markets, it's beneficial, and hopefully over time that should prove to be a positive.

"The income we're receiving in the portfolio is now growing very quickly, as we're seeing a sharp recovery in income. We've seen one or two of our peers cut or rebase dividends. We've not had to do that, and we have still achieved one of the best total returns in the peer group, despite the value and the high yield bias which has not been particularly helpful in the last few years."

The shareholders in Merchants therefore seem happy with the policy of raiding reserves to maintain a high and growing dividend, as the shares have been trading at a premium for most of 2021, enabling the trust to issue more equity through secondary issuance. "I think the reason we're trading at net asset value, and have been able to issue new equity in the last 18 months, is that we've got a good story to tell. Most importantly, we explain what we're doing and why we're doing it, and many people believe in that. I don't think it is just about the yield, because there are plenty of other yielding trusts that trade at discounts and don't have the same profile in the market."

Positive about the UK

As for the future, Gergel remains confident that the UK market can continue to outperform other international market in relative terms. "One of the reasons you're seeing so much M&A is because the markets are cheap and there are opportunities. Corporates are spotting value in the UK, particularly now they're getting their confidence back after the pandemic. If professional investors like myself fail to push the market up, then private equity will certainly come in.

"Hopefully, what will happen is at some point global investors will realise that, post Brexit, the UK has not fallen off a cliff, the UK economy is actually doing all right and most British companies are very global anyway. They're not that dependent on the UK economy, whatever your view on the UK economy. Yes, there are some structural issues with the UK market. It has historically had more in what you might call the old-economy, mining, banking, utilities and those types of sectors, which are less exciting than technology. They may grow less.

"But many of those industries have restructured. Banking has completely changed in the last decade since the financial crisis. The mining industry is now very cash generative. The energy industry is transforming itself. You can make a case that some of those industries are going to get more interesting as well. To some extent the discount in the UK versus the world is justified, but even if you adjust for the sector's composition the UK still looks very cheap, and it is no surprise to me that we are seeing a whole raft of takeovers coming through."

DON'T RISK THE INCOME

CHARLES LUKE, *one of the big winners from last year's merry-go-round in the UK equity income sector, explains his low-risk approach to* JONATHAN DAVIS.

MANAGER CHANGE WAS the big story in the UK equity income sector in 2020, with no fewer than three of the bigger trusts in the sector changing their manager after long periods of poor performance, a trend that was obviously exacerbated by the pandemic. Shareholders in Temple Bar (ticker: TMPL), Edinburgh Investment Trust (EDIN), and Perpetual Income and Growth (PIGIT) all found themselves with new managers after their boards called time on the previous incumbents. This followed hard on the heels of the dramatic and well-publicised demise of Neil Woodford's open-ended equity income fund, the largest UK equity fund of all, the year before.

One of the beneficiaries of this all-change period was Charles Luke, the manager of Murray Income (ticker: MUT), an investment trust with a historical pedigree that dates back to 1923. Originally founded as the Caledonian Trust Company,* it is now part of the abrdn stable of trusts, but owes its name to another fund management company, the Glaswegian-based Murray Johnstone, which was bought by Aberdeen Asset Management, as it then was, in 2000 (a reminder that corporate change is nothing new in the investment trust world).

Compared to the combative and outsized personality of Neil Woodford, it would be hard to overstate the contrast with Luke, a quietly spoken and bespectacled 48-year-old economics graduate who has been at the helm of Murray Income since 2006. Anything but flashy, his careful stewardship of the trust over more than 15 years was richly rewarded when the board of Perpetual Income and Growth decided in September last year to merge their trust with his.

In the process, the combination of two roughly similar mid-sized trusts has doubled the size of Murray Income. With net assets of around £1.2bn, the trust now ranks fourth in the 24-strong UK equity income sector, measured by total assets. Mergers are rare in the investment world, for all sorts of reasons, some good and some bad, but this one does appear to have been a win-win outcome for everyone except Invesco Perpetual, the former managers of PIGIT.

---

* Not to be confused with the Caledonia investment trust, set up by the Cayzer shipping dynasty in 1960, originally to manage the family's wealth, and still 48% owned by them.

The fees have come down, liquidity has improved, and both sets of shareholders can, I think, be reassured that their dividends will not be lightly put at risk. Murray Income is one of the AIC's "dividend heroes", having increased its annual dividend every year for 48 years. It is a safe bet that Luke will not be doing anything to jeopardise that status. Somewhat paradoxically, of course, the need to sustain such a consistent dividend track record, while good for marketing purposes, can stifle a manager's room to manoeuvre and thereby risk foregone returns.

Formative lessons

As it happens, Luke has good reason to be wary of taking too much risk with shareholders' money. After studying and obtaining a joint degree in Japanese and economics, he started his career at Framlington in the 1990s, where he was immediately put to work managing two split capital investment trusts. He joined abrdn in 2000, where, still in his twenties, he ran portfolios for half a dozen funds, including several other split capital investment trusts, an area in which abrdn was, for good and ill, one of the biggest and most influential players.

Although it only involved a minority of firms, the subsequent split capital trust debacle, when scores of trusts with multiple share classes imploded under the weight of an intricate circle of interlocking shareholdings, chummy boards and excessive gearing, was a painful episode for the industry as a whole. The bad odour that the split capital trust saga left behind took several years to dissipate. However, it also led directly to the huge improvement in corporate governance standards that has been observable recently, with genuinely independent boards now much more to the fore.

This experience, I suggest to Luke when we meet to discuss the trust, must have been a formative early lesson in the need for boards and managers to take more seriously the risk they are taking with shareholders' money. "Absolutely it was," Luke says now. "It was very painful from a corporate perspective, as all the trusts were eventually wound up. Fortunately, my job was just to manage the portfolios, so I was not directly involved in the structural issues that caused so many problems."

Another formative experience was seeing first-hand how a famous Framlington fund, the Net Net fund, which invested solely in high-flying Internet stocks during the TMT bubble, had come crashing to the ground after rising ten times or so in little more than a year and attracting huge inflows of money at the height of the speculative mania.

These lessons are clearly ones Luke has not forgotten, since his style as manager of Murray Income is a world away from that kind of approach, instead being very much focused on finding sustainable dividends in good-quality companies and monitoring risk carefully. Despite having studied Japanese at university, he was not tempted to do anything other than stick to the UK equity market as his primary focus. "I did spend a year in Tokyo, but I found myself a natural home in UK companies and that's where I settled and have been ever since," he says.

A focus on quality

Luke's style of looking to invest in quality companies and managing for income clearly sits comfortably with his early experience and personality. "I think the quality perspective dovetails well with the temperament you mentioned. I'm naturally quite risk averse. I don't like taking risks; I am always thinking about downside protection and capital resilience.

"Lots of the economic history and the courses I took at the London School of Economics were around competitive strategy, and if you look back over ten, twenty, thirty years and the companies that perform well, virtually all have had some sort of sustainable competitive advantage. That is where quality investment really comes into its own. Patrick Gifford, the former chairman of Murray Income, always used to say: 'If you want to grow your income, you need to grow your capital first.'

"The way I think about that is that if you want to grow your dividends, you need to grow your earnings – and, over the long term, good-quality companies are best placed to do that. So for lots of reasons – empirically, temperamentally, historically – we're well suited to focusing on good-quality companies. If you look at the academic research, it demonstrates that reinvested dividends generate the greatest proportion of total returns over the long term.

"So I think it makes sense for me to be an income investor. I am not, though, an income investor who just looks for companies with high dividend yields. Rather, it is about finding companies that have sensible dividends and can grow their earnings and hence their dividends over time. I'm looking for companies that have sensible dividend yields and just continue to grow, with good-quality characteristics."

This approach is borne out by the performance of the trust over his 15-year stewardship. The 'beta' of the trust, academic jargon for its sensitivity to market movements, is 0.9, meaning that when the UK equity market falls 10%, Murray Income will tend to decline by only 9%. The same applies on the upside. Over the past ten years, the trust has outperformed the index by 0.5% per month during falling markets, and underperformed by 0.1% in rising markets. Over time those seemingly small margins add up to a useful performance edge.

Best performing UK listed companies

Since 1 July 2001

COMPANY	TOTAL RETURN (%)	10Y MEDIAN ROIC
Diploma	9215	18.5%
Domino's Pizza Group	8657	28.3%
Ashtead Group	8554	14.2%
Flutter Entertainment	8505	41.5%
JD Sports Fashion	8102	25.8%
Games Workshop	7462	29.1%
Genus	7448	8.8%
Aveva Group	5355	18.6%
Croda International	4662	22.6%
Spirax-Sarco Engr.	4598	19.7%
Hill & Smith	4171	10.8%
Dechra Pharmaceuticals	4153	6.7%
XP Power (DI)	3549	22.2%
London Stock Exchange	3345	8.1%
Antofagasta	2959	5.7%
Halma	2841	16.6%
Clarkson	2753	8.9%
4Imprint Group	2705	80.6%
Cranswick	2528	13.6%
Avon Protection	2474	31.0%

Since 1 July 1991

COMPANY	TOTAL RETURN (%)	10Y MEDIAN ROIC
Next	88333	55.9%
Ashtead Group	49170	14.2%
Sage Group	24132	14.6%
Cranswick	23959	13.6%
Diploma	19790	18.5%
Antofagasta	17489	5.7%
Spirax-Sarco Engr.	15426	19.7%
Savills	15375	16.2%
Greggs	13479	20.2%
Rotork	11569	17.1%
Croda International	11487	22.6%
Halma	11353	16.6%
St Modwen Props.	8270	6.8%
Bellway	8229	14.7%
Berkeley Group HDG.	7321	20.7%
Hill & Smith	6512	10.8%
British American Tobacco	6363	19.1%
Bunzl	6266	11.5%
Renishaw	6176	26.8%
Spectris	5721	15.4%

I ask what else Luke has learnt in his 15 years at the helm. "One lesson is that you should never take anything for granted. I worry about every holding all the time, to be honest. I'm that kind of character. But if there was only one question that I could ask a company, it would be this one: 'What is your sustainable competitive advantage?' I think that's really important in making sure you don't get negative surprises. You don't want to find, for example, that a company has made an acquisition which destroys capital."

The abrdn process of screening for quality companies focuses on a range of factors – not just sustainable competitive advantage, but also the management team, the financials, the balance sheet. "You need to ensure that you know the management is sensible, have good track records and are good allocators of capital. You need downside protection in terms of the quality of the business, maybe a strong brand, a product that is needs driven and has a strong market share, capable of making good returns".

"Over the last ten to thirty years of the companies that have done really well, their return on invested capital is much higher than their cost of capital. They have something different that enables them to maintain high returns." The manager's job then, in Luke's view, is simply "to maintain the focus on good-quality companies and divorce yourself from the noise in the market." Luke is keen to impress on me that he is a relatively small cog in the Murray Income machine and the dedication and professionalism of the board, all who work on Murray Income at abrdn and the excellent stock research from his team should not be overlooked.

Investment trust advantages

Although Luke also manages open-ended funds, Murray Income is comfortably his largest mandate. What does he think is the advantage of managing an investment trust? "There are positives and negatives on both sides of the ledger, but I think the investment benefits of the investment trusts are very strong. You can buy assets at a discount – the fund is on about 5% or 6% discount at the moment. You have a little bit of gearing, you have the revenue reserves, the charges are also lower on the investment trust, and you have an independent board."

On the latter point, he says that "some people have the idea that non-executive directors turn up, collect some sandwiches, take the money and go home and that's it. But that is not right. The board and the chairman throughout the whole merger process spent hours and hours in meetings, going through everything and doing a fantastic job for shareholders. That is something that the open-ended fund doesn't have. These are all quite significant benefits."

Nearly one year on from the completion of the merger in November 2020, the performance of the trust has been steady, but trailing slightly behind what has been a strong overall upward trend in the UK equity market. That is consistent with the performance characteristics mentioned already. How does he judge the success of the merger so far against the promised benefits? "I think it's really good news for both sets of shareholders. It improves the scale and economies of scale for the trust, lowers the fees, increases the profile – and, now we have been promoted to the mid-cap index, the spread has narrowed. All those good things."

Any capacity constraints? "I did some work last year on the capacity of a quality portfolio like ours and you can easily get it up to £4bn to £5bn. At the moment with the trust and the open-ended fund it is about £1.5bn, so there's huge amounts of headroom. The benefit of the focus on good-quality companies and a buy and hold investment approach is that once you've got a new investment, you don't have the need to trade all the time. Turnover is pretty low."

What lessons, then, does he draw from the demise of the Woodford Equity Income fund, which at one stage was managing more than £15bn and moving ever deeper into venture capital and other illiquid holdings? "It is difficult to tell," is his careful reply. "I've read the book *Built on a Lie,*[*] which was interesting. There may have been a good idea behind investing in the unquoteds, but it's difficult when it's not what you're saying you do and you don't have so much expertise in it. You need a lot of very knowledgeable people in the specific areas to do it well.

"The important thing for me is just sticking to the knitting, rather than necessarily thinking that if I'm good at something then I must be good at anything. Also, it is important not to be doing something where you don't have any experience or particular knowledge, even if it's a good idea. Clearly, the performance of the illiquid funds went against him, and it all became very challenging."

UK versus overseas

Like many UK equity funds, the fund's mandate allows it to invest a proportion in stocks, up to 20%, that are listed not in the UK but in other markets. When Luke took over the fund it did not have approval to invest in overseas stocks, but he has been able to do so now for over ten years. During that period exposure has been as high as 16% but is now back down to 12%. I ask Luke the rationale behind those moves and for his thoughts on the UK market, which has been in the doghouse with international investors ever since the Brexit referendum but more recently has shown signs of recovery in both absolute and relative terms.

"The rationale behind being able to do so is twofold really. The first one is being able to invest in good-quality companies in industries that you can't find in the UK market. So, in the fund, we have companies such as Kone, the elevators company; VAT Group, which is a vacuum valve manufacturer that supplies into the semiconductor industry; and MOWI, which is a salmon fishing company.

"But we also do it to help to diversify risk. Some of the sectors in the UK are quite concentrated, so we own some Novo Nordisk in the pharmaceutical sector, Nestlé, a little bit of TotalEnergies. It has been very helpful over time in helping performance and also providing that diversification. It's worked well, but at the moment it's still a bit lower than it was before. That's probably an indication that the quality UK companies we can invest in are more attractively valued for quality relative to where we were three or four years ago."

What does he think about the outlook for the UK market? "My phrase would be 'increasingly sanguine'. I don't want to get too excited, but I am relatively optimistic.

---

[*] A book about the Woodford saga, by *FT* journalist Owen Walker.

If you look at the vaccine rollout, the stable politics, Brexit in the rearview mirror, pent-up demand: on a relative basis, as you say, valuations are attractive and international investors are underweight. You are also starting to see lots of M&A, in terms of either corporates buying other corporates or private equity doing so.

"The interesting thing is that private equity doesn't necessarily just go for cheap companies; they look at companies that have similar characteristics to quality income – so, strong balance sheets, resilient earnings, decent quality characteristics and so on. They are also looking for an exit, and we've seen bids for the likes of John Laing and Sanne in the portfolio from private equity companies."

Are valuations still looking attractive in absolute terms as well as in relative terms, given an environment of very low interest rates? "With a low discount rate, it can certainly make the companies look attractive, but for me what it comes down to is still the dividend yield. If you're getting a 3.5% or 4% dividend yield, and you can get 5%, 6%, 7% earnings growth in aggregate, then I think that that is an attractive combination.

"If you look at the income for the UK market compared to other regional equity markets, it's a lot higher. And if you look at it compared to what you're getting from a bond or put it in the bank – or, in many cases, from property – then, again, I think that's a positive. When we have our AGM you meet the investors in Murray Income, and it's very clear to me that the income has a very important functional purpose for them."

Tough at the top

You have the burden of being on the list of AIC dividend heroes, I say, and having been there for many years – and you've had to draw on revenue reserves to get through the wave of dividend cuts that followed the pandemic lockdown. Is the pressure to increase the dividend every year a constraint on what you do, and does it make you uncomfortable at times?

"It's a good discipline to have, in many ways. It comes back to what I said earlier: it's important not only to deliver dividend growth but to earn it. What you don't want is to go down a cul-de-sac by investing in high-yielding companies and then find that, for whatever reason, they end up cutting. Three investment trusts in the sector have had to cut dividends in the last year or so. That just helps you to remember to focus on earnings growth as well as just thinking about a high dividend yield."

The yield of the trust now is about 3.9%, lower than some of Murray Income's competitors. What does Luke expect from here? "Well, the last couple of years have been extremely unusual," he says (a fair point!). "We have a five-year model of dividend growth, which suggests that 20% of the portfolio is going to grow its dividend over the medium term at 8% or more; 60% is growing at between 3% and 7%; and 20% is probably between zero and 2%. If you take the average of that, you probably get 5% to 6% dividend growth. That probably gets you to maybe a 10% return, or a high single-digit return. I think that's pretty decent in this world of low interest rates and after what happened last year."

We talk more about the pandemic and his experience. "Income for the trust has been very resilient and has bounced back very quickly. In the year to June 2021 compared to the year to June 2019 (being the year before the pandemic), income fell for the portfolio by around 5% compared to around a 30% fall in the market's dividend income. We expect income to surpass pre-pandemic levels for the portfolio this financial year, compared to the registrar company Link's expectations for the market being 2025. So it has been much, much more resilient than the market as a whole, and that's the benefit of the focus on good-quality companies." Now all we need is for the markets to stabilise and the recovery from the pandemic to persist.

TRUSTS PAST AND FUTURE

SIR JOHN KAY, *knighted this year for services to business, finance and economics, reflects on his 12 years as a director of Scottish Mortgage Trust.*

Investing through history

THE WORLD'S OLDEST example of a collective investment vehicle, the investment trust, came into being before the First World War. These funds allowed middle-class investors in the UK to benefit from British imperialism – economic and political – in Asia, Africa and Latin America. That history survives in the name of the oldest investment trust, Foreign and Colonial, which celebrated its 150th anniversary in 2018 and now prefers the more discreet title F&C.

Scottish Mortgage Investment Trust was formed in 1909, just as Henry Ford was launching his Model T, to raise funds for what seemed attractive opportunities in Malaysian rubber plantations. These would provide materials for the nascent automobile industry. Evidently the demand for rubber plantation finance was more limited than had been thought, so the company broadened its remit. The connection to automobiles remains, however. Scottish Mortgage's largest holding today, and the one every shareholder and financial adviser wants to talk about, is Tesla.

Investment companies were culpably implicated in the Wall Street crash of 1929. The Goldman Sachs Trading Corporation, launched in 1928, was only one of a dizzying range of leveraged investment companies promoted by that bank and others as the Roaring Twenties roared. By 1931, it had lost 99% of its value. The anxiety of small investors to be part of the boom had also led to the creation of the first US mutual funds. These fell too in the crash but did retain some value. US investors have preferred mutual funds ever since.

The mutual fund format was copied in the UK with the brave establishment in 1931 of the first unit trust by M&G. The key difference between an investment trust (a closed-ended investment company) and a unit trust (an open-ended investment company) is that an investor in a closed-ended fund must buy from or sell to another investor. By contrast, the investor in an open-ended fund deals directly with the manager, who must then buy or sell shares from the underlying portfolio. An investment trust may therefore be priced at a discount or (less often) a premium to its net asset value, while an open-ended fund is, in principle at least, always worth its share of the underlying assets.

Unit trusts historically had two marketing advantages over investment trusts: they could be advertised to potential investors, and they could pay commission to intermediaries. Subsequent regulatory changes have largely addressed these anomalies. The advantages were to the promoter of the trust rather than to the investor but, as a result, far more money is today invested in open-ended vehicles.

However, this apparent vote of confidence is not necessarily to the investor's advantage. Retail investors frequently get trapped in daily-traded funds that invest in illiquid assets, such as commercial property or early-stage companies, which cannot easily be sold. This is a problem with which regulators have been grappling for years.

Investment trusts have proved a better structure for holding more esoteric assets – and furthermore, a variety of studies have suggested that closed-ended funds outperform similar open-ended equivalents.

Deep discounts

Nevertheless, for much of the postwar era, the investment trust seemed to be a dying vehicle. Insurance companies and pension funds had once used investment trusts as they began to add equities to the bonds in their portfolios, but they reduced their holdings as they took over direct control of their funds and the shares of most investment companies traded at a discount to their net asset value (NAV).

The investment trust discount tends to reflect the popularity or otherwise of the fund manager – mainly a reflection of relative recent performance – and the fashionability of the sector in which the trust is invested.

For most of the time in recent years the shares of Scottish Mortgage have stood at a small premium to its net asset value, and so do most trusts specialising in infrastructure or renewables, which are both in vogue with investors. Investment trusts with an Asian focus, however, typically trade at large discounts to NAV. There are also significant discounts on many real estate investment trusts (commonly known as REITs), particularly those exposed to retail property. These discounts may reflect scepticism about reported asset values in the commercial property sector.

Some investment trusts now profess 'discount management policies' which involve buying back shares when a significant discount emerges and issuing shares when it is possible to do so at a premium. Scottish Mortgage is one of the few to have implemented such a policy successfully, with the result that for several years now the shares have traded close to asset value. This is true even though a significant proportion of the portfolio is illiquid.

So, what is the secret of success? For any investor, successful stock-picking requires the pursuit of a group of related investment themes, and the construction of a concentrated portfolio focused on these themes.

In the case of Scottish Mortgage's fund manager James Anderson and his co-manager Tom Slater, the key investment theme is that the centre of growth in the world economy has shifted to Asia. Everyone understands that a large proportion of the manufactured goods we buy today come from China. But the corollary is the evolution of a Chinese middle class with demand for consumer goods and, more importantly, services. The investment opportunity is in the emergent companies that meet these needs.

New horizons

Fifty years of financialisation produced an emphasis on 'making the numbers' in corporate quarterly earnings reports – which did not, over the long term, create the 'shareholder value' which executives purported to seek. Twenty-five years ago, you might have thought a portfolio containing shares in General Electric and General Motors, ICI, Marks and Spencer, Barclays Bank and Sears Roebuck represented a low-risk, conservative approach to investment. And you would have been spectacularly wrong.

Stock market growth over the period has been considerable, but largely driven by new companies, not established market leaders. This was always true, but a more rapid pace of corporate change has made the dependence of aggregate performance on a small number of outstanding stocks more obvious.

Capitalism, as it emerged in the 19th century, is dead. Businesses have long ceased to finance their investment through equity markets. Net capital raising in public markets is negative. New issues have been smaller than the amounts taken out in share buybacks and acquisitions for cash, and tangible assets, less important than they were, are typically fungible; they need not be owned by the company that uses them and typically are not.

After covid-19 there was a predictable revival of new equity issues by established companies – not to finance new activity, but to restore balance sheets depleted by covid-19 related losses. The same thing happened after the 2008 financial crisis, although most of the fresh equity that time came from government.

Such exceptional periods aside, the principal need for new equity capital now is to fund the operating losses of new businesses as they seek to establish a market position. If asset management is to mean something more significant to the economy and more rewarding to investors than outguessing other fund managers on what AstraZeneca's next quarterly earnings will be, it is in such funding that opportunities are to be found.

Scottish Mortgage is not a venture capital fund, but it has become a provider of capital to growing businesses that are not yet cash-generative and which are not yet – and may never be – interested in a public market listing. That is why a quarter of the fund is invested in unlisted securities.

Such a strategy is only realistically achievable in a closed-ended fund. The failure of the Woodford funds, following the earlier gating of open-ended property funds, provides a warning that the promise of immediate redemption at asset value is possible only if the portfolio is confined to a range of highly marketable securities – shares in highly liquid companies such as AstraZeneca, Unilever, HSBC and Shell (I also hold Shell in my portfolio). Yet if that is your choice, you will be limited to index returns and be better off in a tracker or ETF (exchange traded fund).

The Woodford episode is also a warning of the dangers of running a closed-ended fund alongside an open-ended fund with a similar portfolio, as redemptions in the latter will affect values in the former. In the case of Scottish Mortgage, that required a review of the overlaps between the trust's portfolio and other funds managed by Baillie Gifford.

Finding value

There are far too many investment funds in the UK. The ordinary retail investor has a choice of more than 3,000 open-ended funds – there are more funds than London-listed stocks. In addition, there are more than 400 closed-end funds, or investment trusts. Although charges have fallen in the past decade, they are still too high.

I have provocatively explained the reason elsewhere: as with brain surgeons and estate agents, price competition is not very effective in these markets because it is well worth paying more for a product that is even slightly better, yet it is very difficult to judge whether a product is in fact better. Combine that observation with the existence of economies of scale in managing money – it isn't ten times as expensive to handle a portfolio of £1bn as it is to manage one of £100m – and you understand why the fund management industry is so very profitable.

Should you contribute to that profitability? You should not pay active management fees for a 'closet indexed' fund. If the largest holdings are AstraZeneca, Unilever, Shell and HSBC, you are in effect paying active management fees for an index tracker, and you will do better to buy the index tracker.

It is instructive to divide the quoted management fee by the 'active share' – the total of deviations from the benchmark index. If that active share is 20% and the management fee is 0.75%, then you are in effect paying 3.75% for the manager's (very limited) stock selection on that slice of your holdings. They will have to be very good indeed to recoup that for you. Since most managers are hesitant to move very far from their benchmarks – and regulation tends to discourage them from doing so – that criterion rules out many of the trusts competing for your money.

There are two compelling models for an investment trust. One, followed by a few companies, with the Personal Assets Trust as the standout example, is to offer a complete investment portfolio, designed to be the only security you need. That trust's holdings are conservative and diversified across asset categories, and an investor would have experienced few sleepless nights and earned returns well ahead of those you could expect from a building society.

The other approach, of which Scottish Mortgage has become the standout example, is to pursue a style derived from a well-articulated investment philosophy. Importantly, such a strategy is based on a view about business rather than a view about assets or markets, and on a view about the future of particular firms and products rather than a macroeconomic prediction about the future policy of the Federal Reserve Board.

The future of asset management

Such thinking is, I believe, the future of asset management in the 21st century. However, it will require skills rather different from those that chartered financial analysts currently obtain. It is less about the capital asset pricing model and more about models of product pricing. I recall a conversation with a well-known fund manager who, when I began to talk about business strategy, said: "I don't want to know about competitive advantage; I want to know which stocks are going to go up." I wouldn't place my own money there or bet on the long-term future of his firm.

The Scottish Mortgage strategy which I describe stood up well to the covid crisis; the large holding in Amazon paid off and the much smaller holding in Zoom was taken long before anyone imagined that in 2020 it would become the business tool of choice. For different reasons, Tesla has achieved an all-time high. But there might have been a very different existential crisis – a cyber attack, or a 'Carrington event' which knocked out much of the world's electricity network (the last one was in 1859, just before there was a world electricity network to knock out). These crises would have disproportionately damaged the Scottish Mortgage portfolio.

The lesson I will leave investors with is that the only safe – and even then only relatively safe – investment strategy is one that emphasises wide diversification. There should be fewer investment trusts and many fewer unit trusts. The ones worth investing in are those with a well-argued investment philosophy that chimes with your own. After doing your own research, you will find there are some managers who fall into this category, but too many who simply boast of their prowess at stock-picking. A robust equity investment portfolio might be based on a selection of the former – and for the rest, a tracker will do.

SIR JOHN KAY *is one of the UK's most distinguished business economists. His most recent book is* Radical Uncertainty, *co-authored with Lord (Mervyn) King, the former governor of the Bank of England. See www.johnkay.com for more details. An earlier version of this article first appeared in the* Financial Times.

LET'S GET PHYSICAL

PHILIP WALLER, *manager of the J.P. Morgan Global Core Real Assets trust, explains what real assets are and why their time has come.*

O NE OF THE biggest debates that has dominated the investment world since the autumn of 2020 is whether higher inflation is going to be a permanent or merely a transitory feature of the environment as reopening after lockdown gathers pace. With interest rates at such historically low levels, any investor looking for income has much to fear if inflation does start to pick up and rates fail to keep pace. It will be an environment in which 'real assets', meaning tangible investments that deliver a positive return over and above inflation, will be much in demand.

That is why the great majority of fundraising by investment trusts over the past 12 months has been for specialist property, infrastructure, renewable energy and other types of alternative assets which, while they generally offer only modest expectations for capital appreciation, do hold out the prospect of returns that keep pace with – and ideally can outpace – the current rate of inflation. Because these types of investments tend to be very large, specialist projects, they are by their nature hard for private investors to find and own themselves and, even when found, are often complex and difficult to analyse.

Is there a case, then, for looking to put your money into an investment trust that does have access to the biggest and best projects and can do all the heavy lifting for you? That is the pitch that J.P. Morgan is making with its Global Core Real Assets trust (ticker: JARA). It was launched in September 2019 and after a slow start has begun to gain some traction as we move into the post-covid era. The trust raised £150m at launch but has since grown through further issuance to around £200m at the time of writing.

Real means tangible

What are global core real assets and what are their attractions? The J.P. Morgan definition of core real assets is that they are both physically tangible (the likes of warehouses, power plants and ships) and core in the sense of being fundamental to the workings of modern-day economies. In principle they are among the most reliable ways to generate inflation-linked returns, typically because their activities are the subject of long-term inflation-proofed contracts, frequently regulated, and derive most of their value from the income they generate.

J.P. Morgan has been investing globally in these kinds of assets for more than five decades through its alternatives group and has around $80bn invested in them. The idea behind the investment trust is to give private investors the chance to get a small slice of that action, via a diversified range of assets that are normally only available to the biggest institutions such as pension funds and insurance companies. This is how the trust itself sums up its case: "The real asset strategies to which the company has access would generally not be available to most investors, either because the underlying investments are held through private funds, which are not publicly offered, or because of the size of commitment needed to gain access to these strategies."

The key points, says Philip Waller, are that as well as providing secure inflation-linked returns, historically these types of assets are not correlated to the performance of equity markets, which is an important source of their diversification benefit. "We can go into a plethora of definitions and nuances of what we define as core, but it is really about real assets which derive the majority of their returns from predictable, contracted and regulated income streams." In practice, that means projects that generate a return from high-quality counterparts, such as governments, businesses and energy companies in developed markets.

Real assets compare favourably with other asset classes in terms of expected returns

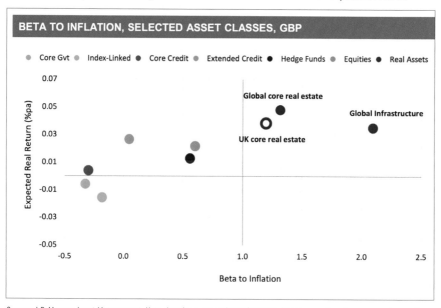

Source: J.P. Morgan Asset Management. Note that these are estimated returns, based on past performance and are not a reliable indicator of current and future results. Provided for discussion purposes only.

High single-digit target returns

The J.P. Morgan trust sees itself therefore as providing a safe way into these kind of assets for two types of investor: (i) those who can't or don't wish to invest directly into specialist infrastructure and real estate trusts; and (ii) those who are looking to increase their exposure to global projects, given that many existing listed infrastructure trusts are primarily focused on the UK. It aims to achieve a target annualised rate of total return of between 7% and 9% net of fees, of which between 4% and 6% will be paid out as a dividend.

The trust was fully invested for the first time in mid-2020 and is on target to pay a 4p dividend for the current 2021/22 financial year, implying a full-year prospective yield of around 4.4% as at the start of Q4 2021. About 60% to 70% of the income is directly and explicitly linked to inflation, meaning that if inflation rises in the countries where the income is generated, the income the trust receives will increase, sometimes after a small lag, by at least the same percentage. The 4.4% dividend yield compares favourably the 1.5%-2.5% income return that J.P. Morgan's capital markets team estimated last year was the expected yield on a traditional bond-equity portfolio, split 60% equities and 40% bonds.

Estimated long-term asset class returns

Key Metrics - 15 yrs	Global Equities	60% Global Equities / 40% Global Debt	Global Listed Infra	Global Listed REITs	JARA
Target Total Return (Net)	5 - 7%	4 - 6%	4 - 6%	6 - 8%	7 - 9%
Target Income Return (Approximate)	2 - 3%	1.5 - 2.5%	3 - 4%	3.5 - 4.5%	4 - 6%
Historical Gross Return	7.7%	6.7%	6.5%	5.2%	10.3%
Historical Volatility	17.1%	10.5%	19.3%	22.4%	9.0%
Gross Return per Unit of Risk	0.5	0.6	0.3	0.2	1.1
Max Drawdown	-38%	-21%	-39%	-48%	-9%
% of Time Over CPI + 3%	77%	77%	54%	62%	100%

Source: J.P. Morgan Asset Management. Note that these are estimated returns, based on past performance and are not a reliable indicator of current and future results. Provided for discussion purposes only.

The JARA portfolio breaks down into two main types of investment. About half the portfolio is in infrastructure (both fixed and moving) and the remainder is in real estate. For the former, says Waller, "We mostly avoid the types of asset that are sensitive to changes in GDP. We typically want ten plus years of visible future cash flow and that means our portfolio is dominated by contracted power projects, primarily renewable energy, and regulated utilities." Around half the infrastructure segment consists of big transport assets operated by well-capitalised counterparties. These are mainly shipping assets, such as container ships and liquefied natural gas carriers. Aircraft leasing, where the counterparties are financially weaker and more volatile and exposed by comparison, are a smaller part of the transport sub-segment.

JARA portfolio weightings by sector

Sector	% Allocation
Industrial / Logistics	16%
Office	13%
Residential	10%
Other Real Estate	5%
Retail	6%
Total Real Estate (private % / public %)	51% (37% / 14%)
Utilities	12%
Renewable Energy	5%
Liquid Bulk Storage	3%
Fixed transportation Assets	2%
Conventional Energy	1%
Total Infrastructure (private % / public %)	22% (17% / 6%)
Maritime	12%
Energy Logistics	5%
Aviation	4%
Rolling Stock	2%
Total Transportation (private % / public %)	22% (18% / 3%)
Total Invested Portfolio	95%

On the real estate side, the investments are into all the main types of commercial property, with a particular focus on the US and the bigger Asian markets, such as Australia, Japan and Singapore, which UK investors can less easily access than the domestic market, which is already well served in the investment trust space. Waller emphasises that the investment trust is investing in all its core projects alongside much bigger institutional investors and on the same terms, apart from a small additional 0.05% asset allocation fee. The real estate assets generate a lower yield (around 4%) than the infrastructure and transport assets (where the yield is closer to 8% on average) and the blend of the two is needed to produce the target dividend yield and leave scope for some modest potential capital appreciation.

"THERE ARE A LOT OF OPPORTUNITIES OUT THERE IN REAL ESTATE, INFRASTRUCTURE OR TRANSPORT..."

— PHILIP WALLER

Vulnerable to sterling strength

It is fair to observe that despite the trust now being fully invested, the target returns have yet to be fully achieved. The last reported net asset value as at 31 August 2021 was 91.48p and the trust has since then paid or declared 7p in dividends, bringing the total return up to 98.48p, just a fraction under the issue price. The primary reason for this flat performance is that JARA's shares are sterling-denominated and therefore vulnerable to fluctuations in exchange rates, given that it is a global portfolio with significant foreign currency exposure.

Key sensitivities

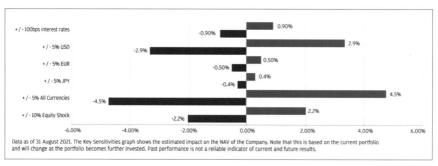

Data as of 31 August 2021. The Key Sensitivities graph shows the estimated impact on the NAV of the Company. Note that this is based on the current portfolio and will change as the portfolio becomes further invested. Past performance is not a reliable indicator of current and future results.

Around 60% of the portfolio is invested in dollar-based assets. The 12% gain in the value of the pound since launch has therefore dragged down the sterling reported figures. In dollar terms the trust has delivered on its target rate of return, but sterling-based investors have yet to see the full benefit. Within a diversified portfolio, however, having exposure to dollar-linked assets need not be a bad thing, but rather a deliberate decision to diversify currency as well as asset class risk. If the pound weakens again, the shares will benefit accordingly.

When I ask why the currency exposure is not hedged, Waller says that when J.P. Morgan was planning the launch it consulted potential shareholders and the majority said that, as the assets themselves were mostly dollar-denominated, and given the cost of hedging, they preferred to manage the currency risk themselves. Nonetheless it is a factor of which potential investors need to be aware. As the chart shows, however, the performance of the portfolio, according to the managers, has limited sensitivity to other factors, underlining its credentials as a lowly correlated defensive asset class.

Early days

Reflecting on performance to date, Waller says: "As we have managed to grow the vehicle by issuing new shares, there has obviously been some market demand. Clearly, we were impacted by covid from a share price perspective for a period of time, but generally we have been trading at a single-digit premium, with some periods of volatility." There is an element of judgement involved in calculating the exact discount/premium at any specific point in time, as NAVs are reported only once every quarter, and therefore can become out of date over subsequent weeks. In common with other trusts that invest in relatively illiquid assets, the regulators require J.P. Morgan to monitor a 'live' NAV and inform the market if there is a material change in portfolio valuations (though there have been no cases of that so far). Broker analysts make their own adjustments for clients.

"Launching in September 2019, just ahead of the pandemic, was clearly somewhat of a baptism of fire. The biggest impact was that our deployment of the IPO funds was delayed. We had set out in our prospectus an investment target of six to 12 months to become fully invested, but you draft these prospectuses with a lot of headroom for the worst-case scenarios. We needed that headroom because of covid, and it took us the full 12 months to get fully invested."

Given the ease with which many specialist alternative trusts have been able to raise new funds, the trust clearly hopes to raise more money once it has proved its proposition can deliver the targeted returns. "There are a lot of opportunities out there in real estate, infrastructure or transport, and each team is putting a lot of capital to work across the sectors. We want JARA to be part of that – it would help our diversification further, and growing the vehicle clearly benefits the investors in terms of liquidity and reduced costs." There are few capacity constraints in a market where the planned expenditure by governments and companies on big infrastructure projects is set to rise significantly over the next few years.

Issues for investors to consider

Because the trust invests into funds and segregated accounts managed by J.P. Morgan's alternative strategies team on virtually the same fee basis, that does not directly leave investors in the trust at a disadvantage to bigger institutions. The management fees on the trust itself are 0.97% per annum, with a performance fee on some of the underlying investments, so not cheap given the target returns. Clearly, it would be helpful if the trust could grow in size: the management fee will reduce to 0.91% if the trust grows to between £500m and £1bn and will dip further if it hits the £1bn mark.

Two issues that would-be shareholders in the trust need to consider carefully are gearing and liquidity. Like most property and infrastructure investments, the underlying assets in the portfolio are leveraged, on an average loan-to-value basis of 40%, but no additional leverage is added at the level of the investment trust. As the trust invests in both privately owned and publicly listed assets (around 20% of the total), there is clearly some liquidity risk too, but this is carefully managed, for example by investing in different classes of security, not just the highest-risk equities. "We have been managing these real asset strategies since 1998, and you can count on one hand the number of times when there have been delays in getting liquidity out of our private assets," he says.

While the long-term outlook for the asset class looks promising, both in absolute terms and as a portfolio diversifier, it may take some time – and a period of stronger performance – for the momentum to build behind what is an interesting differentiated alternative asset product. Quite often a new investment trust has to wait to build a three-year track record as a listed company before its shares start to take off. Many wealth managers only become more comfortable about investing when a trust has reached a minimum size of £300m. A period of sterling weakness, boosting the reported returns, and maybe a change in the inflationary climate, would also be useful.

PHILIP WALLER *has been the manager of the J.P. Morgan Global Core Real Assets trust since its launch.*

BUILDING ON HISTORY

JONATHAN DAVIS *talks to* MATTHEW TILLETT, *lead manager of The Brunner Investment Trust, about the challenges of managing a global equity portfolio.*

I T IS PROBABLY lost way back beyond the memories of many investors today, but there was a time when ICI (Imperial Chemical Industries) was one of the biggest companies in the world, a multifaceted chemicals giant that made everything from ammonia to paint. Its origins in turn dated back to the heroic efforts of industrial pioneers in the chemicals business, such as Ludwig Mond and Sir John Brunner, whose company Brunner Mond, the developer of soda ash, was the largest of the four industrial companies that joined together in 1926 to form ICI.

The Brunner Investment Trust (ticker: BUT) was established the following year, in 1927, to manage the wealth of the Brunner family after it sold its shares in ICI. The family remains a significant shareholder and, in the person of Jim Sharp, who is related to the Brunner family by marriage, maintains representation on the board. As with many other long-running investment trusts originally endowed with the fruits of a successful business career, the Brunner trust has long since evolved into an independent entity with some £500m in assets and a broad range of investors, including institutions and private investors.

Management of the trust's investments has been delegated to Allianz Global Investors for many years. The trust sits in the global equity sector and advertises itself as offering "a one-stop shop for investors looking for a global and UK equity portfolio with a quarterly dividend". It has a mixed benchmark, made up of the FTSE World Ex UK (70%) and the FTSE All-Share index (30%), and is another senior member of the AIC's 'dividend hero' list, having increased its dividend for 49 years in succession.

No spreadsheets, thanks

Matthew Tillett, who took over as lead manager in 2020 after four years as co-manager of the trust, is a lifelong employee of Allianz Global Investors. After reading history and economics at university, he turned his back on both academia and the then fashionable option of a career in banking after reading a book about successful investors and becoming hooked on the idea of an investment career. "Today, everybody wants to go and work in the technology industry, but back then we wanted to be an investment banker – to me that just seemed an absolute nightmare, working until three in the morning on spreadsheets. Instead, this whole world opened up which was completely different, combining qualitative and quantitative analysis, and also bringing in other disciplines like psychology and behaviourial finance. That was what really caught my imagination".

Tillett's experience at AllianzGI, formerly RCM, has mostly been on the UK equity desk, launching a UK equity fund with an unconstrained all-cap mandate, among other products. That was the reason he was first co-opted to help manage Brunner in 2016, to balance the international expertise of its long-serving manager Lucy Macdonald, who was head of global equities until her departure from the firm in 2020. Over the years, the target UK weighting in Brunner's benchmark has been reduced in stages from 60% to its present level of 30%.

Why the change? Tillett says it was partly because Brunner seeks to grow its dividend over the long term and it had become clear that the trust was too dependent on a few large UK stocks with little or no growth prospects, which did not sit well with his preference for higher-quality small and mid-sized companies. It was partly also because a greater global component increases diversification and opens up new sources of income.

The new approach has helped to make the portfolio more resilient than it was five years ago and turned out to be useful last year during the covid-inspired market collapse. The shares still fell by 35% during the month-long sell-off in March 2020 – before bouncing back to reach their current all-time high – but Tillett says, "We would have had a much bigger hit last year if we hadn't done that." Since taking over as lead manager, he has co-opted two colleagues with global expertise and a growth style to complement his own broad experience and specialist knowledge of UK equities and income investing.

The global management challenge

By the time Tillett has finished explaining the many overlapping ways in which he and his colleagues work together, I confess that my head is starting to spin. As well as being the manager of Brunner and his open-ended fund, Tillett is a member of three teams within AllianzGI – the UK, global and value/income teams, many of whose members work in different offices around the world. How do he and his colleagues manage a portfolio with what sounds like a highly complex set of interlocking relationships?

"We get a lot of idea input from the various teams I serve on, and I'm there to make sure we're seeing all of the ideas that are appropriate and can be considered for the portfolio. The three of us, as the portfolio management team, talk all the time.

We have a weekly meeting where we talk specifically about the Brunner portfolio and what we're doing – any new ideas that are coming through, issues with existing holdings, problem stocks, all the kinds of things that you'd expect us to discuss."

The firm's greatest source of ideas, Tillett says, is the global growth team, which is the biggest equity team within AllianzGI and runs the most assets on the equity side. "That's where a lot of the stock debate will happen. Obviously, not every idea that is presented there will be relevant to Brunner, though most of them will be, and the three of us will look at those in our meeting and decide whether or not we think it's worth taking further from a Brunner perspective. I'd say probably 60% to 70% of the holdings in the portfolio are sourced from that team."

Apart from Brunner, that team does not have any other portfolios with an income mandate. They are all growth portfolios. "That's where Brunner is slightly different. I've always been very clear that this is a different portfolio with a different approach, one that promises both income and growth. We want to recognise that. So we source some ideas from other areas – the emerging markets team had a stock that we added recently which actually came through our emerging Europe specialist – and make sure that we're factoring the income-generating objective into the investment process."

It sounds like there is a danger of information overload, I say. That, says Tillett, is certainly "one of the changes in my career. When I started there was a lot of information around, but it's got to the point now where finding information is not really the problem. It's filtering it out and managing your time in the best way; also recognising that there's no way that you can do everything. You have to surround yourself with people who are good at things that not necessarily you're not good at, but just to have knowledge and expertise in areas that you don't have the same level of knowledge and expertise.

"We have loads of good people working around the world for us, running all sorts of different funds. Much of what I do is about networking with those people, understanding what they're doing, what they're looking at, how their views are shifting, making sure I don't miss things. We also have a very useful central information resource, called Salesforce Chatter – or the Global Communication System, as our previous CIO wanted us to call it, because Chatter doesn't sound quite as impressive!" Salesforce is a sophisticated information management system in which Allianz Technology Trust, the AllianzGI stablemate trust profiled in the 2021 handbook, owns shares. The equity teams have been using it for almost ten years now.

The reason it is needed, as has become clear, is that the firm's investment teams are spread right around the world, in London, Paris, Frankfurt, Hong Kong, San Francisco, and so on. "What this system does, it is a kind of push and pull system that gives you all the things that you need to see. Every stock in the world has its own page, every portfolio manager has their own page, every fund has its own page. You can comment on company results, you can put an investment case up, and then you can link other people into it; other people can make comments. You can put a lot of portfolio information up there, as is all of our ESG credentials, plus plenty more." The process relies heavily on Bloomberg, but AllianzGI also draws on external research from the likes of Bernstein, Morningstar and Redburn.

How would he cope if he had to pick stocks without this network of data sources and idea-generating colleagues dotted around the world, I ask – as some fund managers, such as Max Ward, the manager at Independent Investor, still do. "Well, if the board turned around to me tomorrow and said, 'We just want you to do it on your own with no help from anyone,' I could do that, but the thing that would be different is we'd probably have to hold a lot fewer stocks, more like 30 to 40 stocks, maybe fewer, rather than the 60 to 70 that we have at the moment."

Moving on from the past

As often happens with trusts of a certain longevity, there have been legacy issues to deal with – the large family shareholding, a big overhang of stock held by insurance company Aviva, and some expensive fixed-rate debt taken out in a previous high-interest-rate era. The Brunner family shareholding makes little difference to the running of the trust and their influence there is positive, Tillett insists. "They're very supportive. If the discount goes to 15%, they're not phoning me up asking me: 'Why, why?' They're long-term holders. In any event, if you look at the family shareholding, it is basically trickling down every year." At the last reporting date, the family owned 28% of the shares.

A more troublesome legacy has been the 20% shareholding that was originally held by insurance company Friends Provident and inherited by Aviva after its takeover of Friends Provident in 2014. In common with most large insurance companies, which until 15 years ago often used investment trusts to manage their equity investments, Aviva wanted to dispose of its holding but found it hard going. With such a large known seller, the shares in Brunner drifted out to a 20% discount at one stage and it was not until 2020 that Aviva finally found a way to start reducing its holding. It was only in 2021 that the company finally got rid of its last shares, reducing the overhang.

The discount at which Brunner shares trade remains an issue that the trust is working hard to resolve. While some of Aviva's old shares have gone to an arbitrageur looking to profit from the discount narrowing, the majority have gone to the platforms and retail investors, as well as some of the smaller wealth management firms. "We are happy with that, as we think that our proposition should be appealing to smaller investors who are looking for something that's robust and reliable, has a bit of the UK but is mostly invested overseas, does growth and income, has a long track record, sensible balance sheet and a long-term-oriented board and shareholders. Aviva has been a real millstone around our necks and a discussion point at every board meeting for about four years. So we are really pleased that it has been resolved."

While it remains an issue for the board, Tillett says that the discount, which is still around 10%, does not influence the way that the portfolio is managed. "As a portfolio manager, we barely discuss it. What we're doing is trying to pick the right stocks to deliver on our two objectives. Obviously, the discount is something that comes up when we talk to investors, so we get quite a lot of questions about it and it is my job to explain why we think it shouldn't trade at a discount and what we have to do in order to get the share price to NAV."

Key to that, in his view, will be to increase the amount of the share register that is in the hands of the platforms and their retail clients. Having greater private shareholder representation will improve liquidity and should help to bring the discount down. "We're going to have to go through that cycle a few times, I think, but I'm hopeful – now that Aviva has gone – that we won't go to 20% again. As long as we can find the demand to pick up those shares, we can make further progress."

The next challenge

As always, good performance is the most important factor that will determine whether this objective is met. Tillett is keen to emphasise that growth is just as important as yield in constructing the portfolio. "We don't go out looking for high-yielding stocks. If we wanted to, we could create a portfolio that had a much higher yield than it does now. We don't want to do that." (The yield on the trust is around 2% but has been growing at 5% per annum over the last five years.)

"What we want to do is buy companies that are going to outperform on a total return basis and have the quality growth characteristics that we're looking for. We construct the portfolio in a way that delivers the objective that the board have set us, which is that the portfolio needs to deliver a yield in line with the benchmark. As they don't want us to be making decisions purely based on yield, the rough parameter is to be within about 10% of the benchmark yield."

Meeting the twin investment objectives of a market yield and growth from a basket of quality stocks will not be a challenge, Tillett says, "as long as we're picking the right stocks and we deliver growth. The dividend should grow as well, because dividends tend to grow with the share price most of the time. In terms of other constraints, the main thing that we aim to do in terms of the risk is to be sure that any difference in performance against the benchmark is driven by our stock selection and not by some massive bet, like the oil price or sterling."

That means that the trust's portfolio has a high active share, meaning it is very different in composition from the benchmark, but also relatively low turnover. "It's not going to be massively volatile versus the index, just because of the kind of approach that we have. In that sense, it's almost a little bit old-fashioned in some ways because that's how everybody ran portfolios 10 or 15 years ago. We just carry on doing what we've always done; it has worked over the long term and we think that shareholders are happy with it, so why change it?"

The third legacy issue the trust has been dealing with is its inheritance of expensive fixed-rate debt, which was "a real problem" that Tillett thinks may well have deterred investors in the past. The board has refinanced two long-term debt instruments in the past five years and now has access to a mixture of structural and flexible debt finance. The philosophy towards gearing is to have enough to make a difference to returns over time, but not so much as to put the trust at serious risk in the event of a bad market. Having a flexible debt facility is there to take advantage of opportunities if and when sell-offs occur.

Selling a mixed mandate

The board therefore has been doing its job by making some sensible moves to clear up the legacy issues. This process and the drive to find new investors following the departure of Aviva, coupled with a period of solid performance, has had a positive impact on the rating. The NAV per share has grown by 72% over five years and 248% over ten years (as at 7 October 2021), while the discount has roughly halved from the peak of 20%, boosting the shareholder returns. Although changes to the benchmark can mean comparison with peers is not that simple, the discount movement strongly suggests that the trust is on an upward trajectory.

Tillett says his team are hopeful of outperforming the benchmark over time. The current 70:30 mandate is reviewed at regular intervals. "People who are buying into us as a portfolio management team are getting something that they couldn't get if they tried to replicate our portfolio of global equities themselves: a huge resource base and loads of very experienced investors based all round the world, which we then distil into this balanced portfolio that aims to deliver two things in one – some outperformance and a decent income as well."

HEALTHCARE AFTER COVID

GARETH POWELL AND JAMES DOUGLAS *of the Polar Capital Global Healthcare trust explain why they are optimistic about a recovery in their specialist area of healthcare stocks.*

What is the objective of your trust?

GP: When Dan Mahony and I launched the healthcare team at Polar Capital, we started with the open-ended fund that I still run, the Healthcare Opportunities Fund, which invests in companies of all sizes. The rationale for launching the investment trust was that I felt, back in late 2009, that pharmaceutical companies were so out of favour that there was a good opportunity to buy into the area. Dividend yields were really high.

So we devised the idea of a trust with the objective of buying pharma stocks; we thought there was a really good turnaround story there, and you were getting paid to own these stocks at 6% yields. We set it up as an income vehicle. It was a call to arms – because when you have these investment ideas, you need to act quickly.

We went live with that in mid-2010, and we kept the income profile through to 2017. After the elections in the US in 2016, healthcare derated again because there were fears over Hillary Clinton winning the election. Healthcare, relative to the market, again looked as attractive as it did in mid-2010 when we launched the trust. This time, however, we said let's reduce the focus on income, move away from pharma and switch to a growth, not an income mandate.

Pharma had rerated higher during the life of the trust, and investors had generated a decent double-digit return compounded over the life of the trust in its first iteration. It was now a lower-volatility fund compared to biotech or small-cap healthcare, and that's what investors were keen on at that point. We have kept the profile since June 2017.

How does your trust compare to the other large healthcare investment trusts out there?

JD: Some of our peers have a smaller-cap focus; some are a bit more biased towards biotechnology and therapeutics. If we are differentiated, it's that we're further up the market capitalisation scale. Depending where we are in the cycle, it means we provide a more defensive and slightly lower-volatility profile. We also have a ZDP (zero dividend preference) share as structural debt, and that's another differentiator.

So, you're offering choice – that's the idea?

GP: Yes, that's what we've always tried to do and what Anthony Milford, my original boss at Framlington, always used to do. He would not launch a product just because it was a hot area and you could raise a lot of assets very quickly. He'd only try to launch a product when he thought the opportunity was good. That had a big impact on me, and I've always tried to follow that with the funds we've launched at Polar Capital.

Apart from the very large drug companies, do you think healthcare generally is still a growth sector?

GP: Yes, but it depends on the maturity of the companies. The mega-cap pharma companies are mature; they're high cash-flow businesses paying dividends. They're lowish-growth, though it is still better than GDP, but they're basically mature. In biotech, which you'd think of more as a nascent industry, there are lots of small- and mid-cap companies, and there are also growth companies out there in the large-cap end.

If you look at all the different sub-sectors in healthcare, going down to the lowest level, the good news is that there is such a huge universe of different things to invest in, whether it be a company outsourcing cleaning, another selling medical equipment, all the way up to very high-tech radiotherapy.

Has the pandemic been net positive or net negative for the sector?

GP: We need to distinguish between short- and longer-term effects. Even if we get to a good position with regard to covid next year, I do think there'll be a reluctance from people generally to go to big hospitals or places where they deem it a risk to get infected. That will be a prolonged effect, even if we get to some kind of herd immunity, but it will also be positive for alternative care options, such as outpatient settings, smaller centres and suchlike.

The big impact that has been felt already is on R&D. Everyone can see how critical the biotech pharma companies have been in this crisis. Research and development will be seen as crucial from now on, and that will have an impact on the equipment and service companies and the life science tools companies. Collaboration has become an important and powerful new factor.

If we'd had this conversation pre-pandemic, I would have said to you that areas such as vaccines were seen as really boring – old businesses that are dominated by some of the big pharma companies and they just used them to generate cash rather than for any significant growth. That has now changed. The same goes for diagnostic companies. Yet look at how important the diagnostic companies have been in this crisis. Venture capital companies aren't really investing in those areas, apart from in some very niche stuff. It is an area that's really under-invested. So there's a better outlook there.

JD: On the positive side, I think 2020 was a year of phenomenal innovation for our industry. The companies had the DNA of the virus in January, and by the end of that calendar year the regulators were authorising the vaccines. That is pretty remarkable, particularly given the historical context.

Secondly, you had this huge mobilisation of resources: companies making the testing kits, companies manufacturing the vaccines, providing the needles, the vials, and so on. The healthcare industry deserves a huge amount of credit for what they managed to do during 2020.

Not everything is positive. If you ran a private hospital, then you weren't getting patients through your doors because they were deferring elective procedures. We saw the medical device companies who provide the equipment suffer because there were fewer patients coming through. The pharma industry was impacted as well, because diagnosis rates fell quite dramatically last year. People were just afraid to access the healthcare system. That's really quite troubling, if you think about the implications.

Another thing that we think has happened during covid-19 is that it showed up the fact that a lot of healthcare systems globally just had poor infrastructure when it comes to diagnostics. Some of those systems have accelerated their investment in diagnostics, and what we're hoping is that, with that installed base expanded, people take diagnoses more seriously, recognise disease and get patients on the right treatment path sooner. That is clearly hugely positive for patients, but also for healthcare systems as well because you can save money down the road.

Investors always worry about regulation and political intervention, particularly in the US where most of your companies are. How do you deal with that?

GP: It's a great question, because you are right: it does come round every four years in the US. The majority of pharma and biotech companies are in the US, and even if you try to invest in those types of companies outside of the US, the US market is obviously still their most important one. When it comes to the election cycles, you try to position accordingly, but you never really know, obviously – as 2016 and 2020 proved – what is ultimately going to happen.

The way we try to think about it is that the market tends to exaggerate too much one way or the other and so political anxiety periodically offers good opportunities. The pharma stocks in particular get derated heavily if there are fears of a Democrat-controlled Congress with a big majority. That scares people more than who is president. As polls have shown, however, it's incredibly difficult to predict the outcome. That's when portfolio management comes in, rather than stock-picking.

JD: You can always be surprised, but if you look at the makeup of Congress and what's been said publicly, we think that the chances of really draconian measures on the drug-pricing side are probably quite slim. The other important point to make is that when Joe Biden became president he was very clear that he was going to maintain the current infrastructure that was put in by Obama back in the beginning of 2010. So I think you will see support for the Affordable Care Act. Biden wants to get access to healthcare to more people.

When Obamacare was going through, did you have any worries about that?

GP: Yes, absolutely. You just don't know how it's going to turn out. When we launched the original trust, you had pharma companies trading on seven times earnings. It was totally ridiculous. The companies could have bought themselves back in just four or five years! So there was a real value opportunity there. Obamacare was an enormous change; he broadened healthcare access to 30 million people, but ironically when it finally went through it began the next bull market in healthcare and biotech.

If you were in charge of healthcare in the States, what would be the best thing you could do?

GP: The US market is a mess in terms of drug pricing. It's a ridiculous situation. The problem is mostly around the supply chain and the middlemen in the US. That's the bit that needs sorting out, because they take a huge chunk of the profit and also drive the direction of pricing. The consumer gets hit with the impact.

We met one company which charged an enormous price for a drug that didn't warrant it, but when I suggested to the CEO that he could dramatically lower the price so that the drug could be used much more widely, he said that the middlemen didn't want him to reduce the price, and that's because they take a slice of the profit. I presume that sounds absurd to you – and it genuinely is.

What needs to happen in the US is they need to change the rebating system and the way the supply-chain middlemen work. The problem is that the politicians don't understand it, and so all they do is say, "Oh, drug prices are too high," which sounds like a good thing to politicians, but is way too simplistic.

What you need to do is take away the barriers to effective competition. I would have two things: I would stop rebating in the drug system, so you make it genuinely competitive, but I'd also measure quality outcomes, rather like an Ofcom. That would be a very easy way to save an awful lot of money, but you'd still have to make sure that the consumer felt the benefit.

Is the UK system any better?

GP: It's very difficult to get any system right. The NHS has its major challenges. If you were suddenly to get ill in some way, would you want to be treated here or in the US? It's very expensive in the US, but generally if you've had an incident your outcome is likely to be better in the US than it is over here. But that's an average measure. It's not going to be across the board. The NHS is the third-biggest employer in the world, and so will have its challenges on efficiency.

In a way all this washes out as far as you're concerned as an investor, presumably, because wherever the money ends up in the chain, you can invest in it.

GP: Yes, I think there are always opportunities. While some areas are getting pressured, there are opportunities elsewhere. The thing I find most fascinating about healthcare is that it's so dynamic. Every day there's always some news flow that affects one company or another. It can be quite dramatic in its impact, and so there's always excitement. I say that now, but when people start losing any interest because they're worried about politics in the US, it's no fun.

If you look at the data, healthcare over the very long term – say, 30-plus years – has been a good place to be, compared to investing in a general market ETF. But there's volatility; it goes out of favour. The opportunities come and go across the cycle. There's a big discount to the market right now. The S&P 500 Healthcare trades at just under a 20% discount relative to the S&P 500, on a one YR forward P/E ratio basis. It's at the wider end of the normal discount range. Generally that's been a good time to invest, and that's where we find ourselves now – particularly in the large-cap stocks, although there are no guarantees of course when it comes to investment returns.

Where do you see some of the opportunities you mention?

JD: One of the things we are looking at is outsourcing. We are finding more companies within our universe are focusing on their core strengths and outsourcing non-core activities. That might be getting companies to run your clinical trials for you – they're called CROs [contract research organisations] and they can accelerate your revenue profile. We think that's durable.

Another area is those companies which physically make the vaccines or the drugs or make the devices; we've seen an acceleration there. Innovation in health is a strong source of growth; emerging markets are a strong source of growth; and, finally, because healthcare is fragmented, we think mergers and acquisitions will continue to be a theme throughout the rest of the life of the trust.

Another thing that supports a constructive stance is valuations. If you look in the US in particular, on a relative basis valuations are attractive, and we would argue that on an absolute basis they're supportive. Particularly at the large-cap end, we think we can find growth at a reasonable price. Finally – and this is no more than an observation – if you look at mutual fund filings, healthcare seems to be pretty under-owned at the moment, near to ten-year lows.

One of the things we're really focused on is this idea of disrupting the delivery of healthcare. As I'm sure you're aware, most global healthcare systems are under pressure. We're trying to find technologies, services and products that offer you an alternative delivery route. That might be tele-health, where you can have a chat to the doctor over the phone or over Skype. It might be delivering healthcare in the home versus a hospital, or delivering it in what they call an Ambulatory Surgery Centre where you walk in, you get your procedure, and you walk out.

What metrics do you mostly use to measure valuations in your sectors?

JD: We look at a variety of metrics. Price to earnings is powerful, particularly when combined with earnings revisions. When you're dealing with companies that have debt on their balance sheets, you need to potentially think about enterprise value as well, so we look at that, particularly in relation to sales growth. We think that's quite useful for medical devices, life sciences and tools. And obviously in deal situations, we'll look at whether companies can generate returns over and above their invested capital.

Do you have a problem with benchmarks in this sector?

GP: They're just the same as any other: they're dominated by the historical winners. If you look at our benchmark for this, Johnson & Johnson is the biggest company. Pharma is about 45% of the index, biotech large-cap is at about 12%. But it has changed a lot. Going back 20 years, pharma was 80% of the index. It has changed, as you've seen medical devices, healthcare services, biotech become more important.

Style rotation has not been such a helpful factor for you in the last two years?

GP: We got asked a lot: "Why aren't you in small-caps, biotech, and all this?" This year, their kind of stocks peaked in the first two months of the year and are down heavily, and you've seen that in the difference in the performance of the trust this year. It is always the way. People are very late in knowing what's going on.

You've got another continuation vote coming up – does that influence the way you are managing the trust?

GP: No, not at all. The continuation vote is in Q1 2025.That's something that is obviously up to the board and ultimately investors to decide, because of the high vote level required. On the other hand, we're not that far away from the vote; even if the returns are flat and there is no continuation, you will still get a reasonable return as the discount narrows.

How do valuations compare to where they were five or ten years ago?

GP: I'm going to give you my methodology first, because I think it's very important to be transparent. In the innovation portfolio, you can be dealing with companies that don't have any earnings. If you look at the growth portfolio, I derive the yield of those stocks relative to their size within the portfolio. Even within that part of the portfolio, there are some companies that don't have earnings, so I remove them because they completely distort everything.

After that, the portfolio's P/E is on around 20x next year's earnings, and roughly 13x EBITDA. For that, using consensus data, you will hopefully get double-digit earnings growth, plus a little bit of yield as well. That's where we are today, and that's why we think we are getting growth at a reasonable price.

What is the trust's approach to the discount?

GP: We've bought back shares on occasion when it gets really stretched. We find it doesn't help dramatically; it is performance that makes the real difference. When our particular area of healthcare gets into vogue, that will pull the discount in. In hindsight the performance was held back because of the income requirement in the first life, and then we lagged a bit when we switched over to our new strategy in mid-2017. We are working hard to resolve that difference in performance.

How do you assess the outlook as we recover from lockdown?

JD: As I'm a glass-half-full person, I'm going to say it's been a positive. The global co-ordination between academia, industry and regulators is a positive. The way some healthcare systems have realigned how they deliver their services, trying to generate more efficiencies, is also a positive. Sadly, I do think that some other things are going to crop up over the near to medium term that will create challenges. I think misdiagnoses of certain things may be a problem and, unfortunately, mental health will also be a challenge.

GP: It depends a lot on what happens with small caps and biotech. You'd think that they were in a proper bear market, given where sentiment is and how a lot of those stocks are acting. There'll definitely be opportunities along the way. It depends on your risk appetite. The volatility of our trust is much lower than some of our peers and, in my opinion, the current environment is more favourable for our strategy.

GARETH POWELL *and* JAMES DOUGLAS *are co-managers of the Polar Capital Global Healthcare trust (ticker: PCGH) and also manage two UCITs funds for Polar Capital.*

ANALYSING INVESTMENT TRUSTS

by JONATHAN DAVIS

FINDING OUT MORE

By JONATHAN DAVIS

THERE WAS A time when getting hold of good data and information about investment trusts was quite difficult. Brokers' research was not widely available, as well as variable in quality, and investment platforms did not offer much coverage of closed-ended funds. Magazines and newspapers published weekly or monthly prices and some other bits of information, but often not much more.

Specialist data websites such as Trustnet (which originated many years ago as a broking firm's investment trust data centre), Morningstar and Digital Look continue to provide lots of data, but while all of them are very useful, and they do provide news and analysis these days as well as numbers, they have not always been the easiest sites to navigate. Citywire also carries data and has an excellent news and commentary service about investment trusts, but you need to subscribe to one of several services they offer in order to access it.

The good news is that the industry's trade body, the Association of Investment Companies, has taken it upon itself to maintain an excellent and comprehensive database of investment trust information, sourced from Morningstar and Financial Express (the owner of Trustnet). The AIC website (theaic.co.uk) is updated continuously with news and performance data, as well as providing a link to the relevant website of fund management groups and (where they have their own) the trust's own websites.

The AIC website also carries a news feed from Citywire and this year started a separate listing for podcasts which feature investment trusts, including – to declare an interest – the weekly *Money Makers* investment trust podcast that I put together each week with the help of Simon Elliott, head of investment trust research at Winterflood Securities, one of the main corporate broking firms that specialise in investment trusts.

Growing private investor demand

All of this reflects the fact that everyone in the fund business recognises that increasing numbers of private investors are becoming interested in investment trusts as an option for their savings and investments. Research shows that investment trust shareholders tend to have larger sums to invest and are also more sophisticated than the average investor in open-ended funds. They (or should I say you?) are not afraid to do their own homework.

179

More and more of these so-called self-directed investors use platforms such as Hargreaves Lansdown (the market leader), Interactive Investor and AJ Bell to hold their ISAs and SIPP money. Consolidation is underway in the platform business however, with Interactive Investor in particular taking the lead in acquiring the Alliance Trust's old platform and, in a further deal in 2020, that of the retail specialist firm The Share Centre as well.

The platforms in turn have responded by adding more information about investment trusts, including interactive charting tools, but for commercial or other reasons don't offer a huge amount of research. An exception can be made here for Interactive Investor which also recently purchased *Money Observer* magazine. It has subsequently decided to close down the printed versions of the monthly magazine, as well as its investment trust quarterly, while keeping on a number of their regular and better known contributors to write articles for its website.

How this will play out over time remains to be seen, but while consolidation generally reduces choice, for the moment it has certainly expanded the choice of weekly news and analysis of trusts that is available for free to investors. Among specialist financial magazines, *Money Week*, the *Investors Chronicle*, *Shares* magazine and *Master Investor* all carry articles about investment trusts, while the long-running *Investment Trusts* newsletter is another subscription option.

Among national newspapers, *The Times* and the *Telegraph* stand out for the breadth of their coverage of funds. Recommended also is the subscription-based portfolio monitoring service run by John Baron, a former City professional now known to a wider audience through his regular columns in the *Investors Chronicle* and his contributions to the *Handbook*.

Other types of research

If you are looking for some basic information about an investment trust, presented in a standardised form, it is worth looking at some of the newer web-based research firms that cover investment trusts. Of these the best known are QuotedData, Trust Intelligence and Edison Research. Be aware however that all three firms have business models which rely on commercial relationships with fund management firms, including clients which sponsor research and use them for promotional events.

It is important to take note therefore whether the research on individual trusts you read there is sponsored or not, since if it is it can no longer be deemed to be independent and that inevitably raises a question about its value. These research firms, unlike broking firms, are not allowed by the regulator to publish specific buy and sell recommendations, but concentrate mainly instead on descriptive articles about specific trusts and broader thematic analysis, which will usually include at least one or more trusts run by clients of the firm. The latter are often more useful, in my experience.

Both QuotedData and Kepler Intelligence have former City investment trusts analysts among their founders and that experience carries over into a well-presented level of professional research. Bear in mind that the only reason these firms exist is that broker research is now restricted to professional and wealthier clients, so they are filling a gap for basic analysis that private investors will struggle to find filled elsewhere, certainly if they are unwilling to pay for the privilege. My advice is to make full use of the research these sites provide for information and news, but do so with your eyes open. Don't make investment decisions about individual trusts without doing additional research.

When looking for a high level of detail about an individual investment trust, I also make regular use of the subscription share analysis service Stockopedia (www. stockopedia.com), which is based (as it happens) here in my home town of Oxford. Stockopedia does not yet offer a specific investment trust service, unfortunately, although I keep pressing them to do so and Ed Croft, the founder, tells me they are keen to do so and may be starting one at some point.

For the moment the splendidly clear and well laid out company-by-company data pages are not adapted to show the specific data points that are of particular interest to investment trust shareholders. They only highlight share price performance, for example, and not the net asset value per share, which is of limited value in tracking discounts/premiums. However, once you find out how to get around the paywalled site, it is invaluable in quickly tracking dividend payments for example. I also use it, as well as Trustnet, to monitor the real and model portfolios which I run.

One of my complaints about most investment trust research sites is that they generally don't show historical performance over long enough periods. This is unhelpful because it is important to know how an individual fund manager has performed in past jobs, which may well have been at different firms, and during bull and bear markets. Trusts change their managers all the time and it is no use looking at the historical performance if some of it was during the tenure of another manager with a completely different style or success rate.

Fortunately sites such as Citywire and Trustnet do however rate individual fund managers, if you know where to look, and often provide a summary of their track record over the full course of their careers. If you are prepared to dig deeper into some of these details, it will help prevent you from being misled by the shorter term performance on which, unfortunately, so much buying and selling of funds seems to be based. It cannot be emphasised enough that you need to look at the performance of any fund over the whole market cycle.

Using the AIC website

In the 2020 edition of the *Handbook* I included several pages describing the initial steps that a potential investor in investment trusts might take to make best use of the information available on the AIC website. In the 2021 edition I outlined ten steps a private investor could follow to research a potential investment, using not just the AIC website but the other sites I mentioned earlier.

I don't propose to repeat those sections again this year, but you will be able to find an online version of both pieces on the *Money Makers* website, together with the explanatory videos I promised last year. Instead I add here some notes on the new statistics, features and improvements that the AIC has added to its website this year.

The AIC website has the most comprehensive database and range of information and it is clear that a lot of thought has gone into how the material is presented. Nevertheless there is always scope to make any data service more user friendly – some aspects of the AIC site I have found a bit clunky in the past – and some of the latest changes are definite improvements.

The first change is the creation of an investment company screener tool. This allows you to screen the investment trust universe using your own own choice of data points, such as charges, yield, performance and so on, to find the specific trusts that meet your specified criteria. Here is a simple example, the result of searching for UK equity income trusts that have the following characteristics: (1) a yield above 3%; (2) a market capitalisation of more than £100m; (3) are trading at a discount; and (4) no more than 10% gearing.

Chart 1: Setting the search criteria

Chart 2: Results of the initial screen

Name	ISIN	AIC sector	Market Cap. (£m)	Discount/Premium (%)	Gearing (%)	Ongoing charge (%) (exc Perf fee) ⓘ	Dividend Yield (%)
BMO Capital and Income Investment Trust Plc	GB0003463287	UK Equity Income	346.54	-2.66	6	0.58	3.62
Diverse Income Trust	GB00B65TLW28	UK Equity Income	408.04	-2.3	0	1.06	3.32
Dunedin Income Growth Investment Trust	GB0003406096	UK Equity Income	477.09	-0.96	8	0.64	3.98
Edinburgh Investment Trust Plc	GB0003052338	UK Equity Income	1,060.65	-9.85	7	0.44	3.90
Murray Income Trust Plc	GB0006111123	UK Equity Income	1,036.68	-7.73	9	0.46	3.89
Temple Bar Investment Trust Plc	GB0008825324	UK Equity Income	730.80	-7.01	9	0.51	3.50
The City of London Investment Trust Plc	GB0001990497	UK Equity Income	1,721.45	-0.86	9	0.38	4.98

Chart 1 is an example of these input criteria, although there are several more you can add by clicking the 'show more' button. Chart 2 shows the first page of the output with the characteristics I had identified. You can then look at other characteristics of the trusts by looking at a number of other tabs. Chart 3 shows more detail, if you need it, about the dividend, such as the 5-year growth rate and the dividend cover.

Chart 3: Drilling into dividends

Name	ISIN	Dividend Frequency	Dividend Yield (%)	5yr dividend growth (%) p.a.	Dividend Cover (years) ⓘ
BMO Capital and Income Investment Trust Plc	GB0003463287	Other	3.62	2.63	0.94
Diverse Income Trust	GB00B65TLW28	Quarterly	3.32	6.02	1.12
Dunedin Income Growth Investment Trust	GB0003406096	Quarterly	3.98	2.34	1.24
Edinburgh Investment Trust Plc	GB0003052338	Other	3.90	-0.29	1.49
Murray Income Trust Plc	GB0006111123	Quarterly	3.89	1.36	0.66
Temple Bar Investment Trust Plc	GB0008825324	Quarterly	3.50	-0.59	0.51
The City of London Investment Trust Plc	GB0001990497	Quarterly	4.98	3.74	0.44

A second feature in the screener is the ability to select up to five investment companies and bring them into the 'investment compare' function which displays a whole range of data side by side, together with a ready made performance graph (see Chart 4). A second graphing package also allows you to compare returns between up to five companies, plus market indices and sector averages, over different periods – useful if you want to compare performance since a new manager took over a trust, for example.

Chart 4: Comparing five trusts

	Diverse Income Trust Ord	Murray Income Trust Ord	Temple Bar Ord	City of London Ord	Edinburgh Investment Ord
	GB00B65TLW28	GB0006111123	GB0008825324	GB0001990497	GB0003052338

Key Information
Close

AIC Sector	UK Equity Income	UK Equity Income	UK Equity Income	UK Equity Income	UK Equity Income
Benchmark	No benchmark	FTSE AllSh TR GBP	FTSE All-Share	FTSE AllSh TR GBP	FTSE AllSh TR GBP
Market Capitalization	408.04m	1.04b	730.8m	1.72b	1.06b
Net Assets	418.33m	1.12b	785.05m	1.74b	1.18b
Gearing (%)	–	9	9	9	7
Discount/Premium (%)	-2.46	-7.78	-6.91	-0.93	-9.85
Dividend Yield (%)	3.32	3.89	3.50	4.98	3.90
Dividend Frequency	Quarterly	Quarterly	Quarterly	Quarterly	No Dividend
Ongoing Charge	1.06	0.46	0.51	0.38	0.44
Ongoing Charge Date	2021-05-31	2021-06-30	2020-12-31	2021-06-30	2021-03-31
Equity Style Box	Small Value	Large Core	Large Value	Large Value	Large Core
Prospectus Objective	To provide shareholders with an attractive and growing level of dividends coupled with capital growth over the lon ...**more**	To achieve a high and growing income combined with capital growth through investment in a portfolio principally ...**more**	To provide growth in income and capital to achieve a long-term total return greater than the benchmark FTSE ...**more**	The Company's objective is to provide long-term growth in income and capital, principally by investment in eq ...**more**	The Company aims to invest primarily in UK securities with the long-term objective of achieving an increas ...**more**
Manager	Gervais Williams	Charles Luke	Nicholas Purves	Laura Foll	James de Uphaugh

The second new feature is a data and news alert function which allows you to opt to receive an email when specified changes occur to an investment company you are interested in. A common example is when a market price or discount reaches a certain level, or a new dividend or annual report is released. If you have an investment trust on your watchlist that you know has a discount control mechanism, for example, this can be a useful way of finding out when the target is close to being hit. You can also choose to receive notifications of London Stock Exchange news announcements for story types that interest you.

There have also been some improvements to the popular compare companies function, which is the one that I use most myself. I regularly want to check how the performance and rating of the trusts I follow compare to others in their sector. By using the advanced compare function (formerly known as the interactive statistics function) you can also save the search criteria you use regularly.

Finally, with ESG disclosure and analysis being all the rage, the AIC has added a glossary of ESG terms (to explain the difference, for example, between sustainable and social impact investing) and says that 75% of companies in its universe have submitted details of their ESG approach and these have been added to their profile pages. How enlightening, or how important, this information is for investors remains a much debated question, but this is at least a tentative first disclosure step for those who want the information and links to the relevant part of the company's "stewardship report".

As with all data sites it takes time to get used to how they work but this AIC site, in my experience, is fast to load and while there are occasional glitches (do feel free to let the AIC know if you come across one), it remains an invaluable first stop on your research journey. The income builder functions and the compare investment companies features are the ones that I use most, along with Citywire (the best for news and comments) and Trustnet (best for generating long term charts and comparisons between trusts, open-ended funds and – less satisfactorily – market indices).

GETTING HELP

Recognising that it takes some time to get the measure of the AIC's comprehensive statistics section, the AIC statistics department says it welcomes enquiries from private investors; just fill out the email enquiry form on the AIC website.

The AIC has also made some further changes to its sector classifications. Three new sectors, China/Greater China, India and Property (UK Logistics) were launched in March 2022. In addition, three country specialist sectors (Asia Pacific ex Japan, Europe ex UK and Latin America) were merged into a single sector called Country Specialist, while the Asia Pacific Income sector was renamed Asia Pacific Equity Income.

STAY INFORMED

For portfolio updates, market commentary, interviews with top professional investors, performance data and links to topical research, Jonathan Davis now writes a regular subscription newsletter for *Money Makers* (See www.money-makers.co for how to subscribe).

RESEARCHING TRUSTS

STUART WATSON *has been investing in investment trusts for 25 years and contributes regular in-depth fund profiles to the Money Makers subscription service. Here he explains what he looks for when researching new holdings.*

I NVESTMENT TRUSTS HAVE been the mainstay of my portfolio for much of my time in finance. A few years ago, as semi-retirement loomed, I decided I wanted to learn a lot more, both about the trusts I already held and about the sector as a whole.

They say one of the best ways to learn about something is to write about it. So that was what I did, setting up a blog called itinvestor.co.uk with the aim of publishing a new piece every week.

My early blog posts were a little simplistic, but they got a lot longer and more detailed as the months went by and I built up a broader understanding of the sector. I started using a template to give my articles a more consistent framework.

Then the opportunity came up to join Jonathan Davis at Money Makers, and I now write weekly fund profiles for the Money Makers website (money-makers.co). Here I am going to break down the template I use, to provide a little colour around what I look at in these profiles and why.

What I look for in a trust

My preferred investing style is a mixture of a little caution, a lot of stubbornness, and a side helping of lethargy.

I am comfortable with some risk, but I don't feel the need to significantly beat the market each and every year. I am happy to give managers time to work through what appear to be temporary issues, such as their style dipping out of favour for a while. I prefer trusts that I can hold for several years without worrying that they will significantly change their underlying strategy. As one of my former work colleagues was fond of saying, "Don't change horses mid-stream."

The fund profiles are written with this philosophy in mind, so I tend to avoid short-term discount plays and generally steer clear of both regional and country specific trusts, preferring to concentrate on a few big themes and global equity trusts.

A little bit of history

An investment trust has the ability to completely reinvent the way it does business, getting rid of its managers and totally changing its investment focus. In some instances, this means a trust's history may have little if anything to do with its prospects today. Other trusts have had the same manager and broadly the same investment style for many decades.

Therefore the first step I take is to see what a trust has done in the past and consider how far back you can meaningfully go when looking at its track record.

I look for manager changes, at both individual and firm level, and also for major strategy or benchmark changes. That said, older reports rarely mention individual managers by name – often the first time you come across them is when they retire and are thanked for their service!

Most investing websites only have data that goes back ten years, but a trust's own website often has accounts dating back to the early 2000s. Looking at old ten-year summaries can pretty quickly give you a three-decade overview of how a trust has performed. How the presentation of key data has changed over time can be revealing as well. I prefer trusts that have consistently used the same metrics over a long period.

Companies House is another great resource and often has accounts going back to the mid-1970s, although the quality of the photocopying becomes ever more suspect the further back you go.

Sometimes a trust's history will surprise you. For example, looking at Scottish Mortgage reveals how little of its portfolio was in technology stocks prior to the financial crisis, even though James Anderson first took charge in 2000, several years before sub-prime mortgages wrecked the banking system. Indeed, many trusts that you would instinctively think of as being widely globally diversified today were heavily UK-focused until quite recently.

In truth, it would be nice if I didn't have to dig through old reports to get a lot of this information. It seems like the sort of thing that should be set out clearly on a trust's website or in its accounts.

Key statistics

Once a trust has been properly introduced, I like to summarise a few key numbers. A lot of this information is widely available, but it's handy to skim down items like price, size, discount, sector, performance, benchmark, managers, number of holdings, charging structure and so on in one swoop. Quite often I find this process highlights some of the areas I want to examine in greater depth.

Investment policies

Each trust will have a set of guidelines on what it can invest in, usually specifying maximum amounts for certain types of holding and position sizes. I check these against what the trust is actually invested in, to see whether it is bumping up against these limits or whether they seem to have little relevance in practice. Looking back at how this has changed over time can also be revealing.

ESG policies are becoming increasingly common, although they tend not to be something I focus on explicitly. The trusts I prefer often fall into the quality camp, so by default their investments tend to be more sustainable businesses.

Inside the portfolio

I like to get a feel for what I am invested in at the company level, although I rarely delve into lots of detail on individual positions as that tends to be very time-consuming. Rather, I am looking for obvious red flags, a feel for the overall level of diversification across sectors and geographies, and the types of company held. No investor gets everything right, so I don't feel the need to agree with every single position a manager has taken. With specialist trusts, it can be hard to get much information about the underlying holdings anyway.

I prefer more concentrated portfolios of, say, fewer than 30 positions as I believe that provides more opportunity to outperform. But individual positions greater than 10% can make me a little twitchy, especially when they represent a significant proportion of that particular company's issued share capital, potentially making them more difficult to sell.

Looking at a trust's portfolio can also tell me how much it overlaps with trusts I already own. There are significant shared holdings across many Baillie Gifford trusts, for example. I try to keep my own portfolio below 20 trusts, to keep things more manageable, so I often avoid trusts that duplicate a lot of what I already have.

Portfolio turnover is something else I like to examine, and lower is generally better in my opinion. Sometimes a manager will provide commentary on this, and sometimes you need to look at the cash flow statement and compare the amounts bought and sold relative to the size of the trust's assets.

Paid-for broker notes from the likes of Edison, Kepler and QuotedData can be useful sources of information, as they often go into detail about how managers construct their portfolios and size their positions, which is something often not discussed in their reports and presentations.

Another useful source of information, especially for newer trusts, is a prospectus for an IPO or a recent placing. These can run to a few hundred pages, but there is usually a chapter or two covering the market opportunity and investing strategy and these often provide a lot more background detail than you see in a set of accounts.

Finally, the tone of how a manager talks about their holdings and performance can also be revealing. I prefer the modest and understated approach, owning up to bad decisions but not getting too carried away when times are good.

Performance

Assessing a trust's performance is a dark art, at best. Changes to a management team or strategy may mean there is only a limited period you can look back through and still make a sensible comparison. And the further back you go, the harder it is to get good-quality information.

I like to look for consistency of outperformance, preferring my trusts to be frequently good rather than occasionally great. That suits my hands-off investing style and should make a trust easier to hold onto when the markets hit a rough patch.

One thing I am a fan of is how some J.P. Morgan trusts break their performance for each period down into factors like stock selection, currency, gearing and charges. It would be good to see this approach more widely adopted.

Each trust has a different objective, though, and it is important to compare its performance against a sensible yardstick. Sometimes a trust's stated benchmark seems completely inappropriate. HgCapital Trust, a tech-focused private equity trust that I have held for many years, still compares itself against the FTSE All-Share, one of the major indices with the least amount of technology exposure. For many years up until March 2020, Murray International used a mixed benchmark with a 40% weighting to UK stocks although its typical UK weighting was a fraction of that.

It is worth comparing a trust against others in its sector, although even within a sector there can be a number of different styles. The flexible sector is probably the most diverse in this respect. Typically, the more trusts there are in a sector, the more it will make sense to cherry-pick from the most similar trusts. With many of the newer alternative asset trusts, the income and total return expectations outlined in their IPO prospectus make another useful comparator.

I also like to see how trusts perform when markets go through big declines, like the financial crisis, the last quarter of 2018 and the first quarter of 2020. This can give a sense of how defensive they might be when the next bear comes along on.

Directors and managers

I am probably more interested in a trust's managers than in its directors, but I do like to see a board that has a good mixture of industry and investment trust experience. Length of service and how many other directorships they hold can also be revealing. You want to be comfortable they are not too cosy with the managers and can devote sufficient time to the trust.

I do look at how many shares the directors hold, but it's hard to know how meaningful any position is in respect to any individual's net worth. Often directors will buy shares over time, so those who recently joined may have much smaller positions. While I like to see alignment with shareholders, I have grown warier of very large stakes held by key individuals as that may give them a bit too much control and lead to persistent large discounts.

I consider the stakes held by a trust's managers to be more important, although reporting this is voluntary and, disappointingly, many trusts do not mention it at all.

Another piece of information you often have to dig around for is how old the managers are, so you can estimate how close they may be to retirement. What other funds they manage and how large a trust is relative to the management firm's overall assets under management can also give a sense of where the trust might sit in their list of priorities.

Succession is an issue I have been looking at more and more, and I like to see a clear indication that there is a team behind the main man or woman and that a suitable deputy can step in if needed. Firms like Baillie Gifford seem particularly good at smooth transitions from one manager to the next, but at smaller investment houses it is often unclear how deep their bench is. This is another area where I feel some standardised disclosure would be helpful.

Discount control and rating

Some trusts are very keen to minimise their discount or premium and have a clear discount policy control, while others show little if any interest in the subject. It is useful to know where a trust sits on this spectrum.

For smaller trusts on a discount, there is often little they can do – as reducing the size of the trust via buybacks or tender offers may make it less attractive to investors and worsen the problem. Other trusts, like Lindsell Train Investment Trust, have structural issues that make it unfeasible to buy back or issue shares.

Regardless of what a trust says it aims to do, it can be instructive to look at how its discount has moved over time and how regularly it is either bought back or has issued new shares. Comparing a trust's current discount to others in the sector can give an idea of how well it is perceived by other investors, although it can be difficult to get historical comparisons for this.

It is rare to find a trust that has not been on sale at some point, so getting a feel for how its rating has moved over time can be helpful if you want to build up a position gradually and snap up a bargain while doing so.

Furthermore, the rise of alternative asset trusts has meant we are seeing an increasing proportion of trusts that are valued on only a quarterly or semi-annual basis. Some hybrid trusts include a mixture of quoted and unquoted investments, with the former valued daily and the latter much more infrequently. Understanding the valuation cycle helps get a better feel for how valid the latest stated net asset value actually is.

Charges

Charges vary a lot between trusts. There are flat percentage fees, tiered fees, fees on total assets, fees on net assets, fees on market value – and then the hornets' nest of performance fees. Before writing about trusts on a regular basis, I would have said I was fairly indifferent to performance fees, but I have definitely cooled towards them in recent years.

In some cases performance fees can massively outweigh the basic fee, and it is rarely clear exactly how they have been calculated, where the high-water marks are, and exactly how much has been paid out over the long term. You never see a simple table explaining what is due, merely being presented with the total amount.

Some performance fees are as low as 10%, while others are 15% or even 20%. The hurdle to be jumped is often the trust's benchmark index, but sometimes it is a relatively low fixed amount that is very easy to beat.

In terms of the basic management fee, I like to see if the rate charged has moved lower over time or if tiers have been introduced so that the average rate falls as the trust grows in size. Tiered fees are particularly important in the case of alternative asset trusts, given how they seem to grow so quickly in size. The concern with flat fees is that managers have a much greater incentive to hoard more and more assets rather than focusing on the quality of what they are buying.

Dividends

I am more in the total return camp when it comes to investment returns, but it is still handy to look at the dividend track record and to get an understanding of whether a trust only pays out from the income it receives or whether it is regularly dipping into capital. We have also seen an increasing number of trusts adopt so-called enhanced dividend policies where a fixed percentage of net assets is paid out each year.

When it comes to trusts with an income focus, it is good to see that any dividend targets laid out are consistently met and are increased over time as you would expect.

Gearing

Gearing is another area where investors could do with a little more clarity. It is easy to find the current level of gearing, but not so simple to get data on historical movements.

I also find it useful to consider gearing and performance together. A more highly geared trust should, over longer periods, do better than a more lightly geared one. Of course, in times of market stress, highly geared trusts are likely to see their net asset values fall more sharply.

Closing thoughts

The way I look at trusts has changed quite a lot in the last few years, and I suspect it will continue to evolve. That is a key reason why I like producing these profiles. There is always something new to learn about the sector and, if anything, the rate of change seems to be accelerating, with the wide variety of new trusts we have seen in recent years including areas as diverse as music royalties and space exploration.

Writing these profiles has spurred me to make a few changes to my portfolio – although not too many, I am pleased to say. Being exposed to a wider number of trusts has definitely helped me reassess what I already own and how well it fits within my broader portfolio. It is all too easy to build up a large and unwieldy collection of holdings, and therefore some judicious pruning can make a lot of sense.

I produce a new fund profile pretty much every week at Money Makers, and we are always happy to receive suggestions about what to cover in future.

I track my returns quarterly on my website and from the start of 2018 to 30 September 2021, I'm just ahead of my chosen benchmark which is an all-equity global index tracker. I'm very pleased with the progress so far, given all the markets have thrown at us the last few years, but I'm also conscious that it's over a relatively short period of time.

MONEY MAKERS

You can find Stuart Watson's profiles by becoming a member of the Money Makers circle – go to money-makers.co for more details.

Trusts that have been covered recently include:

- Baillie Gifford US Growth
- Fundsmith Equity
- Law Debenture Corporation
- Montanaro European Smaller
- Supermarket Income REIT

- Bluefield Solar Income Fund
- HgCapital Trust
- Lindsell Train Investment Trust
- Odyssean Investment Trust
- TR Property

Stuart's current top ten holdings are:

Investment trusts

- BlackRock Smaller Companies
- J.P. Morgan Global Growth & Income
- RIT Capital Partners
- Worldwide Healthcare Trust

- HgCapital Trust
- Keystone Positive Change
- Smithson

Other types of fund

- Fundsmith Equity
- Vanguard FTSE All-World ETF

- Lindsell Train Global Equity

EXPLAINING DISCOUNTS

Understanding discounts and premiums is key to knowing how investment trusts behave, as EMMA BIRD, *analyst at Winterflood Securities, explains in this Q and A.*

1. What do we mean by a discount/premium?

A discount or premium shows the relationship between an investment trust's net asset value (NAV) and its share price. If a trust's share price is higher than its NAV per share then it is said to be trading at a premium, while a trust is said to be trading on a discount if its share price is below its NAV per share.

2. How are they calculated?

A discount or premium is calculated by dividing the share price by the NAV per share and taking away 1 to give a percentage figure. A positive number gives a premium and a negative number gives a discount. For example, as at 30 September 2021, Alliance Trust's share price was 1,014.00p and its NAV per share was 1,072.50p, meaning that it was trading on a 5.5% discount (1014.00 ÷ 1072.50 − 1 = -0.055 = -5.5%).

3. How often do NAVs get published?

The frequency of NAV publications varies depending on an investment trust's underlying asset class. Long-only equity funds and those investing in publicly traded bonds will generally publish daily announcements of their NAVs as at the close of the previous business day. In contrast, funds investing in illiquid asset classes that are not publicly traded, such as property, private equity or infrastructure, tend to publish monthly or quarterly NAVs, with a time lag of about a month.

4. How reliable are NAV calculations?

For long-only equity investment trusts, NAV calculations can be expected to be very reliable, as they are based on the publicly available closing share prices of the underlying shares. For alternative assets without a set market price, valuations are usually produced or validated by third-party specialists. However, by the time these NAVs are published, they are already out of date, and the rating is therefore likely to reflect the market's expectation of the current asset valuations rather than the last published NAV.

5. Why do different sources sometimes give different figures?

Discount figures can vary from different sources if they use different NAVs in the calculation. Some data providers use the NAV including income ("cum-income"), while others use a figure excluding income ("ex-income"). In addition, if an investment trust has long-term debt, this can either be reflected in the NAV at par value (the amount of money that the fund will repay at the maturity date of the bond) or at fair value (the market price an investor would currently be willing to buy the debt for).

For example, Alliance Trust's cum-income NAV with debt valued at fair value was 1,072.50p at 30 September, resulting in a 5.5% discount when compared to share price of 1,014.00p. However, its ex-income NAV with debt valued at par was 1,080.90p, giving a discount of 6.2%. When looking at discount figures you need to look carefully at the basis on which they have been calculated. The industry standard is to use the cum-income NAV with debt at fair value.

6. What are the main factors that drive discounts/premiums?

Discounts and premiums are driven by both an investment trust's share price, which rises or falls depending on the amount of demand for the shares, and its NAV, which reflects the performance of the underlying portfolio of assets. In addition, investment trust boards can choose to intervene in the market to buy back shares to help narrow the discount, or issue new shares in order to stop the premium extending too far.

7. How common are zero discount policies?

Some investment trusts have a zero discount policy, committing to buy back shares at a discount and issue shares at a premium, in an attempt to maintain the share price very close to the underlying NAV per share. However, these are relatively rare, with only a handful of trusts committing to this mechanism. Of these the best known is probably Personal Assets, which has been successfully implementing a zero discount policy for many years.

8. How many trusts have hard discount controls?

While zero discount policies are reasonably uncommon, numerous investment trusts have stated discount control mechanisms committing to maintain the discount at narrower than a certain level, say 5% or 10%, through the use of share buybacks. We estimate that approximately 45 trusts, or around 15% of the investment trust universe, have a firm discount target.

9. How effective are share buybacks at controlling discounts?

Share buybacks can help to control discounts by reducing the number of shares in issue and increasing the share price. A proven commitment by a board to repurchase shares if the discount widens past a certain level can also help to provide a natural floor. However, if underlying demand for the fund's shares remains weak, buybacks are unlikely to provide a long-term solution. Large and regular share buyback programmes will also cause the fund to shrink in size, which in turn may make it less appealing to a number of investors and therefore exacerbate the problem.

10. What are the arguments for controlling premiums if you are an investment company?

Excessive premiums can make an investment company less appealing to new investors, as they would be knowingly paying significantly more per share than the underlying portfolio is worth. Issuing shares to prevent the premium from extending too far can therefore help to ensure new investors remain willing to invest. Furthermore, issuing shares at a premium adds to the NAV per share for existing investors as the fund raises new money at the prevailing share price and reinvests it in the portfolio at cheaper valuations.

11. Why do big discounts persist (for years in some cases)?

Large discounts can persist for prolonged periods if the fund, or the asset class in which it invests, is out-of-favour with investors. Boards may choose not to intervene if they believe that natural demand remains weak and share buybacks will therefore not lead to any significant re-rating. However, some boards may propose tender offers, a mechanism which allows a certain proportion of shareholders to redeem their shares closer to NAV, or suggest an orderly wind-up of the fund, if the engrained discount is thought to reflect a sustained or permanent lack of demand for the offering.

12. How quickly can discounts move to premiums and vice versa?

Investment trusts can move from trading on a discount to a premium, and vice versa, depending on the level of demand for the vehicle. Catalysts for a re-rating are often a change of investment objective, strategy or manager. The move from a discount to a premium can either be fairly quick in reaction to an announcement of an upcoming change, or can be steady over a longer period of time as a fund's shareholder base evolves. A recent example is Baillie Gifford China Growth, previously called Witan Pacific, which announced its appointment of Baillie Gifford as manager and a move from a pan-Asian mandate to a China growth equity strategy in July 2020. The day prior to the announcement the fund's discount stood at 7.9%, but less than two months later the trust was trading on a premium.

13. How should shareholders think about discount/premiums when contemplating portfolio moves?

On the face of it, buying an investment trust at a discount means you are accessing it cheaply, whilst buying at a premium implies paying more than the underlying portfolio is worth. However, shareholders only receive the share price return and so buying at a discount does not guarantee a successful investment, for example if the discount widens further. One way to identify potentially attractive value opportunities is to look at the current rating compared with the fund's own historical discount or premium, as well as compared with its peer group. The presence, or lack thereof, of discount control mechanisms can also give an idea of the amount of potential downside discount risk. With some specialist trusts where the NAVs are reported with a lag, and therefore out of date, an investor may decide that paying a premium is justified when set against the estimated current NAV.

14. Discounts generally have narrowed in recent years – why and can they persist?

The investment trust sector average discount has been narrowing over recent years and indeed decades. This reflects the prevalence of buybacks since April 1999 (when the tax rules changed to make them a practical reality), increased corporate activity and strong performance records. All these trends have attracted new buyers to the sector. In addition, the low interest rate environment that has persisted since the global financial crisis has coincided with a wave of new investment trust launches focusing on alternative income. The demand for this income has led to these types of fund often trading on premiums, or at worst small discounts, which has helped to narrow the overall sector average discount.

We would expect the average discount level to remain tighter than its long-term historical average, supported by increased retail investment in the sector and boards taking a more active approach to the repurchase of shares. However, we would also note that the level of discount will continue to reflect the overall market backdrop, with discounts widening sharply in periods of equity market volatility, as was seen during the global financial crisis and again in the pandemic-induced sell-off in March 2020.

A year of discount moves

Discount

Fund	Ticker	Now	Previous	Change	Fund	Ticker	Now	Previous	Change
Electra Private Equity	ELTA	17.8%	-56.7%	74.5%	APQ Global	APQ	-54.9%	-14.0%	-40.9%
KKV Secured Loan C	KKVX	-19.1%	-88.7%	69.6%	Myanmar Investments	MIL	-52.7%	-14.9%	-37.8%
KKV Secured Loan	KKVL	-37.8%	-91.1%	53.3%	Seed Innovations	SEED	-39.4%	-1.9%	-37.5%
GCP Student Living	DIGS	18.3%	-30.8%	49.1%	Global Resources	GRIT	66.7%	91.0%	-24.3%
Industrials REIT	MLI	25.0%	-14.8%	39.7%	Syncona	SYNC	2.1%	20.8%	-18.7%
Secure Income REIT	SIR	3.6%	-33.5%	37.1%	NB Distressed Debt - Global	NBDG	-33.3%	-14.8%	-18.6%
Empiric Student Property	ESP	-16.1%	-46.9%	30.9%	Gabelli Merger Plus	GMP	-38.9%	-21.9%	-17.1%
Secured Income Fund	SSIF	-19.9%	-49.8%	29.9%	Assura	AGR	24.2%	39.1%	-14.9%
PRS REIT	PRSR	6.6%	-22.9%	29.5%	Civitas Social Housing	CSH	-19.3%	-4.6%	-14.7%
Picton Property Income	PCTN	-5.1%	-34.1%	29.0%	Georgia Capital	CGEO	-51.1%	-36.5%	-14.7%
Schroder European Real Estate	SERE	-15.5%	-43.9%	28.4%	Manchester & London	MNL	-16.1%	-2.3%	-13.7%
Ediston Property	EPIC	-17.7%	-44.8%	27.0%	JLEN Environmental Assets	JLEN	9.2%	22.4%	-13.2%
BMO Commercial Property	BCPT	-23.0%	-49.3%	26.2%	JPMorgan Global Core Real Assets	JARA	-1.6%	9.2%	-10.8%
Regional REIT	RGL	-12.9%	-38.1%	25.2%	NB Distressed Debt Investment	NBDD	-20.0%	-9.9%	-10.1%
Raven Property Group	RAV	-30.0%	-55.0%	25.0%	JPMorgan China Growth & Income	JCGI	-6.7%	3.4%	-10.1%

The table shows the biggest change in discounts over the 12 months to 30 September 2021. If the change is positve it means the discount on the shares has narrowed or gone from a discount to a premium. If it is negative it means that the discount has widended or moved from a premium to a discount. Source: Numis Securities.

The largest equity sectors

AIC SECTOR	NET ASSETS (£M)	MARKET CAP (£M)	MARKET CAP (£M) 2016	NUMBER OF COMPANIES	% INDUSTRY NET ASSETS	5 YR MARKET CAP % GROWTH	AVERAGE GEARING %
Global	38,802	38,417	19,774	16	15.7%	94.3%	7
Flexible Investment	14,678	11,791	6,822	21	5.9%	72.9%	5
UK Equity Income	11,819	11,383	9,341	21	4.8%	21.9%	8
Global Emerging Markets	7,728	7,009	4,996	13	3.1%	40.3%	2
Global Smaller Companies	8,038	7,550	215	5	3.3%	3,411.8%	1
UK Smaller Companies	8,025	7,371	3,853	24	3.3%	91.3%	8
UK All Companies	5,222	4,849	4,701	9	2.1%	3.1%	12
Europe	4,664	4,363	2,690	7	1.9%	62.2%	7
Asia Pacific	3,878	3,671	4,700	6	1.6%	-21.9%	5
North America	4,306	3,798	1,494	6	1.7%	154.2%	6
Global Equity Income	3,804	3,685	2,856	6	1.5%	29.0%	9
Country Specialist	3,554	2,957	n/a	6	1.4%	n/a	0
China / Greater China	2,508	2,291	n/a	3	1.0%	n/a	22
Japan	3,136	2,943	1,336	6	1.3%	120.2%	13
European Smaller Companies	2,660	2,407	1,308	4	1.1%	84.1%	4
Asia Pacific Equity Income	2,348	2,192	n/a	5	1.0%	n/a	3
Japanese Smaller Companies	1,509	1,484	663	5	0.6%	123.9%	6
India	1,517	1,331	n/a	4	0.6%	n/a	4
Asia Pacific Smaller Companies	1,223	1,114	n/a	3	0.5%	n/a	4
North American Smaller Companies	468	437	637	2	0.2%	-31.3%	0
UK Equity & Bond Income	321	309	2,069	2	0.1%	-85.1%	13
Financials	435	446	176	1	0.2%	153.0%	8
Latin America	186	166	199	2	0.1%	-16.7%	n/a

Source: AIC/Morningstar, data to 30/09/21

There are no fixed rules for what an investment trust can invest in. The trust's strategy does, however, have to be outlined in a prospectus and approved by shareholders if, as does happen, the board wishes to change that objective at a later date. For convenience, and to help comparative analysis, trusts are grouped into a number of different sectors, based primarily on their investment focus. These are listed here and on the following two pages. It has become conventional to list highly specialised investment trusts in separate categories.

The majority of the sector categories are self-explanatory. It is worth noting, however, that individual trusts within each broad sector category will often have somewhat different investment objectives and benchmarks. The 'flexible investment' sector is a relatively new one that includes a number of trusts which invest across a broad range of asset classes, not just equities. Most of these were previously included in the global sector.

These sectoral classifications are reviewed at regular intervals by a committee of the Association of Investment Companies. In 2019 the AIC introduced a number of changes to its categorisation of Asian trusts and specialist trusts in particular. In 2020 utilities was changed to infrastructure securities. By tradition the sectoral breakdown distinguishes between trusts that invest primarily in large cap stocks and those that focus on mid and smaller companies, whatever their regional focus.

The table on this page summarises the sectors which, together with healthcare, financials and technology, are known as conventional equity trusts, as opposed to alternative assets. With the latter proving very popular in recent years, the conventional trusts today account for only about 50% of the industry's total assets. Before the global financial crisis, it was notably higher.

A notable feature of the table is that only around 20% of these conventional equity trusts have the UK as their primary investment focus. Investment trusts from the very earliest days have always had a bias towards investment outside the UK. The aim of the very first trust to be launched, Foreign & Colonial (now known simply as F&C), was to enable its shareholders to diversify their portfolios by investing in bonds issued by companies outside the UK.

An external focus remains one of the key attractions of trusts today. It is one of the principal reasons why investment trusts have on average performed significantly better than the FTSE All-Share index over recent years (and dramatically so during the pandemic year 2020). Since November 2020 however, with Brexit uncertainty eliminated, the UK's successful vaccination programme reviving the economy, and many UK stocks cheap by comparison to international peers, the UK market has outperformed and the pound has strengthened. The investment trust sector index has therefore lagged the UK equity market for the first time in several years. ∎

Specialist sectors

AIC SECTOR	NET ASSETS (£M)	MARKET CAP TODAY (£M)	MARKET CAP (£M) 2016	NUMBER OF COMPANIES	% INDUSTRY NET ASSETS	5 YR MARKET CAP % GROWTH	AVERAGE GEARING %
Private Equity	23,795	24,020	16,989	17	9.64%	41.4%	4
Infrastructure	12,497	13,853	9,291	8	5.06%	49.1%	1
Renewable Energy	11,793	12,626	2,862	19	4.78%	341.1%	11
Hedge Funds	12,950	9,509	6,054	7	5.24%	57.1%	0
Biotechnology & Healthcare	6,363	6,172	1,834	7	2.58%	236.5%	2
Technology & Media	5,228	4,821	1,268	4	2.12%	280.1%	0
Growth Capital	3,457	4,191	n/a	5	1.40%	n/a	3
Debt - Direct Lending	2,789	2,635	n/a	7	1.13%	n/a	10
Debt – Structured Finance	2,192	1,980	n/a	8	0.89%	n/a	66
Commodities & Natural Resources	1,851	1,629	1,797	8	0.75%	-9.3%	8
Debt – Loans & Bonds	1,818	1,728	n/a	10	0.74%	n/a	4
Music Royalties	1,878	1,915	n/a	2	0.76%	n/a	0
Leasing	1,406	1,111	990	7	0.57%	12.2%	100
Environmental	1,610	1,686	499	3	0.65%	237.9%	1
Infrastructure Securities	251	249	167	2	0.10%	48.5%	n/a
Insurance & Reinsurance Strategies	198	162	637	2	0.08%	-74.5%	0
Liquidity Funds	9	9	10	1	0.00%	-3.8%	n/a

Source: AIC/Morningstar, data to 30/09/21

The specialist sectors are also clearly identified by their name. Unlike the conventional trusts, which are mainly defined by their regional focus, the specialist sectors are mostly grouped by industry. The specialist sector is worth looking at in more detail to get a flavour of the wide (and expanding) range of investment strategies which are available once you look beyond the conventional equity asset trusts.

The market value of private equity, infrastructure and renewable energy trusts has grown by 50% over the last five years, thanks to good performance, the arrival of several new entrants and secondary share issuance. Along with those investing in commercial property, they make up the majority of the so-called 'alternative asset' sector.

The biotechnology and healthcare sector has also seen a significant expansion in size and rating. Along with financials and technology, they qualify as specialist trusts by virtue of being narrowly focused on one particular sector of the listed equity market. Unlike alternatives, their appeal is mostly to do with the potential for capital growth rather than their ability to generate solid and reliable dividend income streams.

A number of new specialist sectors have appeared in the last three years. One is music royalties, which currently consists of two trusts, Hipgnosis Songs (SONG) and Round Hill Music Royalty (RHM). Another newcomer is growth capital, a new category consisting of six trusts which invest part or all of their capital in unlisted securities. The three biggest ones are Schroder UK Public Private (SUPP), formerly the Woodford Patient Capital Trust, Schiehallion (MNTN) and Merian Chrysalis (MERI).

The way the universe of listed trusts looks can and does change significantly from decade to decade, reflecting both the changing market environment and investor appetite. Investment trusts run by hedge fund managers were popular before the global financial crisis but with three notable exceptions (Pershing Square, Third Point and BH Macro) have mostly disappeared, while trusts investing in assorted types of debt and insurance are also in retreat after underperforming. The most recent newcomers include a space industry trust, two shipping investment vehicles, two energy storage companies and two digital infrastructure funds. ■

Property sectors

AIC SECTOR	NET ASSETS (£M)	MARKET CAP (£M)	MARKET CAP (£M) 2016
Property – UK Commercial	6,258	5,546	3,838
Property – UK Logistics	4,285	4,843	n/a
Property – UK Residential	3,343	3,237	n/a
Property – Europe	1,865	1,853	2,275
Property Securities	1,506	1,492	994
Property – Debt	1,039	989	n/a
Property – UK Healthcare	1,065	1,098	n/a
Property – Rest of World	223	127	501

Top 15

COMPANY NAME	TICKER	AIC SECTOR	MANAGEMENT GROUP
Tritax Big Box REIT	BBOX	Property – UK Logistics	Tritax Management
TR Property	TRY	Property Securities	BMO Global Asset Management
UK Commercial Property REIT	UKCM	Property – UK Commercial	abrdn
Tritax Eurobox	BOXE	Property – Europe	Tritax Management
BMO Commercial Property	BCPT	Property – UK Commercial	BMO Global Asset Management
GCP Student Living	DIGS	Property – UK Residential	Gravis Capital Management
Supermarket Income REIT	SUPR	Property – UK Commercial	Atrato Capital
LXI REIT	LXI	Property – UK Commercial	LJ Capital
Civitas Social Housing	CSH	Property – UK Residential	Civitas Investment Management
Regional REIT	RGL	Property – UK Commercial	Toscafund Asset Management
Target Healthcare REIT	THRL	Property – UK Healthcare	Target Fund Managers
PRS REIT	PRSR	Property – UK Residential	Sigma Capital
Warehouse REIT	WHR	Property – UK Logistics	Tilstone Partners
Triple Point Social Housing REIT	SOHO	Property – UK Residential	Triple Point Investment Management
Custodian REIT	CREI	Property – UK Commercial	Custodian Capital

Source: AIC/Morningstar, data to 30/09/21

	NUMBER OF COMPANIES	% INDUSTRY NET ASSETS	5 YR MARKET CAP % GROWTH	AVERAGE GEARING %
	15	2.5%	44.5%	23
	3	1.7%	n/a	8
	7	1.4%	n/a	28
	4	0.8%	-18.6%	33
	1	0.6%	50.1%	n/a
	5	0.4%	n/a	3
	2	0.4%	n/a	n/a
	2	0.1%	-74.6%	0

% YIELD	% 5 YEAR DIVIDEND GROWTH	% GEARING	ONGOING CHARGE INCL PERF FEE %	% 5YR SHARE PRICE TOTAL RETURN	% 5 YEAR NAV TOTAL RETURN	TOTAL ASSETS (£M)	NET ASSETS (£M)
3.0%	2.5%	0	0.8%	90.0	86.2	4,501	3,220
3.0%	11.2%	15	1.4%	74.5	49.9	1,801	1,506
3.5%	-8.4%	7	1.9%	13.9	26.6	1,398	1,150
3.8%		31	2.0%	n/a	n/a	1,325	984
4.4%	-14.4%	29	1.7%	-2.5	11.1	1,249	941
0.5%	1.9%	25	1.3%	71.2	66.3	1,175	889
5.1%		27	1.3%	n/a	n/a	1,169	868
4.4%		0	0.9%	n/a	n/a	1,084	897
6.3%		30	1.4%	n/a	n/a	942	673
7.2%	45.0%	51	4.7%	24.0	31.3	859	503
5.9%	1.7%	19	1.5%	38.1	50.7	835	685
4.0%		40	1.8%	n/a	n/a	822	491
4.2%		32	1.2%	n/a	n/a	793	574
5.5%		33	1.6%	n/a	n/a	616	421
5.4%	-4.4%	28	2.5%	17.6	31.9	567	418

VCT sectors

AIC SECTOR	NET ASSETS (£M)	MARKET CAP (£M)
VCT Generalist	4,843	4,544
VCT AIM Quoted	1,236	1,136
VCT Specialist: Environmental	159	149
VCT Generalist Pre Qualifying	79	73
VCT Specialist: Media, Leisure & Events	19	13
VCT Specialist: Healthcare & Biotechnology	21	21
VCT Specialist: Environmental Pre Qualifying	13	13
VCT Specialist: Technology	21	19

Top 15

COMPANY NAME	MANAGEMENT GROUP	AIC SECTOR	TOTAL ASSETS (£M)
Octopus Titan VCT	Octopus Investments	VCT Generalist	1,289
Unicorn AIM VCT	Unicorn Asset Management	VCT AIM Quoted	371
Amati AIM VCT	Amati Global Investors	VCT AIM Quoted	307
Baronsmead Second Venture Trust	Gresham House Asset Management	VCT Generalist	250
Hargreave Hale AIM VCT	Hargreave Hale	VCT AIM Quoted	224
Baronsmead Venture Trust	Gresham House Asset Management	VCT Generalist	223
Octopus Apollo VCT	Octopus Investments	VCT Generalist	227
Octopus AIM VCT	Octopus Investments	VCT AIM Quoted	187
ProVen Growth & Income VCT	Beringea	VCT Generalist	157
Foresight VCT	Foresight Group	VCT Generalist	164
Pembroke VCT B shares	Oakley Investment Managers	VCT Generalist	155
ProVen VCT	Beringea	VCT Generalist	147
Octopus AIM VCT 2	Octopus Investments	VCT AIM Quoted	134
Northern Venture Trust	Mercia Asset Management	VCT Generalist	117
Foresight Enterprise VCT	Foresight Group	VCT Generalist	132

Source: AIC/Morningstar, data to 30/09/21

MARKET CAP (£M) 2016	NUMBER OF COMPANIES	% VCT INDUSTRY NET ASSETS	5 YR MARKET CAP % GROWTH
2,208	37	75.8%	105.8%
560	7	19.3%	102.9%
173	5	2.5%	-13.7%
142	1	1.2%	-48.8%
36	1	0.3%	-63.9%
4	1	0.3%	447.8%
7	-	0.2%	96.7%
13	4	0.3%	49.4%

MARKET CAP (£M)	NET ASSETS (£M)	NET ASSETS 2016 (£M)	LAUNCH DATE	YIELD %	% SPREAD
1,214	1,289	307	28/12/2007	4.6%	2.8%
327	371	150	05/04/2007	3.0%	0.0%
283	307	38	22/02/2001	5.1%	1.0%
241	250	143	29/01/2001	7.6%	0.0%
212	224	47	29/10/2004	3.9%	0.0%
215	223	154	02/04/1998	8.2%	0.0%
217	227	142	17/10/2006	5.1%	4.1%
177	187	95	17/03/1998	7.7%	2.4%
147	157	73	31/05/2001	5.2%	0.0%
148	164	96	02/11/1999	5.1%	4.1%
145	155	12	01/04/2015	2.7%	0.0%
136	147	104	10/04/2000	5.0%	0.0%
127	134	61	25/01/2006	4.4%	2.1%
113	117	70	01/11/1995	5.7%	5.0%
114	132	42	16/03/1998	7.1%	0.0%

Property sectors

One important distinction in the property sector table is between trusts that invest directly in property (that is, buy, sell and lease out the bricks and mortar themselves) and those that invest primarily in the shares or debt of other listed property companies. The former by their nature are less liquid than the latter. Buildings such as offices, shops and factories can take many months to purchase and cannot be sold in a hurry, whereas shares in a property company can be bought and sold within minutes.

The two types of property investment trust therefore have very different characteristics as investments. TR Property is the last remaining example of a trust that invests almost exclusively in the shares of other property companies (in its case scattered across the whole of Europe). The trust's own shares therefore trade very much like other types of share, rising and falling much more markedly from day to day than those of trusts which invest directly in their own property assets.

Until a few years go most of the biggest trusts in the property sector were so-called generalist commercial property trusts, the likes of BMO Commercial Property and Standard Life Property Income, funds managed by the big fund management companies. They own a well diversified portfolio of assets in all three of the main property categories, namely shops, offices and industrial buildings. They have been supplanted in popularity more recently by a range of trusts that specialise in smaller, niche sectors of the market, such as social housing, doctors' surgeries and warehouses.

That trend can be seen in the table of the 15 largest property trusts. Tritax Big Box, which invests in the huge distribution warehouses used by Amazon and other retailers to move products around the country, only came to the market in 2013 but is now, through good performance and multiple issues of new shares, the single largest trust in the sector. Its sister company Tritax Eurobox did not exist until five years ago.

Many of these new look property companies trade on notable premiums to net asset value, reflecting the appeal of above average dividend yields and long term, often wholly or partially inflation-linked income streams. This is in marked contrast to the shares of many of the conventional property trusts, whose shares tumbled dramatically during the pandemic and which, while recovering strongly in 2021, still trade on quite substantial discounts. ∎

VCT sectors

Venture capital trusts are specialist investment companies that exist to support companies at an early stage of their development, in return for which shareholders in the VCTs are offered potentially attractive tax breaks. Most of these trusts will be investing in unlisted securities, although an exception are the AIM VCTs, which own mostly shares listed on the Alternative Investment Market.

By their nature, most VCTs are designed to be relatively small in size and are inherently riskier than conventional equity trusts. Some of the first VCTs to be launched have grown however to become substantial and mature businesses. Of these Octopus Titan is comfortably the largest and best known, having been early investors in at least four companies which have gone to become so-called "unicorns", meaning companies which are valued at $1bn or more.

The trust was launched in 2007 and now itself has a market value of more than £1 billion, while the Octopus management company has also subsequently followed up with a number of other VCTs and a renewable energy infrastructure trust. The AIC now breaks down VCTs into ten different sub-sectors, reflecting the kind of business that they were set up to invest in. Many of these have yet to generate a five-year history.

Although the purpose behind giving tax breaks to investors in VCTs is to encourage the financing of early stage businesses, many higher rate taxpayers in the first VCTs found the tax-free dividends a particularly strong attraction. The criteria VCTs must meet in order for their shareholders to qualify for the tax benefits have subsequently been tightened to make sure that they are genuine higher risk early stage ventures.

As the demand for VCTs shows however, the appeal of the tax-free dividends remains and several of the older trusts have also generated notable capital gains as well, as noted by Alex Davies in his annual review of the sector earlier in the *Handbook*. ■

Key sector metrics

AIC SECTOR	NUMBER OF COMPANIES	MARKET CAPITALISATION (£M)	10YR NAV TOTAL RETURN %
Global	16	38,417	392.8%
Private Equity	17	24,020	284.9%
Infrastructure	8	13,853	164.0%
Renewable Energy Infrastructure	19	12,626	
Flexible Investment	21	11,791	143.8%
UK Equity Income	21	11,383	151.3%
Hedge Funds	7	9,509	98.9%
Global Smaller Companies	5	7,550	390.4%
UK Smaller Companies	24	7,371	297.5%
Global Emerging Markets	13	7,009	126.6%
Biotechnology & Healthcare	7	6,172	454.0%
Property – UK Commercial	15	5,546	94.3%
UK All Companies	9	4,849	247.8%
Property – UK Logistics	3	4,843	
Technology & Media	4	4,821	
VCT Generalist	37	4,544	119.5%
Europe	7	4,363	273.2%
Growth Capital	5	4,191	
North America	6	3,798	343.5%
Global Equity Income	6	3,685	173.4%
Asia Pacific	6	3,671	232.1%
Property – UK Residential	7	3,237	
Country Specialist	6	2,957	270.1%
Japan	6	2,943	300.8%
Debt – Direct Lending	7	2,635	
European Smaller Companies	4	2,407	362.3%
China / Greater China	3	2,291	361.9%
Asia Pacific Equity Income	5	2,192	172.4%
Debt – Structured Finance	8	1,980	
Royalties	2	1,915	
Property – Europe	4	1,853	
Debt – Loans & Bonds	10	1,728	89.3%
Environmental	3	1,686	
Commodities & Natural Resources	8	1,629	18.6%
Property Securities	1	1,492	
Japanese Smaller Companies	5	1,484	345.3%
India	4	1,331	163.6%
VCT AIM Quoted	7	1,136	221.4%
Asia Pacific Smaller Companies	3	1,114	188.5%

5 YEAR NAV TOTAL RETURN %	DIVIDEND YIELD %	% 5 YEAR DIVIDEND GROWTH (ANNUALISED)	DISCOUNT / PREMIUM %	DISCOUNT / PREMIUM % 2016	ONGOING CHARGE EXCL PERF FEE %	ONGOING CHARGE INCL PERF FEE %
144.3%	0.8%	5.0%	-0.7%	-7.4%	0.5%	0.5%
97.9%	2.9%	11.5%	5.8%	-2.8%	1.4%	1.4%
47.3%	4.8%	2.4%	11.3%	15.5%	1.1%	1.1%
49.6%	5.6%	2.2%	7.2%	7.3%	1.2%	1.2%
47.7%	1.8%	2.2%	-11.6%	-10.3%	1.6%	1.6%
33.6%	3.8%	4.0%	-3.4%	-4.2%	0.6%	0.6%
151.6%			-24.2%	-15.5%	1.6%	10.4%
126.9%			-5.4%		1.0%	1.0%
84.5%	1.8%	8.2%	-8.0%	-12.9%	0.9%	1.2%
60.5%	2.4%	11.0%	-9.3%	-11.1%	1.1%	1.1%
64.8%	1.5%	3.5%	-3.0%	-6.2%	1.2%	1.2%
24.1%	4.9%	-0.5%	-7.7%	-5.9%	1.9%	1.9%
69.2%	2.0%	6.2%	-7.1%	-9.3%	0.7%	0.7%
	3.1%		13.0%		0.9%	0.9%
			-7.5%		0.9%	1.6%
44.0%	6.0%	-2.4%	-6.0%	-8.1%	2.4%	3.2%
79.0%	1.3%	-1.2%	-6.2%	-10.9%	0.9%	0.9%
			21.0%	n/a	0.7%	4.8%
111.6%	2.0%	9.8%	-7.6%	-5.8%	0.8%	0.8%
49.7%	3.7%	8.7%	-2.8%	-0.9%	0.7%	0.7%
86.0%	0.9%	6.2%	-4.7%	-10.3%	0.9%	1.1%
	3.8%		-1.9%	n/a	1.6%	1.6%
114.9%	2.8%	20.4%	-16.4%	n/a	1.9%	1.9%
86.8%	1.0%	15.2%	-6.1%	-10.0%	0.8%	0.8%
46.3%	7.5%		-5.6%	n/a	1.5%	1.9%
92.4%	2.2%	14.8%	-9.2%	-14.1%	0.9%	0.9%
79.3%	2.1%	29.1%	-8.6%	n/a	1.0%	1.0%
48.4%	4.9%	14.6%	-6.5%	n/a	0.9%	0.9%
35.9%	9.1%	-1.9%	-8.7%	n/a	1.2%	1.2%
			2.1%	n/a		
	3.6%		0.1%	-12.6%	2.2%	2.2%
25.9%	5.6%	-1.5%	-3.9%	n/a	1.2%	1.2%
107.2%	0.4%		5.5%	-14.6%	1.1%	1.1%
7.3%	3.9%	-1.3%	-10.7%	-13.4%	1.7%	1.7%
99.6%	2.7%		-1.4%	-11.3%	1.0%	1.0%
44.0%			-12.0%	n/a	1.1%	1.6%
83.7%	4.6%	3.4%	-7.9%	-7.7%	2.1%	2.1%
45.2%	1.1%	13.4%	-8.7%	n/a	1.0%	1.0%

AIC SECTOR	NUMBER OF COMPANIES	MARKET CAPITALISATION (£M)	10YR NAV TOTAL RETURN %
Leasing	7	1,111	
Property – UK Healthcare	2	1,098	
Property – Debt	5	989	
Financials	1	446	
North American Smaller Companies	2	437	15.3%
UK Equity & Bond Income	2	309	12.8%
Infrastructure Securities	2	249	
Latin America	2	166	
Insurance & Reinsurance Strategies	2	162	
VCT Specialist: Environmental	5	149	96.3%
Property – Rest of World	2	127	-5.8%
VCT Generalist Pre Qualifying	1	73	
VCT Specialist: Healthcare & Biotechnology	1	21	
VCT Specialist: Media, Leisure & Events	1	13	
VCT Specialist: Environmental Pre Qualifying	0	13	
Liquidity Funds	1	9	
VCT Specialist: Technology	4	19	10.5%

Source: AIC/Morningstar, data to 30/09/21

Different sectors have very different characteristics, reflecting the different kinds of asset in which they invest. You can see this by looking at some of the key metrics for more than 40 sectors and sub-sectors. This table excludes the very large trust 3i. Trusts are ranked by their 10-year average share price total returns. Note that these figures are weighted averages, giving most impact to the largest trusts, and individual trusts within each sector may have significantly different characteristics.

Some interesting trends can be discerned, however. For example, the most expensive trusts, as measured by OCRs (ongoing charge ratios) are to be found in VCTs, commercial property, hedge funds and private equity, where performance fees are most often still to be found. The cheapest sectors on average are to be found in the two main UK equity sectors (equity income and all companies) and the global trusts. Fees generally have been falling in recent years.

The highest yields are found among VCTs and in the equity income, property and infrastructure sectors. Looking at the performance figures it is evident that there is something of an inverse relationship between yield and NAV total returns over 10 years.

5 YEAR NAV TOTAL RETURN %	DIVIDEND YIELD %	% 5 YEAR DIVIDEND GROWTH (ANNUALISED)	DISCOUNT / PREMIUM %	DISCOUNT / PREMIUM % 2016	ONGOING CHARGE EXCL PERF FEE %	ONGOING CHARGE INCL PERF FEE %
7.3%	25.5%	0.2%	-9.4%	17.1%	9.2%	9.2%
				n/a		
36.3%	6.2%	1.3%	-4.3%	n/a	1.6%	1.6%
	5.8%		-17.1%		1.7%	1.8%
12.8%			-15.1%	-14.0%	1.3%	1.1%
6.2%	5.9%	2.4%	0.3%	-2.4%	1.1%	1.1%
			-16.3%	-6.9%	7.8%	7.8%
25.4%	7.1%	6.6%	-6.0%	-7.1%	3.7%	3.7%
-6.7%			-26.9%	n/a	8.3%	8.2%
	3.5%		-7.5%	-0.5%	3.1%	3.1%
				-18.6%		
				-11.2%		
-29.9%			-4.3%	-34.9%	3.4%	3.4%

Even though trusts with higher yields have attracted a disproportionate amount of the capital that has flowed into the investment trust sector, the potential capital gains which are foregone by opting for higher yielding trusts has been significant in the last 10 years.

However, this has been masked to a considerable extent by the tighter discounts on which higher yielding trusts tend to trade. Compare for example the average discount in the UK equity income sector (3.4%) with that in the UK smaller companies (8.2%) and the UK all companies sectors (6.2%). On a positive note, the discounts on all three sectors have narrowed in the last 12 months as the UK equity market has come back into favour.

Looking at the level of discounts more generally, it can be seen that there is a correlation between the risk of a sector and the level of the discount. It is generally wider for specific country trusts, smaller company specialists and less liquid asset classes. Of the larger sectors trading on premiums, infrastructure, renewable energy and some specialist property trusts stand out, while biotechnology/healthcare trusts, which were trading at a premium in 2020, have moved to a discount, largely on fears of regulatory moves by the incoming Democrat administration in the United States. ■

Largest management groups

MANAGEMENT GROUP	NUMBER OF COMPANIES	TOTAL ASSETS (£M)	NET ASSETS (£M)
Baillie Gifford	13	33,620	31,474
J.P. Morgan Asset Management	20	15,079	14,004
abrdn	23	12,383	11,131
BMO Global Asset Management	10	12,113	10,686
3i Group	1	11,116	10,141
Pershing Square Capital Management	1	8,509	7,086
Janus Henderson Investors	12	8,429	7,765
Fidelity	5	6,010	4,962
Frostrow Capital	5	5,923	5,728
Tritax Management	2	5,483	3,861
InfraRed Capital Partners	2	5,329	5,329
BlackRock Investment Management (UK)	9	5,226	4,613
Polar Capital Holdings	3	4,661	4,570
RIT Capital Partners	1	4,536	4,166
Greencoat Capital	2	4,251	3,101
Schroder Investment Management	9	3,986	3,720
Willis Towers Watson	1	3,843	3,502
Fundsmith	2	3,521	3,521
Allianz Global Investors	3	2,741	2,623

Source: AIC/Morningstar, data to 30/09/21

The management groups with the most trust mandates are listed here. The trust sector is a competitive one, in which no management group has a dominant position. There has however been some notable consolidation in the last few years. The 20 largest groups manage 60% of total industry assets, up from 47% five years ago, but still only five firms out of roughly 400 in total manage more than 10 trusts.

In 2018 Baillie Gifford, a private partnership based in Edinburgh, became the largest player in the investment trust sector for the first time, overtaking 3i and J.P. Morgan, and has since further consolidated its lead through a combination of exceptionally strong performance, notably by its flagship trust, Scottish Mortgage, and new mandate wins. It now accounts for one eighth

MARKET CAP (£M)	AVG MARKET CAP (£M)	% TOTAL ASSETS 2021	TOTAL ASSETS 2016 (£M)	% TOTAL ASSETS 2016
31,424	2,417	12.7%	7,822	5.1%
12,998	650	5.7%	10,175	6.6%
10,001	435	4.7%	6,812	4.4%
9,815	982	4.6%	8,274	5.4%
13,017	13,017	4.2%	5,138	3.3%
5,209	5,209	3.2%	3,135	2.0%
7,435	620	3.2%	5,700	3.7%
4,772	954	2.3%	3,509	2.3%
5,546	1,109	2.2%	2,913	1.9%
4,831	2,415	2.1%	1,439	0.9%
5,989	2,995	2.0%	2,914	1.9%
4,437	493	2.0%	3,194	2.1%
4,265	1,422	1.8%	1,594	1.0%
4,191	4,191	1.7%	2,994	1.9%
3,316	1,658	1.6%	726	0.5%
3,460	384	1.5%	2,474	1.6%
3,251	3,251	1.5%	n/a	-
3,558	1,779	1.3%	236	0.2%
2,460	820	1.0%	1,269	0.8%

of the investment trust sector's assets. Other notable gainers in asset terms over the past five years include Pershing Square, Tritax, InfraRed Capital and Polar Capital.

Aberdeen Standard Investments (now given, in a fit of branding machismo, a new and vowel-challenged name, abrdn) has the largest number of trusts, slightly ahead of J.P. Morgan. The biggest firms typically launch and market their own trusts, as well as providing portfolio management and administrative functions, often centralising them. Smaller firms, by contrast, especially those managing specialist trusts, may only have one or more funds that they look after and will often sub-contract more services. ■

The largest trusts

COMPANY NAME	MANAGEMENT GROUP	AIC SECTOR	TOTAL ASSETS (£M)
Scottish Mortgage	Baillie Gifford	Global	21,073
3i Group	3i Group	Private Equity	11,116
Pershing Square Holdings	Pershing Square Capital Management	Hedge Funds	10,380
F&C Investment Trust	BMO Global Asset Management	Global	5,626
RIT Capital Partners	RIT Capital Partners	Flexible Investment	4,622
Tritax Big Box REIT	Tritax Management	Property – UK Logistics	4,501
Alliance Trust	Willis Towers Watson	Global	3,731
Polar Capital Technology	Polar Capital Holdings	Technology & Media	3,665
Greencoat UK Wind	Greencoat Capital	Renewable Energy Infrastructure	3,416
Monks	Baillie Gifford	Global	3,412
Smithson	Fundsmith	Global Smaller Companies	3,056
HICL Infrastructure	InfraRed Capital Partners	Infrastructure	2,950
Mercantile	J.P. Morgan Asset Management	UK All Companies	2,656
Renewables Infrastructure Group	InfraRed Capital Partners	Renewable Energy Infrastructure	2,590
Worldwide Healthcare	Frostrow Capital	Biotechnology & Healthcare	2,560
HarbourVest Global Private Equity	HarbourVest Advisers L.P.	Private Equity	2,493
Templeton Emerging Markets	Franklin Templeton Investments	Global Emerging Markets	2,457
International Public Partnerships	Amber Infrastructure Group	Infrastructure	2,444
Caledonia	Caledonia Investments	Flexible Investment	2,431

MARKET CAP (£M)	NET ASSETS (£M)	NET ASSETS 2016 (£M)	LAUNCH DATE	YIELD %	% SPREAD	ONGOING CHARGE INCL PERF FEE %	ONGOING CHARGE AS AT DATE
20,160	18,062	4,265	17/03/1909	0.2%	0.1%	0.3%	31/03/2021
12,472	9,109	5,138	01/04/1945	3.0%	0.0%	1.3%	31/03/2021
7,188	7,292	3,135	13/10/2014	1.1%	6.8%	11.7%	31/12/2020
4,560	4,813	3,049	19/03/1868	1.4%	0.7%	0.5%	31/12/2020
4,003	3,986	2,619	01/08/1988	1.4%	0.8%	0.7%	31/12/2020
3,658	2,893	1,062	09/12/2013	3.0%	0.1%	0.8%	31/12/2020
3,159	3,329	3,347	21/04/1888	1.5%	0.2%	0.7%	31/12/2020
3,284	2,427	1,087	16/12/1996	0.0%	0.2%	0.8%	30/04/2021
2,565	3,409	622	27/03/2013	5.5%	0.2%	1.0%	31/12/2020
3,287	3,205	1,230	06/02/1929	0.1%	0.6%	0.4%	30/04/2021
3,107	2,997	n/a	19/10/2018	0.0%	0.6%	1.0%	31/12/2020
3,227	2,273	2,115	29/03/2006	5.0%	0.2%	1.0%	31/03/2021
2,105	2,624	1,820	08/12/1884	2.5%	0.9%	0.5%	31/01/2021
2,796	2,697	800	29/07/2013	5.5%	0.3%	0.9%	31/12/2020
2,372	2,346	1,036	28/04/1995	0.6%	0.3%	0.9%	31/03/2021
1,869	2,466	1,084	06/12/2007	0.0%	0.4%	0.4%	31/01/2021
2,126	2,390	1,927	12/06/1989	3.2%	0.4%	1.0%	31/03/2021
2,763	2,366	1,480	09/11/2006	4.7%	0.5%	1.2%	31/12/2020
1,882	2,020	1,726	18/07/1960	1.8%	0.3%	1.0%	31/03/2021

COMPANY NAME	MANAGEMENT GROUP	AIC SECTOR	TOTAL ASSETS (£M)
Tetragon Financial Group	Tetragon Financial Management	Flexible Investment	2,363
3i Infrastructure	3i Investments	Infrastructure	2,346
Fidelity China Special Situations	Fidelity	China / Greater China	2,308
Witan	Witan Investment Services	Global	2,262
Finsbury Growth & Income	Frostrow Capital	UK Equity Income	2,106
Pantheon International	Pantheon Ventures	Private Equity	2,099

Source: AIC/Morningstar, data to 30/09/21

While a small minority of investment trusts are managed directly by the board of directors, the great majority delegate the management of their portfolios to specialist fund managers, employed on annual or multi-year management contracts with a mandate to meet the trust's investment objectives. Those objectives are set by the board of directors and need to be approved by shareholders before any significant changes can be made.

The investment trust with the greatest total assets, Scottish Mortgage (SMT), had an extraordinary year in 2020, making a return of more than 100% in 12 months, as the big technology stocks it has owned for years soared during the lockdown. At 30 September 2020 this one trust accounted for 12.5% of the industry total, compared to 7.5% a year earlier.

The 20 largest individual trusts on this measure accounted for just over 40% of total industry assets. In contrast, more than 100 trusts had less than £50m in assets, although this figure includes a large number of venture capital trusts, which are invariably much smaller on average. The largest trusts tend to have the best liquidity, meaning they are easier to buy and sell in size. The

MARKET CAP (£M)	NET ASSETS (£M)	NET ASSETS 2016 (£M)	LAUNCH DATE	YIELD %	% SPREAD	ONGOING CHARGE INCL PERF FEE %	ONGOING CHARGE AS AT DATE
817	2,228	1,457	19/04/2007	4.4%	0.7%	5.4%	31/12/2020
2,710	2,209	1,714	13/03/2007	3.4%	0.3%	1.5%	31/03/2021
1,627	2,030	1,157	19/04/2010	1.5%	1.9%	1.0%	31/03/2021
1,855	2,050	1,681	17/02/1909	2.2%	0.2%	0.8%	31/12/2020
1,971	1,801	936	15/01/1926	1.9%	0.1%	0.6%	30/09/2020
1,627	1,681	1,250	18/09/1987	0.0%	0.5%	1.2%	31/05/2021

spread between bid and offer prices is typically well below 0.5%. Economies of scale also make it easier for the biggest trusts to accept reduced annual management fees, with Scottish Mortgage, boasting an OCF of just 0.36% again a prime example.

A majority of the largest trusts in the sector have been operating for many years, but that is by no means universally the case. Smithson (SSON), whose IPO in 2018 was the largest launch in investment trust history, Pershing Square (PSH), Greencoat UK Wind (UKW) and Tritax Big Box (BBOX) have all been launched or listed on the London market in the last 10 years and grown quickly and moved to a high ranking.

At the same time there are regular departures from the investment trust universe, as funds either close down or return capital to shareholders, typically (though not invariably) as a result of indifferent performance, or where the trust has a predetermined wind-up date. Once again the diversity of the investment trust universe is well demonstrated in this table. ∎

Vintage investment trusts

COMPANY NAME	AIC SECTOR	LAUNCH DATE	MARKET CAP (£M)
F&C Investment Trust	Global	19/03/1868	4,560
Investment Company	Flexible Investment	14/11/1868	14
Dunedin Income Growth	UK Equity Income	01/02/1873	482
Scottish American	Global Equity Income	31/03/1873	873
J.P. Morgan American	North America	18/06/1881	1,334
Mercantile	UK All Companies	08/12/1884	2,105
J.P. Morgan Global Growth & Income	Global Equity Income	21/04/1887	696
Scottish Investment Trust	Global	27/07/1887	490
Henderson Smaller Companies	UK Smaller Companies	16/12/1887	916
Bankers	Global	13/04/1888	1,452
Alliance Trust	Global	21/04/1888	3,159
BMO Global Smaller Companies	Global Smaller Companies	15/02/1889	942
Merchants	UK Equity Income	16/02/1889	676
Edinburgh Investment	UK Equity Income	01/03/1889	1,050
AVI Global	Global	01/07/1889	1,042
Law Debenture Corporation	UK Equity Income	12/12/1889	941
City of London	UK Equity Income	01/01/1891	1,726
Aberdeen Diversified Income & Growth	Flexible Investment	05/01/1898	309
TR Property	Property Securities	05/05/1905	1,492
BlackRock Smaller Companies	UK Smaller Companies	02/05/1906	1,006
Baillie Gifford China Growth	China / Greater China	24/01/1907	233
Murray International	Global Equity Income	18/12/1907	1,399
Witan	Global	17/02/1909	1,855
Scottish Mortgage	Global	17/03/1909	20,160
Hansa Investment Company	Flexible Investment	01/01/1912	174
Hansa Investment Company	Flexible Investment	01/01/1912	89

NET ASSETS (£M)	TICKER	YIELD %	% SPREAD	1YR AVG DISCOUNT / PREMIUM %	ONGOING CHARGE INCL PERF FEE %	ONGOING CHARGE AS AT DATE
5,037	FCIT	1.4%	0.7%	-7.1%	0.5%	31/12/2020
17	INV	0.7%	0.0%	-9.2%	2.9%	30/06/2021
478	DIG	3.9%	1.5%	-3.5%	0.6%	31/01/2021
857	SAIN	2.4%	1.2%	3.0%	0.7%	31/12/2020
1,379	JAM	1.0%	1.0%	-5.1%	0.3%	31/12/2020
2,312	MRC	2.5%	0.9%	-4.8%	0.5%	31/01/2021
671	JGGI	3.0%	0.7%	2.9%	1.6%	30/06/2021
561	SCIN	3.1%	0.8%	-10.2%	0.5%	31/10/2020
1,003	HSL	1.9%	1.5%	-5.9%	1.0%	31/05/2021
1,544	BNKR	2.0%	0.9%	0.5%	0.5%	31/10/2020
3,346	ATST	1.5%	0.2%	-5.6%	0.7%	31/12/2020
1,027	BGSC	1.1%	0.6%	-8.0%	0.8%	30/04/2021
671	MRCH	5.0%	1.1%	0.1%	0.6%	31/01/2021
1,156	EDIN	3.9%	0.7%	-8.0%	0.4%	31/03/2021
1,120	AGT	1.6%	0.2%	-8.5%	0.9%	30/09/2020
955	LWDB	3.7%	1.0%	0.6%	0.6%	31/12/2020
1,709	CTY	5.0%	0.4%	2.4%	0.4%	30/06/2021
369	ADIG	5.5%	2.0%	-16.7%	0.6%	30/09/2020
1,506	TRY	3.0%	1.6%	-6.6%	1.4%	31/03/2021
1,059	BRSC	1.6%	1.0%	-4.6%	0.8%	28/02/2021
249	BGCG	1.9%	0.9%	7.2%	0.8%	31/01/2021
1,509	MYI	5.0%	0.5%	-1.7%	0.6%	31/12/2020
2,001	WTAN	2.2%	0.2%	-6.8%	0.8%	31/12/2020
19,484	SMT	0.2%	0.1%	-1.4%	0.3%	31/03/2021
266	HANA	1.5%	7.3%	-33.3%	1.1%	31/03/2021
133	HAN	1.4%	5.4%	-33.1%	1.1%	31/03/2021

COMPANY NAME	AIC SECTOR	LAUNCH DATE	MARKET CAP (£M)
Murray Income	UK Equity Income	07/06/1923	1,028
Finsbury Growth & Income	UK Equity Income	15/01/1926	1,971
Temple Bar	UK Equity Income	24/06/1926	710
Brunner	Global	01/01/1927	440
J.P. Morgan Japanese	Japan	02/08/1927	1,071
Monks	Global	06/02/1929	3,287
J.P. Morgan European Growth	Europe	15/03/1929	259
Shires Income	UK Equity Income	31/03/1929	83
Canadian General Investments	North America	15/01/1930	815
Henderson Far East Income	Asia Pacific Equity Income	30/05/1930	448
3i Group	Private Equity	01/04/1945	12,472
Henderson European Focus	Europe	01/01/1947	340
Keystone Positive Change	Global	19/09/1954	213
Caledonia	Flexible Investment	18/07/1960	1,882

Source: AIC/Morningstar, data to 30/09/21

The first investment trust, F&C (FCIT), was formed in 1868 and continues in existence today. It celebrated its 150th anniversary in 2018. A number of other investment companies have also been around for many years. Twelve can trace their histories back to the 19th century. This is a list of some of the oldest vintage trusts which are still in existence.

A number of these trusts were started by wealthy families looking to invest their fortunes in a tax-efficient manner, but have since expanded to include outside investors as well. The first Scottish investment trust, Dunedin Income Growth (DIG), for example, was founded to provide a home for the savings of wealthy textile merchants in Dundee. Caledonia (CLDN) was founded by the Cayzer shipping dynasty and Brunner, profiled elsewhere in this year's *Handbook*, by one of the families whose chemical businesses combined to form ICI in 1926.

There is no obvious correlation between age and size or quality of trust, although the mere fact of having survived for so long indicates that a trust

NET ASSETS (£M)	TICKER	YIELD %	% SPREAD	1YR AVG DISCOUNT / PREMIUM %	ONGOING CHARGE INCL PERF FEE %	ONGOING CHARGE AS AT DATE
1,111	MUT	3.9%	0.7%	-4.3%	0.5%	30/06/2021
2,070	FGT	1.9%	0.1%	-1.0%	0.6%	30/09/2020
777	TMPL	3.6%	0.9%	-6.6%	0.5%	31/12/2020
480	BUT	2.0%	1.0%	-12.6%	0.6%	30/11/2020
1,151	JFJ	0.7%	1.0%	-3.8%	0.7%	30/09/2020
3,271	MNKS	0.1%	0.6%	2.1%	0.4%	30/04/2021
287	JETG	1.2%	1.9%	-11.5%	1.0%	31/03/2020
88	SHRS	5.1%	1.9%	-4.8%	1.0%	31/03/2021
1,208	CGI	2.2%	7.0%	-32.5%	1.5%	31/12/2020
452	HFEL	7.9%	0.8%	1.7%	1.1%	31/08/2020
10,141	III	3.0%	0.0%	24.2%	1.3%	31/03/2021
371	HEFT	2.0%	10.1%	-9.2%	0.8%	30/09/2020
215	KPC	3.3%	0.6%	-5.1%	0.5%	30/09/2020
2,431	CLDN	1.8%	0.3%	-23.0%	1.0%	31/03/2021

Spread = (offer-bid)/mid(close)

has at least successfully established a niche in the market. The wide range of average discounts illustrates the disparity in their liquidity, performance and popularity. Trusts with a founding family often take on third party investors over time, surrendering their control in return for a broader asset base, but a long history is no guarantee that the trust will survive without new management.

A number of these trusts have changed investment manager in recent years. In 2020 the boards of Witan Pacific, which moved to Baillie Gifford as Baillie Gifford China Growth (BGCG), Edinburgh Investment Trust (EDIN), Temple Bar (TMPL) and Perpetual Income and Growth (PLI), which merged with Murray Income (MUT), all chose to move from one management firm to a different one. Keystone (now KPC) has done the same in 2021 and Scottish Investment Trust (SCIT), one of the oldest of them all, will shortly go the same way. ■

Long-serving managers

COMPANY NAME	TICKER	AIC SECTOR
Capital Gearing	CGT	Flexible Investment
Rights & Issues	RIII	UK Smaller Companies
Lowland	LWI	UK Equity Income
City of London	CTY	UK Equity Income
Herald	HRI	Global Smaller Companies
J.P. Morgan Emerging Markets	JMG	Global Emerging Markets
Aberdeen Standard Asia Focus	AAS	Asia Pacific Smaller Companies
British & American	BAF	UK Equity Income
Atlantis Japan Growth	AJG	Japanese Smaller Companies
Atlantis Japan Growth	AJG	Japanese Smaller Companies
BMO Capital & Income	BCI	UK Equity Income
J.P. Morgan UK Smaller Companies	JMI	UK Smaller Companies
J.P. Morgan European Discovery	JEDT	European Smaller Companies
Chelverton UK Dividend	SDV	UK Equity Income
BMO Private Equity	BPET	Private Equity
Scottish Mortgage	SMT	Global
BlackRock World Mining	BRWM	Commodities & Natural Resources
Independent Investment Trust	IIT	UK All Companies
European Opportunities	JEO	Europe
Finsbury Growth & Income	FGT	UK Equity Income
HgCapital	HGT	Private Equity
Lindsell Train	LTI	Global
International Biotechnology	IBT	Biotechnology & Healthcare
Aberforth Smaller Companies	ASL	UK Smaller Companies
J.P. Morgan Russian Securities	JRS	Country Specialist
Impax Environmental Markets	IEM	Environmental
Impax Environmental Markets	IEM	Environmental
Henderson Smaller Companies	HSL	UK Smaller Companies
Schroder UK Mid Cap	SCP	UK All Companies
Artemis Alpha Trust	ATS	UK All Companies
Law Debenture Corporation	LWDB	UK Equity Income
Bankers	BNKR	Global

MANAGER NAME	EFFECTIVE FROM	YEARS IN SERVICE	10 YEAR NAV TOTAL RETURN %
Peter Spiller	01/01/1982	39 years 9 months	86.5
Simon Knott	01/01/1984	37 years 9 months	405.5
James H Henderson	01/01/1990	31 years 9 months	153.6
Job Curtis	01/07/1991	30 years 3 months	132.0
Katie Potts	16/02/1994	27 years 7 months	407.5
Austin Forey	01/06/1994	27 years 4 months	190.0
Hugh Young	19/10/1995	25 years 11 months	201.2
Jonathan Woolf	03/01/1996	25 years 9 months	110.5
Edwin C Merner	10/05/1996	25 years 4 months	262.2
Taeko Setaishi	10/05/1996	25 years 4 months	262.2
Julian Cane	01/03/1997	24 years 7 months	147.5
Georgina Brittain	02/01/1998	23 years 9 months	396.2
Francesco Conte	01/11/1998	22 years 11 months	310.3
David Horner	12/05/1999	22 years 4 months	300.3
Hamish Mair	01/02/2000	21 years 8 months	228.9
James K. Anderson	01/04/2000	21 years 6 months	1,078.9
Evy Hambro	01/09/2000	21 years 1 month	26.8
Maxwell Ward	18/10/2000	20 years 11 months	268.1
Alexander Darwall	22/11/2000	20 years 10 months	304.3
Nick Train	11/12/2000	20 years 9 months	263.3
Nic Humphries	01/01/2001	20 years 9 months	343.1
Nick Train	22/01/2001	20 years 8 months	638.4
Kate Bingham	01/05/2001	20 years 5 months	481.9
Euan R MacDonald	14/05/2001	20 years 4 months	253.0
Oleg Biryulyov	09/01/2002	19 years 8 months	171.9
Bruce Jenkyn-Jones	22/02/2002	19 years 7 months	371.0
Jon Forster	22/02/2002	19 years 7 months	371.0
Neil Hermon	01/11/2002	18 years 11 months	425.2
Andy Brough	30/04/2003	18 years 5 months	272.8
John Dodd	01/06/2003	18 years 4 months	77.7
James H Henderson	01/06/2003	18 years 4 months	201.8
Alex Crooke	01/07/2003	18 years 3 months	265.2

COMPANY NAME	TICKER	AIC SECTOR
abrdn UK Smaller Companies	SLS	UK Smaller Companies
EP Global Opportunities	EPG	Global
Miton Global Opportunities	MIGO	Flexible Investment
Murray International	MYI	Global Equity Income
Schroder Real Estate	SREI	Property – UK Commercial
BlackRock Greater Europe	BRGE	Europe
Aberdeen New India	ANII	India
BMO Commercial Property	BCPT	Property – UK Commercial
Biotech Growth	BIOG	Biotechnology & Healthcare
JPEL Private Equity	JPEL	Private Equity
JPEL Private Equity	JPEL	Private Equity
J.P. Morgan American	JAM	North America
J.P. Morgan China Growth & Income	JCGI	China / Greater China
BMO Global Smaller Companies	BGSC	Global Smaller Companies
J.P. Morgan European Income	JETI	Europe

Source: AIC/Morningstar, data to 30/09/21

Some individual trusts are also notable for having long-serving managers who have been running the trust's investments for many years. In some cases the managers also have significant personal shareholdings in the trust. This is typically regarded as a good omen for other shareholders, since it should establish a close alignment of interest between the manager and the shareholders. See the Skin in the Game page (page 226) for some others, including some where it had not worked out quite like that.

Because fund management is an extremely well-paid profession, the fact that a manager continues to manage a trust after many years in harness can be interpreted also as demonstrating exceptional commitment to the business. While some successful fund managers retire early to do other things, those who remain in post for decades are typically such enthusiasts for investing that they cannot think of anything more interesting or rewarding to do with their time (look at Warren Buffett, still running Berkshire Hathaway in his 90s).

MANAGER NAME	EFFECTIVE FROM	YEARS IN SERVICE	10 YEAR NAV TOTAL RETURN %
Harry Nimmo	01/09/2003	18 years 1 month	346.8
Sandy Nairn	15/12/2003	17 years 9 months	143.6
Nick Greenwood	06/04/2004	17 years 5 months	167.4
Bruce Stout	16/06/2004	17 years 3 months	127.4
Nick Montgomery	15/07/2004	17 years 2 months	102.2
Sam Vecht	20/09/2004	17 years 0 months	370.0
Kristy Fong	09/12/2004	16 years 9 months	213.5
Richard Kirby	17/03/2005	16 years 6 months	92.2
Geoffrey Hsu	19/05/2005	16 years 4 months	605.5
Troy Duncan	30/06/2005	16 years 3 months	51.5
Gregory Getschow	30/06/2005	16 years 3 months	51.5
Eytan Shapiro	01/07/2005	16 years 3 months	431.3
Howard Wang	01/07/2005	16 years 3 months	397.6
Peter Ewins	31/07/2005	16 years 2 months	303.2
Michael Barakos	02/08/2005	16 years 2 months	179.9

Against that sometimes situations arise where managers have such a large personal shareholding in a trust that they effectively control the running of the company, and as a result may not always make the interests of other shareholders as high a priority as they should. They are effectively being paid to look after their own money, often with a longer-term perspective that makes them worry less about short-term performance or the persistence of a wide discount. The fallout this year between the board and managers of Gabelli Value Plus (GVP), who controlled around a quarter of the shares, is a good case in point.

That said, there is a reason that many of the trusts in the *Handbook* portfolio are managed by names in this list. Experience is a vital quality when it comes to choosing someone to manage your money. From those included in this list a year ago, notable names who have announced retirements include James Anderson at Scottish Mortgage (SMT) and Matthew Dobbs at Schroder Asia Pacific (SDP) and Schroder Oriental Income (SOI). The longest serving manager still managing a trust now remains Peter Spiller at Capital Gearing Trust (CGT). ∎

Skin in the game

Why it matters

T HE EXTENT TO which the interests of the directors and managers of a company are aligned with the interests of the shareholders is an important factor for investors. Other things being equal, it is comforting to know that those overseeing the company managing its investments stand to gain or lose in the same way as those providing the capital for the business (which is what shareholders effectively do). 'Skin in the game' matters.

Directors of investment trusts are required to disclose at least once a year in the company's annual report and accounts the extent of their holdings in the trusts on whose boards they serve. It is also a stock exchange listing requirement they notify the market within 24 hours of any further dealings in their trust's shares. All significant shareholders must also notify the market if they own more than 3% of the share capital in any trust.

While directors' interests are always publicly available, it is less easy to discover how much the portfolio managers have invested in their trusts. They only have to disclose their shareholding if it exceeds 3% of the total issued share capital of the trust. Some choose to do so voluntarily and more probably should.

Alan Brierley, an investment trust analyst at Investec, periodically compiles a summary of the shareholdings of directors and managers (where the latter can be ascertained). His latest research on this topic, based on analysing 298 trusts, was published in June 2021. Earlier reports appeared in 2019, 2018, 2017, 2014, 2012 and 2010, making it easy to spot some of the most striking trends in board composition.

Some headline findings

- The total investment by boards and managers in the 2021 report was £4.8bn. While changes in the number of trusts make comparisons of limited value, and equity markets have been strong, this is materially higher than the total of £3.4bn in 2019, £1bn in 2014 and £687m in 2012. It represents about 2% of the total value of the universe.

- 51 chairmen/directors have an individual investment in their trusts of more than £1m, and 78 managers or management teams a personal investment of at least that amount. 39 investment trusts have boards where all the directors on a board can claim the same.

- On the other hand 8% of directors have no investment at all in their trusts (vs 14% in 2018 and 16% in 2014), while 44 chairmen with more than five years sitting on the board have shareholdings worth less than their annual fees.

- 95% of boards can be deemed to be independent in corporate governance terms, meaning they have no business or close personal relationship with the fund manager of the trust. This is a big change from the past when boards were often very 'chummy', with many directors facing conflicts of interest that potentially inhibited their ability to act solely in the interests of shareholders.

Progress on diversity

A very notable trend is that there has been a sharp increase in the percentage of women directors on boards, Mr Brierley reports. As the chart indicates, women now represent 34.5% of all investment company directorships, compared to just 8.0% in his first Skin in the Game report back in 2010.

Significant growth in women's representation on Investment Company Boards (% of total board positions)

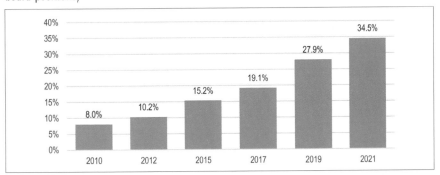

Source: Investec Securities analysis

"Looking forward" he says, "we expect further progress, as directors from the more mature and male-dominated vintages retire and through new appointments." Since the beginning of 2020, 52% of new directors have been women. In terms of the top job, the number of women chairing boards has risen to 59 out of 298 (19.8%). In 2010 there were just nine out of 238 (3.8%) in 2010.

The number of women on trust boards in 2021 for the first time now stands comparison with the (voluntary) 33% target for UK listed companies set by the Hampton-Alexander corporate governance. 23 trusts without female representation remain, while 95, around third of the total, have one woman only on the board. There are no all-male boards left in the FTSE 350 index.

Managers with a personal investment in excess of £1m at COB 1 June 2021

COMPANY	MANAGER	INVESTMENT VALUE (£'000)
Pershing Square Holdings	Bill Ackman, Nicholas Botta & Management team	1,315,016
Tetragon Financial Group	Reade Griffith/Paddy Dear & Management team	243,467
Apax Global Alpha	Management team	236,711
Scottish Mortgage	Management team	200,000
North Atlantic Smaller Companies	Christopher Mills	167,022
Manchester & London	Mark Sheppard/Richard Morgan	132,010
Third Point Offshore	Management team	104,873
Boussard & Gavaudan	Management team	63,100
Utilico Emerging Markets	Management team	60,842
New Star	John Duffield	55,444
Smithson Investment Trust	Management team	53,203
HgCapital Trust	Management team	46,500
Lindsell Train	Michael Lindsell/Nick Train/Team	34,151
Finsbury Growth & Income	Nick Train/Alastair Smith	31,745
Jupiter European Opportunities	Alex Darwall	28,090
Warehouse REIT	Management team	24,690
JZ Capital Partners	Jay Jordan/David Zalaznick	24,688
Value and Indexed Property Income Trust	Matthew Oakeshott	24,557
Capital Gearing	Peter Spiller/team	21,948
Mobius Investment Trust	Mark Mobius/Carlos Hardenberg	21,234
Montanaro UK Smaller Companies	Management team	19,722
Tritax Big Box	Management team	19,261
Gresham House Energy Storage	Ben Guest/Bozkurt Aydinoglu	18,878
Montanaro European Smaller Companies	Management team	18,031
Mid Wynd International	Simon Edelsten	17,799
Riverstone Energy	Management team	14,373
International Public Partnerships	Management team	13,844
Odyssean Investment Trust	Management team	13,440
Artemis Alpha Trust	John Dodd/Kartik Kumar	13,190
VinaCapital Vietnam Opportunity Fund	Management team	11,799
Fundsmith Emerging Equities	Terry Smith/Mike O'Brien	11,630
Honeycomb Investment Trust	Management team	10,635

Source: Investec Securities analysis

Too much skin in the game?

It is not always the case that skin in the game is a force for good as far as shareholders are concerned. A number of recent examples highlight the problems that can arise when the managers of a trust have such a significant shareholding in the company that it gives them an effective blocking power, or even a veto, over a board's ability to make decisions.

The protracted struggle between the board and the management company of the Gabelli Value Plus investment trust (GVP) turned into one of the longest running stories in 2020–21. After several years of poor performance in both absolute and relative terms, the board of Gabelli Value Plus decided in July 2020 to support the liquidation of the trust, a move that was supported by two thirds of the trust's shareholders at its AGM.

However the proposal was resisted by the trust's investment management company, which held a 27% shareholding in the trust, and is indirectly controlled by the American fund manager Mario Gabelli whose name the trust had adopted when it launched. This amounted to a blocking stake as a liquidation proposal requires a 75% shareholder majority to pass. It was only after a year of standoff and protracted argument between the board and the management company, running up hefty legal fees, that the decision to liquidate the trust was finally approved.

A related but slightly different situation has also kept the lawyers busy for most of the past year at Third Point Investors, in which the hedge fund manager Dan Loeb has a significant 17% shareholding. In this case the board and Mr Loeb are agreed on the need to try and bring in the wide discount at which the shares have traded for several years, but they have been unable to agree with one of their shareholders, an activist investment group, Asset Value Investors, about what is required to achieve that. That dispute rumbles on.

An even more egregious example can be found at JX Capital Partners, an investment trust that ranked 747 out of 747 UK listed trusts and open-ended funds for its performance over 20 years in the summer of 2021, losing about 765 of its value. In this case two of the founders own 27% of the shares between them, but that has been insufficient to prevent its dismal performance. Since 2008, however, according to Mr Brierley's calculations, the management firm has received $189m in fees and incentives since 2008 – a handsome reward for such little return (and rewards that have certainly not been shared by the remaining shareholders).

The lesson of these cases is that while the board of directors is legally responsible for protecting shareholder interests, cases where the fund managers have too large a stake to give the board the freedom it needs to exercise its duties, alignment of interest can sometimes be a two-edged sword.

A similar problem can arise where a trust is set up with multiple share classes with different voting rights. This can effectively block shareholders from having influence over the destiny of the company. Caveat emptor is the best advice for shareholders here; only get involved if you are aware of and comfortable with this kind of one-sided arrangement.

This year we also include a table showing the trusts where all the directors of a trust have shareholdings that are worth more than one year's fees. The intuition here is that this is a positive sign, as it means that the directors have an obvious incentive to focus on growing the capital value of the trust, and are not just turning up to collect a useful fee for a few days' work a year in retirement. My experience is that the latter categorisation, while not unfair in some cases, is a criticism that cannot be reasonably levied at the majority of trust directors.

Investment companies where all board members have current shareholding equivalent to more than one year's fees

Aberdeen Standard European Logistics	Lindsell Train
Aberforth Smaller Companies	Mid Wynd International
Aberforth Split Level Income Trust	Miton Global Opportunities
Aquila European Renewables Income	Miton UK Microcap
Ashoka India Momentum	Multi Asset Value Trust
Atlantis Japan Growth	Montanaro European Smaller Companies
Augmentum Fintech	Nippon Active Value
AVI Global Trust	NB Private Equity Partners
Baillie Gifford Japan	North Atlantic Smaller Companies
Baillie Gifford UK Growth	Odyssean Investment Trust
Bankers	Pacific Assets
BlackRock Income and Growth	Polar Capital Global Financials
BlackRock World Mining Trust	Regional REIT
Brunner	Ruffer Investment Company
CC Japan Income & Growth	Schroder Asia Pacific
Diverse Income Trust	Schroder Asian Total Return
Dunedin Enterprise	Scottish Mortgage
Fidelity Japanese Values	Smithson Investment Trust
Fundsmith Emerging Equities	Strategic Equity Capital
Greencoat Renewables	Supermarket Income Reit
Gresham House Strategic	Troy Income & Growth
ICG Enterprise Trust	Utilico Emerging Markets
Independent Investment Trust	Value and Indexed Property Income Trust
Invesco Perpetual UK Smaller Companies	Warehouse REIT
J.P. Morgan Multi-Asset	Witan
Jupiter Emerging & Frontier Income	Worldwide Healthcare Trust

Source: Investec Securities estimates

"IT IS NOT ALWAYS
THE CASE THAT
SKIN IN THE GAME
IS A FORCE FOR
GOOD AS FAR AS
SHAREHOLDERS ARE
CONCERNED."

Returning capital

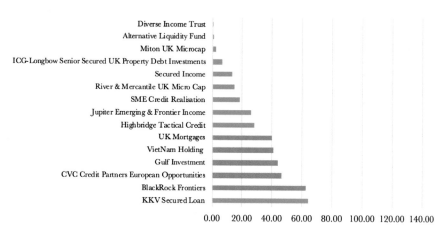

■ Capital returned via tender offer (£m) – to 06/10/21
■ Capital returned via redemption opportunity (£m) – to 06/10/21

Source: AIC/Morningstar, data to 30/09/21
Currently excludes companies that liquidated in their entirety in 2021, excludes buybacks.

Summary of Return of Capital by Fund in 9M 2021 (£m)

Fund	Corporate Action	Buybacks	Return of Capital	Liquidation/ Realisation	Total
Alternative Credit Investments	Acquisition by Waterfall AM at 870p per share	-	-	639.2	639.2
Scottish Mortgage	Buybacks to support discount	465.0	-	-	465.0
Gabelli Value Plus	Liquidation following continuation vote being failed	-	-	169.8	169.8
Witan	Buybacks to support discount	108.5	-	-	108.5
Alliance Trust	Buybacks to protect 5% discount	96.5	-	-	96.5
KKV Secured Loan	Distributions following adoption of wind-down strategy	-	-	94.4	94.4
BH Global	Cash exit option as part of rollover into BH Macro	-	-	73.6	73.6
BlackRock Frontiers	Five-yearly tender offer for 100% of share capital	-	62.7	-	62.7
JPEL Private Equity	Distribution following adoption of wind-down strategy	-	-	62.2	62.2
VietNam Holding	Tender offer for 30% of share capital and buybacks to support discount	1.2	56.7	-	57.9
F&C Investment Trust	Buybacks to support discount	52.8	-	-	52.8
Invesco Income Growth	30% tender ahead of rollover into Invesco Select – UK Equity	-	-	51.0	51.0
SME Credit Realisation	Redemptions as part of managed wind-down	-	-	50.5	50.5
Third Point Investors	Buybacks to support discount	47.8	-	-	47.8
BH Macro	40% tender offer ahead of combination with BH Global	-	47.2	-	47.2
CVC Credit Euro Opps	Quarterly tender mechanism	-	46.7	-	46.7
Gulf Investment Fund	Tender offer for 100% of share capital	-	44.4	-	44.4
Highbridge Tactical Credit Fund	Distribution following adoption of wind-down strategy	-	-	43.5	43.5
UK Mortgages	Two £20m tender offers following asset realisations	-	40.0	-	40.0
Scottish Investment Trust	Buybacks to support discount	39.5	-	-	39.5
River & Mercantile UK Micro-Cap	Mandatory redemptions to control size of fund	-	35.0	-	35.0
Polar Capital Technology	Buybacks to support discount	33.5	-	-	33.5
Jupiter UK Growth	Voluntary wind up with rollover into Brown Advisory Global Leaders	-	-	33.5	33.5
Weiss Korea Opportunity	Tender offer for 100% of share capital	1.7	31.8	-	33.5
TwentyFour Select Monthly Inc.	Quarterly tender mechanism	-	32.2	-	32.2
Other		599.7	29.2	58.3	687.2
Total		1,469.2	425.9	1,276.0	3,171.1

Source: Numis Securities Research

Liquidations/Takeovers/Delistings in 9m 2021

Fund	Ticker	Date	Net Assets £m	Details
Delisted/Liquidated				
RDL Realisation	RDL	10-Feb	10	Delisted following managed wind-down
Alternative Credit Investments	ACI	15-Mar	639.2	Takeover by Waterfall AM at 870p
Jupiter UK Growth	JUKG	27-Mar	27.9	Liquidated with rollover into Brown Advisory Global Leaders
Invesco Income Growth	IVI	26-Apr	52.3	Liquidated following merger with Invesco Select UK Equity portfolio
Invesco Enhanced Income	IPE	19-May	-	Liquidated following merger with City Merchants High Yield
Gabelli Value Plus	GVP	12-Jul	169.8	Liquidated following failed continuation vote
BH Global	BHGG	15-Jul	73.6	Liquidated following merger with BH Macro

Source: Company & Numis Securities Research

There can be a number of reasons why a trust decides to return capital to its shareholders. One is to try and limit the discount at which the shares in the trust are trading. Another is because a trust has decided to liquidate itself or offer an exit to shareholders, typically because of a run of poor performance. In some other cases a trust may decide to make a distribution of capital because of the sale of a significant asset it owns.

Many investment companies now have measures in place with which they attempt to control the discount and/or reduce discount volatility. Some trusts give a specific discount target, a level at which they promise to take remedial action. Others content themselves with a more modest statement of intent to keep the discount in mind.

These measures include buying back shares in the market, making tender offers at periodic intervals (enabling those who wish to sell a chance to tender at least a proportion of their shares at a price close to NAV) and agreeing to hold a continuation vote at some date in the future. It is fairly routine these days for investment companies to adopt the power to buy back their own shares. This requires shareholder approval at a general meeting and more than two-thirds of the companies in the sector have obtained this approval.

In 1999 it became possible for investment companies to hold shares they have bought back 'in treasury', meaning they can be retained without being cancelled and so can be reissued later if and when demand for the shares has grown again. Buybacks have been running at an average rate of around £1.2bn a year over the past 20 years.

As the chart shows, overall figures for the return of capital have been trending higher in recent years. ■

New issues

Number of Investment Company IPOs by Year since 2000

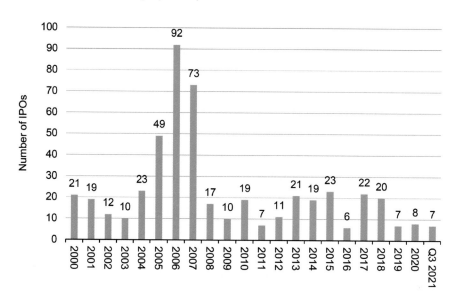

To 30 September 2021. Note: excludes listings where no new capital is raised.

Source: Numis Securities Research

Investment Company IPOs to Q3 2021

Fund	Ticker	£m Gross Proceeds#		Date	Listing	Domicile	Mandate	Target Yield	Target Return	Price TR	
		Total	Cash							Curr	Since IPO*
VH Global Sustainable Energy	GSEO	242.6	242.6	01-Feb-21	LSE	UK	Global renewable energy	5% (1% in Y1)	10%	GBp	2.3%
Cordiant Digital Infrastructure	CORD	362.6	362.6	15-Feb-21	SFS	Guernsey	Digital infrastructure in UK/Eur/ N.Am	4% (3% Y1)	9%	GBp	11.0%
Digital 9 Infrastructure	DGI9	300.0	300.0	26-Mar-21	SFS	Jersey	Global digital infrastructure	6%	10%	GBp	11.9%
Taylor Maritime	TMI	179.2	112.9	24-May-21	LSE	Guernsey	Shipping	7%	10-12%	US$	30.4%
Aquila Energy Efficiency	AEEE	100.0	100.0	01-Jun-21	LSE	UK	European/UK energy efficiency	5% (3.5% in Y1)	7.5-9.5%	GBp	(4.2%)
Literacy Capital	BOOK	96.0	-	25-Jun-21	LSE	UK	UK private equity	-	-	GBp	58.3%
Seraphim Space	SSIT	178.4	150.0	14-Jul-21	LSE	UK	Global private equity	-	20%	GBp	14.7%
HydrogenOne	HGEN	107.4	107.4	30-Jul-21	LSE	UK	Global renewable energy	-	10-15%	GBp	7.0%

Total gross proceeds includes shares issued in return for seed portfolio assets rather than cash. * Total return in traded currency since IPO to 12 October.

Source: Numis Securities Research

Whereas buybacks and tender offers reduce the amount of capital invested in the trust sector, in any year they will be offset by a combination of new and secondary issues by other trusts. New trusts are commonly launched through an IPO (initial public offering), although it is also possible to list a trust on the stock market without raising any new capital.

The IPO process runs to an irregular cycle. Some periods are characterised by a spurt of new issues in a particular segment of the market. Property trusts and hedge funds, for example, were popular in the run up to the financial crisis in 2008. Income-generating trusts operating with alternative assets, notably infrastructure, renewable energy and specialist property sectors, have been particularly popular since then.

After two good years for IPOs in 2017 and 2018, the last three years have been relatively disappointing with just seven new launches successfully completed in 2019, eight in 2020 and seven or eight in the first nine months of 2021 (depending on how you classify them by date). There are however many more potential IPOs being worked on by brokers hoping to take advantage of the buoyant market conditions. Only a handful will make it to the starting line.

This year there has been a record amount of fundraising by investment trusts, but the great majority has been through secondary issuance (see next page). At least seven IPOs that have been announced were subsequently postponed or withdrawn for lack of sufficient support. To have a realistic chance of succeeding, new trusts these days need more than just a manager or an investment approach with a good track record.

They have to be sufficiently differentiated in some way from existing trusts and comparable open-ended funds to attract attention. Nearly all the successful IPOs so far in 2021 have met that criterion. They include three infrastructure trusts (two in the new sector of digital infrastructure), one energy efficiency trust, a shipping fund and three other distinctive investment vehicles trusts, among them an investor in companies linked to space exploration and another planning to invest in the development of hydrogen as a commercial fuel source.

The analysts at Numis Securities summed up as follows: "The bar remains high to get IPOs over the line, with investors requiring ever increasing timescales for due diligence processes and many investors preferring to avoid execution risk by waiting to back funds once (if) they succeed. In addition, recent trends have shown that me too products in crowded sectors may struggle to get away". ■

Secondary issuance

COMPANY NAME	SECONDARY FUNDRAISING 2021 YTD – £M	COMPANY NAME	SECONDARY FUNDRAISING 2021 YTD – £M
Schiehallion	503	Aberdeen Standard European Logistics Income	144
Digital 9 Infrastructure	450	Gore Street Energy Storage	135
Renewables Infrastructure Group	440	International Public Partnerships	135
Smithson	424	Impax Environmental Markets	132
Tritax Eurobox	412	Edinburgh Worldwide	131
SDCL Energy Efficiency Income	410	Worldwide Healthcare	124
Home REIT	350	Polar Capital Global Financials	122
Chrysalis Investments	300	Pacific Horizon	117
Tritax Big Box REIT	300	Sequoia Economic Infrastructure Income	110
Hipgnosis Songs	241	BB Healthcare	109
LXI REIT	225	Urban logistics REIT	108
Cordiant Digital Infrastructure	218	Ruffer Investment Company	108
Capital Gearing	208	Bluefield Solar Income Fund	105
Greencoat UK Wind	198	Gresham House Energy Storage	100
Target Healthcare REIT	185	Monks	97
Personal Assets	180	HgCapital	97
Supermarket Income REIT	153	BlackRock Throgmorton Trust	96
Octopus Renewables Infrastructure	150		

Secondary fundraising (£m)

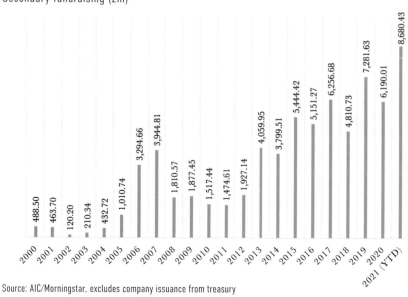

Source: AIC/Morningstar, excludes company issuance from treasury

The picture could not be more different for secondary issuance by investment trusts, which even at the nine month stage this year was already running at a higher level than in any previous year. The seeds for an impressive show of fundraising were sown two decades ago when it became possible for trusts that were proving popular with investors to issue additional shares more easily, without the need to produce an expensive legal prospectus in every case.

The new regime is still nothing like as simple as the daily process by which open-ended funds can issue or cancel units in their funds, but it does enable trusts to tap into additional demand on a regular basis. Scottish Mortgage is the most striking example: it has raised an additional £700m of capital in this way since January 2017. Many of the infrastructure funds have also grown rapidly through this route.

Secondary issues can take a number of different forms. The most common are placings of new shares and so-called 'C-share issues'. These two mechanisms, which are less cumbersome and time-consuming than a new issue, both have the effect of allowing an existing trust to expand its capital base by growing the number of shares in issue.

A C-share issue is typically used when it may take some time for the capital raised to be invested. The shares are then traded separately until the investment process is largely complete and the two shares classes are consolidated into one. Placings are more common and are used when a trust has already identified where it wants to invest the money and can complete the transactions in quick order.

Boards that have bought back their own shares also have the option of reissuing shares that they have not yet cancelled. A number of well-known trusts whose performance or style of investing have become popular in recent years have been able to issue a steady stream of new shares at a premium to NAV. Issuing shares at a higher price than the current NAV per share enables the trust to grow without penalising existing shareholders.

Out of the record total raised to date of more than £9.4bn, secondary issuance in alternative assets so far in 2021 has been led by commercial property trusts (£2.1bn), renewable energy trusts ($2.8bn), private equity (£1.1bn), infrastructure (£850m) and music royalty companies. A number of popular equity trusts have also succeeded in issuing substantial amounts of new shares. ■

Closed-end funds vs open-ended funds

Performance of Closed-End Funds vs Open-Ended Funds (Equity & Property Mandates)

	NAV total returns (annualised) OE funds			NAV total returns (annualised) ICs		
	1 yr	5 yr	10 yr	1 yr	5 yr	10 yr
UK – Equity Income	32.7	4.6	8.5	30.4	5.8	9.6
UK – All Companies	32.1	6.7	9.3	42.4	9.5	11.4
UK – Smaller Company	48.8	13.8	14.3	57.4	13.9	15.6
US – Equity	25.2	15.0	16.3	30.3	14.6	14.5
US – Smaller Company	34.4	15.1	16.5	36.4	12.8	14.7
Global – Equity	23.1	12.3	12.5	32.3	20.0	17.1
Global – Equity Income	21.8	8.6	10.8	24.0	8.6	10.7
Europe – Equity	22.4	9.9	11.6	22.8	12.4	14.1
Europe – Smaller Company	31.2	12.1	14.2	34.8	14.4	16.5
Asia Pacific – Equity	15.4	9.6	10.3	22.2	13.4	13.1
Japan – Equity	16.5	9.2	10.4	15.1	13.3	14.5
Japan – Smaller Company	15.0	10.4	13.7	9.8	14.9	16.2
Emerging – Global	17.2	8.0	7.6	16.7	10.3	8.6
Technology	25.7	22.2	19.3	26.7	25.3	21.6

Source: Numis Securities October 2021

It is not uncommon for the investment managers of trusts to manage other funds outside the investment trust sector at the same time. In fact, a number of fund managers start their careers managing different kinds of fund (typically unit trusts and OEICs, though also hedge funds) and if successful are encouraged to take over or start an investment trust with a broadly similar investment objective.

Adding an investment trust to their responsibilities gives successful fund managers the opportunity to take advantage of the benefits of the investment trust structure, including the use of gearing and freedom from unhelpful forced selling as a result of fund flows. They can also use derivative securities such as futures and options for investment purposes.

These advantages show up regularly in comparisons between the long-term performance of investment trusts and that of open-ended funds with either the same manager or the same investment objective. Where trusts and similar funds can be directly compared in this way, trusts typically show up with superior performance records. Where a trust and an open-ended fund with the same mandate are managed by the same individual, it is rare for the trust not to do better over the longer term.

	Price ICs		
1 yr	**5 yr**	**10 yr**	
33.9	6.1	9.2	
51.4	10.7	12.2	
64.0	15.6	16.7	
30.1	14.9	14.3	
41.7	13.9	13.9	
35.1	20.7	17.9	
21.8	8.1	10.1	
26.1	13.5	15.1	
41.6	16.1	17.2	
22.6	14.6	13.6	
17.4	14.4	15.6	
9.6	15.5	16.9	
19.8	11.0	8.4	
24.3	25.2	21.2	

The degree to which comparable trusts outperform does vary markedly however from sector to sector and is not true every year (2019 being an example when the effect was less marked). The table summarises the difference in the performance of directly comparable trust and open-ended equivalent sectors as at 30 September 2021. The blue-shaded cells show the periods over which trusts in each sector have outperformed.

While the general trend of outperformance continued to hold, the table highlights the relatively poor share price and NAV performance of US trusts over five and ten years and short but not long term underperformance in one or two other sectors, mainly due to adverse discount movements.

It is fair to point out that such simple comparisons can be criticised by statisticians on the grounds that the two samples are very different in size and also may display what is called survivorship bias. In 2018 academics at Cass Business School in London reported that a detailed analysis of investment trust returns between 2000 and 2016 appeared to support their superior performance. However, the study has now been abandoned because of 'data issues', principally the sample size and survivorship bias problems. ■

Interpreting performance data

There is a reason why the regulators insist that every piece of marketing literature issued by any kind of fund provider includes the phrase "past performance is no guarantee of future performance". The reason is that it is true. Performance data – how much money a trust has made for its shareholders in the past – does give you useful information about an investment trust's track record, and the way that it has been investing your money, but that information in isolation is insufficient to tell you whether you should buy or continue to own that trust. It is a starting point for analysis, but not in itself conclusive about the likelihood the past success, or past failure, will repeat.

There are several reasons for that. They include:

- markets move in cycles and are unpredictable

- styles of investing come in and out of fashion

- superior performance in one period often does not repeat in the next

- managers of trusts can be and often are changed, making direct comparisons with earlier periods difficult

- unexpected events, such as political shocks and natural disasters, may throw a hitherto successful strategy off course.

What the regulators are keen to ensure is that less-sophisticated investors are not misled into thinking that a trust which has done particularly well in the past will continue to do so in the future. Their perspective is underpinned by many academic studies. However, that is not the same as saying that past performance information has no value at all. Clearly it is still important for any investor to understand how a trust has performed in the past and to seek to establish why it has the track record it does.

At the very least it is important to understand the following:

- whether (and if so why) the trust's investment manager has changed over the track record period being looked at

- how far the performance of the trust has been affected by gearing

- how the trust performed during periods when markets were rising and when they were falling – it may be very different

- whether or not the trust has done better than a suitable benchmark, including the one chosen by the board

- how much risk the trust is taking relative to other comparable trusts and the markets in which it is investing.

The performance tables that follow should be studied with those factors very much in mind.

The dangers of relying on past performance figures has ironically been underlined by the experience of Key Information Documents (KIDs). These became compulsory for investment companies to issue in 2018 under new fund regulations introduced by the European Union. Despite the regulatory mantra about past performance mentioned earlier, KIDs still require investment companies to illustrate how a trust might perform under a number of different forward-looking scenarios.

Closer analysis revealed that the projections which companies are required to produce are based on a formula which appears in part to be an extrapolation of how the trust in question performed at different points in the past. Not only that, but they also produced very different projected outcomes for similar kinds of trusts, and statements about risk which in places appeared to defy both logic and common sense. The AIC's official response was to advise potential shareholders to "burn before reading".

Given that one scenario trusts were mandated to provide, using a formula over which they had no say, included a market decline similar to that seen in 2008-09, the market fall in March 2020 has provided an obvious opportunity to compare the results indicated in the KIDs with what actually happened. There was very little correlation between the outcome foretold by the KID and the actual share price response. The KIDs appear to be both poorly constructed and potentially misleading, and the Financial Conduct Authority announced in July 2021 it was looking to to improve the regulations. New (and hopefully more sensible) rules will be announced in January 2022.

The Financial Conduct Authority has also conducted a number of studies into the best buy lists which are produced by a number of investment platforms and broking firms. Its conclusion is that there may be some value in them, but investors would be unwise to rely solely on them when making decisions on which funds to buy. Their conclusions can be found on the FCA website.

Best long-term performers

10 years

COMPANY NAME	TICKER	AIC SECTOR	
Scottish Mortgage	SMT	Global	
3i Group	III	Private Equity	
Allianz Technology	ATT	Technology & Media	
Oryx International Growth	OIG	UK Smaller Companies	
Lindsell Train	LTI	Global	
Polar Capital Technology	PCT	Technology & Media	
Baillie Gifford Shin Nippon	BGS	Japanese Smaller Companies	
Biotech Growth	BIOG	Biotechnology & Healthcare	
VietNam Holding	VNH	Country Specialist	
BlackRock Throgmorton Trust	THRG	UK Smaller Companies	
Pacific Horizon	PHI	Asia Pacific	
Electra Private Equity	ELTA	Private Equity	
Montanaro European Smaller Companies	MTE	European Smaller Companies	
Impax Environmental Markets	IEM	Environmental	
International Biotechnology	IBT	Biotechnology & Healthcare	
Rights & Issues	RIII	UK Smaller Companies	
Edinburgh Worldwide	EWI	Global Smaller Companies	
Henderson Smaller Companies	HSL	UK Smaller Companies	
TR European Growth	TRG	European Smaller Companies	
Worldwide Healthcare	WWH	Biotechnology & Healthcare	
J.P. Morgan UK Smaller Companies	JMI	UK Smaller Companies	
VinaCapital Vietnam Opportunity	VOF	Country Specialist	
BlackRock Smaller Companies	BRSC	UK Smaller Companies	
J.P. Morgan US Smaller Companies	JUSC	North American Smaller Companies	
Herald	HRI	Global Smaller Companies	

MANAGEMENT GROUP	£100 INITIAL INVESTMENT (SHARE PRICE TOTAL RETURN)	ANNUALISED %	£100 INITIAL INVESTMENT (NAV TOTAL RETURN)	ANNUALISED %
Baillie Gifford	1,272.0	29.0	1,177.6	28.0
3i Group	998.1	25.9	547.6	18.5
Allianz Global Investors	921.1	24.9	996.3	25.8
Harwood Capital	847.1	23.8	723.8	21.9
Lindsell Train	800.5	23.1	728.2	22.0
Polar Capital Holdings	745.2	22.2	826.1	23.5
Baillie Gifford	727.9	22.0	657.6	20.7
Frostrow Capital	695.1	21.4	724.4	21.9
Dynam Capital	686.1	21.2	506.8	17.6
BlackRock Investment Management (UK)	680.2	21.1	565.0	18.9
Baillie Gifford	667.9	20.9	551.2	18.6
G10 Capital Management	656.4	20.7	251.9	9.7
Montanaro Investment Managers	623.6	20.1	570.1	19.0
Impax Asset Management	621.9	20.1	470.8	16.8
SV Health Managers	616.4	19.9	580.3	19.2
Rights & Issues	613.1	19.9	508.6	17.7
Baillie Gifford	607.1	19.8	587.1	19.4
Janus Henderson Investors	596.6	19.6	525.9	18.1
Janus Henderson Investors	586.0	19.3	538.2	18.3
Frostrow Capital	582.6	19.3	551.1	18.6
J.P. Morgan Asset Management	581.7	19.3	495.8	17.4
VinaCapital Investment Management	576.4	19.1	433.2	15.8
BlackRock Investment Management (UK)	564.5	18.9	498.7	17.4
J.P. Morgan Asset Management	559.3	18.8	539.4	18.4
Herald Investment Management	555.6	18.7	507.5	17.6

20 years

COMPANY NAME	TICKER	AIC SECTOR	
Pacific Horizon	PHI	Asia Pacific	
Scottish Mortgage	SMT	Global	
Aberdeen Standard Asia Focus	AAS	Asia Pacific Smaller Companies	
HgCapital	HGT	Private Equity	
BlackRock Smaller Companies	BRSC	UK Smaller Companies	
J.P. Morgan Russian Securities	JRS	Country Specialist	
BlackRock Throgmorton Trust	THRG	UK Smaller Companies	
Lindsell Train	LTI	Global	
Scottish Oriental Smaller Companies	SST	Asia Pacific Smaller Companies	
J.P. Morgan Emerging Markets	JMG	Global Emerging Markets	

30 years

COMPANY NAME	TICKER	AIC SECTOR	
Rights & Issues	RIII	UK Smaller Companies	
HgCapital	HGT	Private Equity	
Scottish Mortgage	SMT	Global	
ICG Enterprise	ICGT	Private Equity	
Canadian General Investments	CGI	North America	
North Atlantic Smaller Companies	NAS	Global Smaller Companies	
Electra Private Equity	ELTA	Private Equity	
J.P. Morgan European Discovery	JEDT	European Smaller Companies	
TR European Growth	TRG	European Smaller Companies	
Invesco Perpetual UK Smaller Companies	IPU	UK Smaller Companies	

Source: AIC/Morningstar, data to 30/09/21

MANAGEMENT GROUP	£100 INITIAL INVESTMENT (SHARE PRICE TOTAL RETURN)	ANNUALISED %	£100 INITIAL INVESTMENT (NAV TOTAL RETURN)	ANNUALISED %
Baillie Gifford	3,253.2	19.0	2,434.4	17.3
Baillie Gifford	3,152.9	18.8	2,479.4	17.4
abrdn	2,480.8	17.4	2,107.6	16.5
Hg	2,237.2	16.8	1,553.7	14.7
BlackRock Investment Management (UK)	2,153.2	16.6	1,668.6	15.1
J.P. Morgan Asset Management	2,057.4	16.3	2,139.0	16.6
BlackRock Investment Management (UK)	2,036.0	16.3	1,538.4	14.6
Lindsell Train	1,993.1	16.1	1,783.5	15.5
First State Investments	1,957.5	16.0	1,643.0	15.0
J.P. Morgan Asset Management	1,872.8	15.8	1,647.7	15.0

MANAGEMENT GROUP	£100 INITIAL INVESTMENT (SHARE PRICE TOTAL RETURN)	ANNUALISED %	£100 INITIAL INVESTMENT (NAV TOTAL RETURN)	ANNUALISED %
Rights & Issues	9,357.2	16.3	10,856.6	16.9
Hg	8,349.9	15.9	6,477.5	14.9
Baillie Gifford	7,441.7	15.5	5,894.1	14.6
Intermediate Capital Group	6,537.6	15.0	5,281.8	14.1
Morgan Meighen & Associates	5,679.2	14.4	3,638.1	12.7
Harwood Capital	5,577.4	14.3	5,226.6	14.1
G10 Capital Management	4,816.8	13.8	2,206.0	10.9
J.P. Morgan Asset Management	4,706.8	13.7	4,887.1	13.8
Janus Henderson Investors	4,559.5	13.6	4,637.3	13.6
Invesco Asset Management	4,321.1	13.4	3,506.1	12.6

Although the turnover in surviving trusts from one year to the next is high, a good number of trusts have survived long enough to post 20- and 30-year track records. These tables list the best performing trusts over both those periods, as well as the past 10 years, measured as both the value of £100 invested and as a compound annualised rate of return, with dividends reinvested.

Of just under 400 trusts whose data is recorded by the AIC, around a third have been launched in the last 10 years. Another third have compiled 20-year records and only around a fifth have survived long enough to have a 30-year record. This is another indication that there is a Darwinian process at work in the sector, with the weakest trusts eventually being either liquidated, taken over and renamed, or absorbed into another investment trust.

The average annualised rate of return achieved by the top trusts that have survived this long is higher over ten years than it is over 20 or 30 years where the outcomes are very similar, notwithstanding a wide range of outcomes and risk profiles. Because of the magical effect of compounding, any trust that can grow at 10% every year will at least double in value every seven years and quadruple every fourteen.

The longer the period, however, the harder it is to sustain a double-digit rate of return. The 30-year period for example includes two significant bear markets (2000–03 and 2007–09), while until the pandemic-inspired market fall in 2020 the past 10-year performance figures included none of them. The global financial crisis has been followed by what by historical standards is one of the longest and most impressive bull markets, so the 10-year figures for many trusts are still flattered by that.

What is striking looking at the 10-year performance figures is how the pandemic sell-off actually helped to improve the returns of several trusts, as the market divided sharply between those investing in companies, such as online retailing, technology and biotech, which thrived in lockdown, and those whose asset classes were badly affected, such as bricks and mortar retailers, airlines and holiday companies. The 10th best performing trust over ten years now, Blackrock Throgmorton, has an annualised rate of return over the ten years of 21.1%, 2.5% more than the tenth ranked trust a year ago, Edinburgh Worldwide.

That said most of the trusts in the top ten last time we published this table are still there this year, although Baillie Gifford's Japanese smaller companies trust, Shin Nippon, has been knocked off the top spot by the remarkable performance of Scottish Mortgage, which went from strength to strength during the pandemic and now has a remarkable 10-year annualised performance record of over 25% per annum.

Over 20 years the story is not dissimilar, with many of the same names reappearing, but is notable for the stronger showing of Asia Pacific and smaller company trusts this year, including two UK trusts managed by Blackrock. The tenth ranked trust now has a 20-year annualised share price rate of return that it is nearly 3% per annum higher than this time a year ago. Over 30 years the best performing trusts' annualised rates of return remain around the same as their long term average however, with only niche trust, Rights and Issues, achieving more than a 15% per annum compound rate of return.

Comparing the share price and NAV per shares total returns figures, it is evident that some trusts with strong performance records have benefited from favourable discount movements. In some cases that is down to improved performance, but over 30 years in particular, the best trusts have enjoyed the benefit of the vernal narrowing of discounts across the investment trust industry.

It is notable also how little commonality there is between the three tables. Only one trust, Scottish Mortgage, appears among the top 10 in all three periods. The 30-year period includes trusts from no fewer than eight different sectors, suggesting that these trusts do have something special about them, not just the good fortune of operating in the sectors that have performed particularly well. It is also a testament to the breadth and diversity of the investment company sector as a whole. ■

Sector returns by year

Average share price total returns (unweighted)

01/10/2020 – 30/09/2021 TICKER	SPTR	01/10/2019 – 30/09/2020 TICKER	SPTR	01/10/2018 – 30/09/2019 TICKER	SPTR	01/10/2017 – 30/09/2018 TICKER	SPTR
Private Equity	60.95	Global Equities	4.58	VCTs	5.39	Private Equity	12.42
UK Equities	51.72	Other Alternatives	3.63	Global Equities	5.36	Global Equities	8.88
Global Equities	29.63	VCTs	1.02	Private Equity	4.75	UK Equities	6.82
Property	29.51	Private Equity	-10.64	Flexible Investment	2.37	Other Alternatives	6.18
Flexible Investment	27.16	Flexible Investment	-11.41	Other Alternatives	2.03	Flexible Investment	5.48
VCTs	25.8	Property	-11.75	Property	-0.2	Debt	5.08
Debt	23.82	UK Equities	-13.69	Debt	-0.87	Property	4.93
Other Alternatives	17.42	Debt	-14.92	UK Equities	-5.1	VCTs	4.46

NAV per total returns (unweighted)

01/10/2020 – 30/09/2021 TICKER	SPTR	01/10/2019 – 30/09/2020 TICKER	SPTR	01/10/2018 – 30/09/2019 TICKER	SPTR	01/10/2017 – 30/09/2018 TICKER	SPTR
UK Equities	41.04	Global Equities	5.96	Private Equity	9.51	Private Equity	10.91
Private Equity	28.52	Other Alternatives	5.83	Property	5.22	Global Equities	9.18
Global Equities	26.34	Property	1.8	Global Equities	5.11	Property	8.59
VCTs	21.91	Private Equity	0.93	Flexible Investment	4.78	Other Alternatives	7.61
Flexible Investment	21.14	VCTs	-1.2	Other Alternatives	3.44	Flexible Investment	6.99
Debt	13.58	Debt	-3.99	Debt	3.3	UK Equities	5.25
Other Alternatives	13.42	Flexible Investment	-5.69	VCTs	1.62	Debt	5.12
Property	8.59	UK Equities	-10.22	UK Equities	-2.86	VCTs	4.93

Average share price total returns (unweighted)

01/10/2012 – 30/09/2013 TICKER	SPTR	01/10/2011 – 30/09/2012 TICKER	SPTR	01/10/2010 – 30/09/2011 TICKER	SPTR	01/10/2009 – 30/09/2010 TICKER	SPTR
UK Equities	37.98	Debt	18.89	Private Equity	9.28	Debt	52.5
Property	29.37	UK Equities	16.43	Debt	7.69	Flexible Investment	23.04
Private Equity	26.41	Global Equities	14.53	Flexible Investment	7.28	UK Equities	20.52
Global Equities	22.86	VCTs	13.46	VCTs	5.63	Global Equities	18.2
VCTs	18.1	Private Equity	9.11	UK Equities	5.05	Other Alternatives	16.45
Debt	15.65	Other Alternatives	4.96	Other Alternatives	4.82	VCTs	16.4
Flexible Investment	12.49	Flexible Investment	4.74	Property	4.33	Private Equity	13.3
Other Alternatives	11.1	Property	3.75	Global Equities	-6.13	Property	10.37

NAV per total returns (unweighted)

01/10/2012 – 30/09/2013 TICKER	SPTR	01/10/2011 – 30/09/2012 TICKER	SPTR	01/10/2010 – 30/09/2011 TICKER	SPTR	01/10/2009 – 30/09/2010 TICKER	SPTR
UK Equities	28.48	Debt	19.33	Private Equity	11.06	Debt	31.33
Global Equities	18.83	UK Equities	18.57	Flexible Investment	5.45	UK Equities	19.53
Debt	15.02	Global Equities	14.93	Debt	4.8	Global Equities	17.97
Property	11.09	VCTs	9.82	VCTs	3.79	Property	17.04
VCTs	10.99	Flexible Investment	8.77	Other Alternatives	2.4	Flexible Investment	16.18
Private Equity	9.54	Property	7.78	UK Equities	1.72	Other Alternatives	14.27
Flexible Investment	9.36	Other Alternatives	7.46	Property	0.95	Private Equity	12.45
Other Alternatives	7.84	Private Equity	2.19	Global Equities	-6.41	VCTs	3.93

01/10/2016 – 30/09/2017		01/10/2015 – 30/09/2016		01/10/2014 – 30/09/2015		01/10/2013 – 30/09/2014	
TICKER	SPTR	TICKER	SPTR	TICKER	SPTR	TICKER	SPTR
Global Equities	21.31	Global Equities	30.36	Property	11.13	Property	15.48
Private Equity	20.6	Private Equity	21.15	UK Equities	9.66	VCTs	12.58
UK Equities	17.55	Flexible Investment	19.06	VCTs	7.14	Private Equity	11.88
Property	14.11	Other Alternatives	18.81	Private Equity	5.37	Global Equities	9.51
Other Alternatives	13.55	UK Equities	8.97	Flexible Investment	0.29	Flexible Investment	8.48
Flexible Investment	12.78	Property	8.71	Global Equities	-1.03	Other Alternatives	7.9
Debt	10.16	Debt	7.99	Debt	-1.24	Debt	7.35
VCTs	6.56	VCTs	5.36	Other Alternatives	-2.32	UK Equities	6.96

01/10/2016 – 30/09/2017		01/10/2015 – 30/09/2016		01/10/2014 – 30/09/2015		01/10/2013 – 30/09/2014	
TICKER	SPTR	TICKER	SPTR	TICKER	SPTR	TICKER	SPTR
Global Equities	17.74	Global Equities	32.15	Property	11.36	Property	16.19
UK Equities	17.19	Flexible Investment	23.06	Private Equity	9.55	VCTs	9.63
Property	10.59	Private Equity	22.01	UK Equities	8.7	Global Equities	9.37
Private Equity	9.97	Other Alternatives	17.82	VCTs	5.58	Private Equity	9.02
Other Alternatives	9.22	Debt	13.09	Flexible Investment	1.89	UK Equities	8.24
Debt	8.61	UK Equities	10.23	Other Alternatives	0.08	Other Alternatives	8.07
Flexible Investment	7.76	Property	9.18	Debt	-0.15	Flexible Investment	7.98
VCTs	5.25	VCTs	5.84	Global Equities	-0.48	Debt	7.32

01/10/2008 – 30/09/2009		01/10/2007 – 30/09/2008		01/10/2006 – 30/09/2007		01/10/2005 – 30/09/2006	
TICKER	SPTR	TICKER	SPTR	TICKER	SPTR	TICKER	SPTR
Global Equities	21.76	Other Alternatives	-9.26	Other Alternatives	24.34	Property	24.63
Other Alternatives	15.9	VCTs	-9.37	Global Equities	22.07	Private Equity	24.08
Debt	13.38	Flexible Investment	-16.45	Private Equity	18.31	UK Equities	18.76
Property	11.05	Private Equity	-17.23	Flexible Investment	10.94	Global Equities	12.62
UK Equities	8.17	Debt	-25.45	UK Equities	10.34	Other Alternatives	11.59
Flexible Investment	-4.21	Global Equities	-26.34	VCTs	3.07	Flexible Investment	10.57
VCTs	-11.08	UK Equities	-29.97	Debt	2.6	VCTs	4.27
Private Equity	-14.39	Property	-32.09	Property	-9.25	Debt	0.85

01/10/2008 – 30/09/2009		01/10/2007 – 30/09/2008		01/10/2006 – 30/09/2007		01/10/2005 – 30/09/2006	
TICKER	SPTR	TICKER	SPTR	TICKER	SPTR	TICKER	SPTR
Global Equities	19.83	Private Equity	7.23	Other Alternatives	27.84	Property	29.71
Other Alternatives	18.3	Other Alternatives	-7.28	Private Equity	24.8	Private Equity	25.34
UK Equities	8.88	VCTs	-8.45	Global Equities	23.73	UK Equities	18.92
Debt	5.72	Flexible Investment	-11.65	Flexible Investment	13.78	Global Equities	13.49
Flexible Investment	0.41	Property	-14.35	UK Equities	10.69	Flexible Investment	12.22
VCTs	-4.01	Debt	-22.68	Debt	5.53	Other Alternatives	9.86
Private Equity	-13.76	Global Equities	-22.97	VCTs	5.05	Debt	6.78
Property	-16.3	UK Equities	-27.7	Property	2.45	VCTs	5.32

Average share price total returns (unweighted)

01/10/2004 – 30/09/2005		01/10/2003 – 30/09/2004		01/10/2002 – 30/09/2003		01/10/2001 – 30/09/2002	
TICKER	SPTR	TICKER	SPTR	TICKER	SPTR	TICKER	SPTR
Private Equity	46.5	Property	49.72	Other Alternatives	59.86	Property	9.36
Global Equities	44.5	Flexible Investment	24.34	Global Equities	35.87	VCTs	-6.97
Flexible Investment	42.9	Global Equities	16.29	Property	33.74	Debt	-7.49
UK Equities	34.3	Private Equity	15.47	Debt	31.01	Global Equities	-9.48
Other Alternatives	31.57	UK Equities	15	UK Equities	27.98	Flexible Investment	-11.46
Property	22.76	VCTs	11.36	Private Equity	22.82	UK Equities	-16.3
Debt	13.56	Other Alternatives	8.28	Flexible Investment	20.31	Private Equity	-18.93
VCTs	12.25	Debt	7.27	VCTs	-4.4	Other Alternatives	-31.44

NAV per total returns (unweighted)

01/10/2004 – 30/09/2005		01/10/2003 – 30/09/2004		01/10/2002 – 30/09/2003		01/10/2001 – 30/09/2002	
TICKER	SPTR	TICKER	SPTR	TICKER	SPTR	TICKER	SPTR
Global Equities	35.61	Property	46.35	Other Alternatives	41.14	Property	6.07
Flexible Investment	31.62	Flexible Investment	20.46	Global Equities	29.1	Debt	2.51
UK Equities	30.29	UK Equities	17.16	Property	28.44	Global Equities	-8
Private Equity	28.72	Global Equities	13.77	UK Equities	23.95	Private Equity	-8.04
Property	25.29	Private Equity	12.22	Debt	22.79	VCTs	-9.1
Other Alternatives	24.28	Debt	7.17	Flexible Investment	17.22	Flexible Investment	-12.87
Debt	14.35	Other Alternatives	5.82	Private Equity	2.83	UK Equities	-14.51
VCTs	6.3	VCTs	4.9	VCTs	-1.67	Other Alternatives	-25.1

These coloured charts show, in reverse order, the best and worst performing sectors over the past 24 years. Each category aggregates a number of component sectors and subs-sectors into broad asset class groupings. The purpose is to give a broad perspective on the fluctuations that investors inevitably face from year to year.

The data shows the share price and NAV per share total return for each 12-month period ending on 30 September going back to 1997–98. The charts underline not only how sectors rise and fall in popularity from one year to the next, but also illustrate the importance of asset allocation and the benefits of diversification.

To take the most extreme (but impractical) example if an investor had the foresight to know which sector was going to perform best in the following

| 01/10/2000 – 30/09/2001 | | 01/10/1999 – 30/09/2000 | | 01/10/1998 – 30/09/1999 | | 01/10/1997 – 30/09/1998 | |
TICKER	SPTR	TICKER	SPTR	TICKER	SPTR	TICKER	SPTR
Debt	3.27	Other Alternatives	206.64	Global Equities	76.3	Debt	12.49
Property	-1.4	Private Equity	53.72	Other Alternatives	66.86	Private Equity	11.64
Flexible Investment	-14.06	VCTs	36.13	Private Equity	33.86	Flexible Investment	0.84
VCTs	-16.9	Global Equities	30.48	Property	28.16	UK Equities	-4.12
UK Equities	-19.48	UK Equities	29.2	UK Equities	28.06	VCTs	-7.57
Global Equities	-31.21	Flexible Investment	29.12	Flexible Investment	19.67	Property	-10.8
Private Equity	-32.96	Property	24.57	Debt	14.82	Global Equities	-28.16
Other Alternatives	-47.23	Debt	4.96	VCTs	5.29	Other Alternatives	-39.36

| 01/10/2000 – 30/09/2001 | | 01/10/1999 – 30/09/2000 | | 01/10/1998 – 30/09/1999 | | 01/10/1997 – 30/09/1998 | |
TICKER	SPTR	TICKER	SPTR	TICKER	SPTR	TICKER	SPTR
Property	2.86	Other Alternatives	165.85	Global Equities	59.43	Private Equity	17.21
Debt	-0.18	Private Equity	34.39	Other Alternatives	53.48	Debt	11.57
VCTs	-2.83	Global Equities	28.43	UK Equities	27.68	VCTs	6.58
Flexible Investment	-12.67	VCTs	28.08	Property	23.77	Property	-0.4
Private Equity	-17.32	Flexible Investment	24.56	Flexible Investment	20.85	Flexible Investment	-0.66
UK Equities	-19.64	UK Equities	22.1	Private Equity	19.53	UK Equities	-3.4
Global Equities	-29.67	Property	20.66	Debt	12.83	Global Equities	-24.22
Other Alternatives	-41.26	Debt	0.57	VCTs	2.36	Other Alternatives	-25.29

year and allocated all his or her capital to it at the start of the year, an initial investment in 1997 of £1,000 would have grown to more than £300,000 by this year. If instead he or she had chosen the asset class which was going to perform worst each year, that £1,000 would have shrunk to just £149 – quite some difference. Note also how asset classes which do well in one year inevitably also have years when they do poorly, and vice versa.

It is worth studying the behaviour of different types of asset during bad bear markets (as we experienced from March 2000 to March 2003 and from late 2007 to March 2009). The difference between the share price total return and NAV per share total return is largely explained by movements in discounts. ■

Z scores

Z Scores

(current discount - average discount) / volatility of discount

1 year

| Fund | Ticker | Discount | | |
		Current	Average	Z Score
Schroder Asian Total Return	ATR	-3.2	1.0	-4.8
BlackRock Throgmorton Trust	THRG	-2.2	1.2	-3.2
City of London	CTY	-0.9	2.4	-3.2
Bankers	BNKR	-5.3	0.2	-3.1
Monks	MNKS	-3.7	2.0	-3.1
Edinburgh Worldwide	EWI	-6.3	0.9	-2.9
Aquila European Renewables Income	AERI	0.6	7.5	-2.9
Civitas Social Housing	CSH	-19.3	0.2	-2.7
Schroder BSC Social Impact	SBSI	1.6	3.9	-2.5
JPMorgan Asia Growth & Income	JAGI	-6.7	0.8	-2.5
Baillie Gifford European Growth	BGEU	-5.5	0.7	-2.5
Aquila European Renewables Income	AERS	-2.4	4.3	-2.4
Greencoat Renewables	GRP	10.4	16.6	-2.4
Macau Property Opportunities	MPO	-65.3	-58.2	-2.4
Baillie Gifford UK Growth	BGUK	-5.7	0.4	-2.3

| Fund | Ticker | Discount | | |
		Current	Average	Z Score
Schiehallion Fund C	MNTC	28.1	26.1	2.8
JPMorgan Russian	JRS	-8.5	-11.9	2.7
JPMorgan American	JAM	-2.7	-4.9	2.6
Polar Capital Global Healthcare	PCGH	-7.7	-11.0	2.6
KKV Secured Loan C	KKVX	-19.1	-68.8	2.3
BMO UK High Income - Units	BHIU	-2.9	-8.7	2.2
Dunedin Enterprise	DNE	-9.1	-15.9	2.1
Nippon Active Value	NAVF	0.9	-4.1	2.1
Scottish Oriental Smaller Cos	SST	-10.2	-13.2	2.0
Scottish Mortgage	SMT	3.6	-1.2	1.9
Industrials REIT	MLI	25.0	4.8	1.9
Aberdeen Emerging Markets	AEMC	-10.0	-12.9	1.9
VH Global Sustainable Energy Opport	GSEO	6.3	3.4	1.9
India Capital Growth	IGC	-7.9	-13.5	1.9
BMO UK High Income - B Shares	BHIB	1.1	-6.7	1.9

Z-scores measure mathematically how far a trust's current discount or premium has diverged from its average over some previous period (days, months or even a year can be used). Brokers and other professional investors calculate the figures regularly in order to look for trading opportunities or good entry/exit points. A minus figure for a z-score suggests that a trust looks 'cheap' relative to its past discount history; and a positive figure the reverse.

There may, however, be a good reason for the change in sentiment towards a particular trust, so they are a blunt instrument without specialist knowledge and should never be used or relied on by inexperienced investors. If you already have a specific investment trust on your watchlist and are looking for a good moment to buy, then checking the z scores can be a useful guide to timing your purchase. Bear in mind however that discounts widen for a reason; if the z-score is looking attractive, it is often because there is some negative story or headline out there.

If the story is essentially transient, as it often will be, and your belief in the investment trust is that it has a sound strategy for the longer term, then these will be good moments to take the plunge. By the same token, if you are thinking of selling part or all of your holding in a trust, then at the margin it makes most sense to do so when the trust's shares are showing up as 'dear' in the z-score rankings. Since most investors tend to hold the trusts they own for a number of years, these opportunities do not arise very often in practice.

The table that is shown opposite (source Numis Securities) is for illustration only. The data was current at 30 September 2021, but remember that Z-scores by their nature, whether measured over one week or one year, tend to be volatile. Trusts in the upper part of the table, which look 'cheap' at that point on the basis of a negative one-year z-score, could easily appear in the 'dear' section of the table just a few weeks later, having gained in price and seen the discount narrow in the interim. If you happen to see this kind of information, handle with care!

While z-scores can be helpful in timing a sale or purchase, investment trusts do not generally lend themselves to in and out trading and are best held for the longer term. A consistent 15% return over 20 years, if you are smart enough to find such a thing, will be worth far more at the end of the period (nearly 19 times your original investment) than anything bought in the hope of gaining from a short term z-score movement. ■

Who owns investment trusts

TYPE OF INVESTOR	END 2020 %	END 2013 %	CHANGE %
Retail investor			
Platforms	26.14	23.85	2.29
Manager share plans	2.87	9.02	-6.15
Wealth manager	34.1	30.3	3.8
Institutions			
Mutual funds	2.77	1.58	1.19
Asset managers	11.01	10.45	0.56
Pension fund	6.84	9.34	-2.5
Insurance company	5.66	5.16	0.5
Other institutions	4.28	6.1	-1.82

Source: Richard Davies IR, Warhorse Partners, June 2021

TYPE OF INVESTOR	END 2020 %	END 2013 %	CHANGE %
Hargreaves Lansdown (EO)	8.7	2.2	6.5
Interactive Investor (EO)	5.6	1.0	4.6
Rathbones	5.3	5.4	-0.1
Brewin Dolphin	3.5	5.5	-2.0
Investec Wealth	3.2	4.1	-0.9
BlackRock	2.9	2.5	0.4
Charles Stanley	2.7	2.5	0.2
AJ Bell (EO)	2.2	0.3	2.0
City of London IM	2.0	2.1	-0.1
Smith & Williamson	1.9	1.5	0.4
Legal & General IM	1.9	3.2	-1.3
Quilter Cheviot IM	1.7	1.8	-0.1
HSDL (EO)	1.6	1.8	-0.3
abrdn	1.5	2.8	-1.3
Lazard Asset Management	1.4	2.2	-0.7
Fidelity (platform)	1.3	1.0	0.4
Wells Capital Management	1.2	0.4	0.7
JM Finn	1.2	1.0	0.1
Canaccord Genuity Wealth	1.1	0.7	0.4
Vanguard Group	1.0	0.1	0.9

Source: Richard Davies IR, Warhorse Partners

There is no doubt that private investors are becoming an ever more important market for investment trusts. The latest research by two specialist share register analysis and marketing firms (Richard Davies IR and Warhorse Partners) shows how the proportion of shares in investment trusts held by private investors has been rising over the past decade, thanks in part to the appearance of the big platforms such as Hargreaves Lansdown, Interactive Investor and A.J.Bell. The trend is slow but steady rather than dramatic, but evident nonetheless.

It is strongest in the traditional equity sectors of the universe, where few big institutions such as pension funds and insurance companies remain shareholders. They mostly now manage their investment portfolios directly themselves or by hiring the services of specialist fund managers on bespoke terms. The trend is somewhat less marked in the alternative asset classes. The wealth management industry, traditionally the biggest buyer of investment trusts since the institutions departed, has meanwhile been consolidating and for a variety of reasons are no longer relying on investment trusts as mainstays of their client portfolios as much as they did. ■

Platform costs

	£5,000	£15,000
AJ Bell Youinvest	1.05%	0.47%
Aviva Consumer Platform		
Barclays	1.44%	0.48%
Bestinvest	1.00%	0.60%
Charles Stanley Direct	1.40%	0.66%
Close Brothers A.M. Self Directed Service	0.97%	0.49%
EQi	1.09%	0.36%
Equiniti Shareview	1.50%	0.83%
Fidelity Personal Investing	1.70%	0.57%
Halifax Share Dealing	1.25%	0.42%
Hargreaves Lansdown	1.41%	0.62%
iDealing	1.19%	0.40%
IG	2.56%	0.85%
Interactive Investor (Investor Product)	2.40%	0.80%
iWeb	0.90%	0.30%
Santander		
Sharedeal	1.76%	0.59%
Strawberry	1.56%	0.62%
The Share Centre (standard)	1.80%	0.80%
The Share Centre (frequent)	3.72%	1.24%
Willis Owen	1.00%	0.60%
X-O	0.48%	0.16%

Source: AIC/the Lang Cat consultancy

How much does it cost to hold shares in investment trusts on a private investor platform? The table gives an illustrative estimate for most of the largest platforms. The costs are shown as an annual percentage of the value of your portfolio, based on the amount you have invested. The data is collected by the Lang Cat consultancy and published on the AIC website. It is a valuable source of information, albeit with some important caveats.

It is important to note that your investment is assumed to be within an ISA tax wrapper. The figures shown only include ongoing platform fees, additional wrapper charges (if any) and trading charges (where applicable). Other charges involved in investing in investment companies, for example the management charges of the investment companies themselves, are excluded. The data is

	£25,000	£50,000	£100,000	£250,000	£500,000	£1,000,000
	0.28%	0.14%	0.07%	0.03%	0.01%	0.01%
	0.29%	0.15%	0.12%	0.11%	0.10%	0.10%
	0.52%	0.46%	0.43%	0.41%	0.31%	0.25%
	0.53%	0.44%	0.29%	0.11%	0.06%	0.03%
	0.39%	0.32%	0.29%	0.26%	0.26%	0.23%
	0.22%	0.11%	0.05%	0.02%	0.01%	0.01%
	0.56%	0.28%	0.14%	0.06%	0.03%	0.01%
	0.34%	0.17%	0.09%	0.03%	0.02%	0.01%
	0.25%	0.13%	0.06%	0.03%	0.01%	0.01%
	0.37%	0.19%	0.09%	0.04%	0.02%	0.01%
	0.24%	0.12%	0.06%	0.02%	0.01%	0.01%
	0.51%	0.26%	0.13%	0.05%	0.03%	0.01%
	0.48%	0.24%	0.12%	0.05%	0.02%	0.01%
	0.18%	0.09%	0.05%	0.02%	0.01%	0.00%
	0.35%	0.18%	0.09%	0.04%	0.02%	0.01%
	0.49%	0.40%	0.30%	0.24%	0.22%	0.21%
	0.64%	0.52%	0.46%	0.42%	0.41%	0.41%
	0.74%	0.37%	0.19%	0.07%	0.04%	0.02%
	0.52%	0.46%	0.38%	0.27%	0.21%	0.18%
	0.10%	0.05%	0.02%	0.01%	0.00%	0.00%

based on publicly available charging structure information, with some details verified in conversations with platforms.

This table assumes that you only hold investment trusts on the platform. A separate table on the website shows how the figure might vary if you also hold open-ended funds on the platform. The platform charges will generally be higher, at least for portfolios of £50,000 or more, as the platform charges for holding investment trusts are typically lower. Bear in mind however that charges are not the sole, or even the most important, criterion for choosing a platform. The quality of the service – the range of options, the quality of the research and how smoothly and efficiently the platform works – are every bit as relevant. ■

Dividend heroes

COMPANY	AIC SECTOR	NUMBER OF CONSECUTIVE YEARS DIVIDEND INCREASED
City of London Investment Trust	UK Equity Income	55
Bankers Investment Trust	Global	54
Alliance Trust	Global	54
Caledonia Investments	Flexible Investment	54
BMO Global Smaller Companies	Global Smaller Companies	51
F&C Investment Trust	Global	50
Brunner Investment Trust	Global	49
J.P. Morgan Claverhouse Investment Trust	UK Equity Income	48
Murray Income	UK Equity Income	48
Scottish American	Global Equity Income	47
Witan Investment Trust	Global	46
Merchants Trust	UK Equity Income	39
Scottish Mortgage Investment Trust	Global	39
Scottish Investment Trust	Global	37
Value and Indexed Property Income	Property – UK Commercial	34
BMO Capital & Income	UK Equity Income	27
Schroder Income Growth	UK Equity Income	26
Aberdeen Standard Equity Income	UK Equity Income	20

The AIC hit on an excellent marketing idea when it introduced its list of dividend heroes in 2009. To qualify for the list an investment trust has to have increased its annual dividend payout every year for more than 20 years. That is possible because the investment trust structure is sufficiently flexible to allow the boards of trusts to hold back up to 15% of the portfolio income each year to hold as revenue reserves (effectively as 'rainy day' money).

This policy means that the trust can usually call on its reserves during recessions (or indeed pandemics) to continue to pay a dividend. Only during really difficult periods will they be forced to cut the dividend below the previous year's figure. Qualifying as a dividend hero has proved particularly popular with shareholders since the global financial crisis and the subsequent decade of very low interest rates, which in turn has led to minimal yields from cash and bonds.

Dividend hero status is not a guarantee that the income from a trust will persist indefinitely. Three trusts that featured on the list before the pandemic had to take an axe to their dividends and subsequently lost their place in the rankings. Next year the Scottish Investment Trust will fall out of the list as well when it surrenders its independence following its absorption into the J.P. Morgan Global Growth and Income trust.

It is also fair to say that some years trusts are only able to preserve their place on the list by making the tiniest of increases in the dividend. You occasionally also hear mutterings from fund managers that the need to preserve dividend hero status at almost any cost can have an inhibiting effect on their ability to maximise returns. Prioritising income obligations is not always optimal from a total return or taxation perspective.

Nevertheless for many shareholders that does not seem to be much of a concern. Trusts such as the City of London, which can point to its 53 years of successive dividend increases, and heads the list, remains very popular despite not having the best long-term track record on other counts. As the table shows, 18 trusts can claim 20 or more years of consecutive dividend increases and ten of them have been in that camp for more than 40 years.

Coming up behind them are another 28 trusts which have between 10 and 20 years of consecutive dividend increases, including one (Lowland) that was in the original list but subsequently demoted. You can be sure that not all of these will be able to maintain that feat for long enough to move up into the top tier, given the inevitability of another recession/bear market in due course. For the moment however the slogan continues to get results as a compelling marketing proposition and effectively differentiates investment trusts from open-ended funds which do not have the same dividend flexibility. ■

Next generation dividend heroes

COMPANY	AIC SECTOR	NUMBER OF CONSECUTIVE YEARS DIVIDEND INCREASED
Athelney	UK Smaller Companies	18
BlackRock Smaller Companies	UK Smaller Companies	18
Henderson Smaller Companies	UK Smaller Companies	18
Artemis Alpha Trust	UK All Companies	17
Murray International	Global Equity Income	16
BlackRock Greater Europe	Europe	14
Schroder Oriental Income	Asia Pacific Equity Income	13
CQS New City High Yield	Debt – Loans and Bonds	13
Henderson Far East Income	Asia Pacific Equity Income	12
Aberdeen Asian Income	Asia Pacific Equity Income	12
International Public Partnerships	Infrastructure	12
Fidelity Special Values	UK All Companies	11
Lowland	UK Equity Income	11
Law Debenture Corporation	UK Equity Income	11
Invesco Select Global Equity Income	Global Equity Income	11
TR Property	Property Securities	11
Chelverton UK Dividend	UK Equity Income	11
J.P. Morgan Elect Managed Income	UK Equity Income	11
BMO Managed Portfolio Income	Flexible Investment	10
Aberforth Smaller Companies	UK Smaller Companies	10
Dunedin Income Growth	UK Equity Income	10
Fidelity China Special Situations	China / Greater China	10
Fidelity European	Europe	10
Henderson Opportunities	UK All Companies	10
J.P. Morgan American	North America	10
North American Income	North America	10
Lindsell Train	Global	10

PARTNERS

abrdn

About abrdn

We invest to help our clients create more.

More opportunity. More potential. More impact. We offer investment expertise across all key asset classes, regions and markets so that our clients can capture investment potential wherever it arises.

By combining market and economic insight with technology and diverse perspectives, we look for optimal ways to help investors navigate the future and reach their financial goals.

And by putting environmental, social and governance (ESG) considerations at the heart of our process, we seek to find the most sustainable investment opportunities globally. By ensuring the assets we invest in are ready for and resilient to a world in transition, we act as guardians of our clients' assets.

- Operating in over 30 locations worldwide* keeping us close to our clients and ensuring first-hand insight into companies, industries and markets.

- Managing £465.3bn in assets for our clients* on behalf of individuals, governments, pension funds, insurers, companies, charities and foundations across 80 countries*.

- Focus on fundamental research: the combination of our research, thematic thinking, ESG best practice and extensive on-the-ground analysis helps us find the most sustainable future-fit investment opportunities globally.

abrdn.co.uk

invtrusts.co.uk

*All data facts and figures as at 30 June 2021. The value of investments and the income from them can go down as well as up and investors may get back less than the amount invested.

Issued by Aberdeen Asset Managers Limited which is authorised and regulated by the Financial Conduct Authority in the United Kingdom. Registered Office: 10 Queen's Terrace, Aberdeen AB10 1XL. Registered in Scotland No. 108419.

About Allianz Global Investors

Allianz Global Investors is one of the world's leading active investment managers. Understanding our clients' needs in order to act to their best advantage is embedded in our business, using our insightfulness to partner with clients and to drive performance.

Allianz Global Investors works for many clients around the world. From pension funds, large and small, to blue-chip multinationals, from charitable foundations to families, individuals and their advisers. We have created a business that enables us to meet the demands of our clients on a local basis and that empowers our investment managers to focus on achieving strong and consistent investment results.

Allianz Global Investors and its predecessors have been managing investment trusts since 1889, providing investors with access to investment opportunities around the world. Each trust is a company listed and traded on the London Stock Exchange that has its own independent board of directors whose duty it is to look after your interests as an investor.

Established in 1889, The Merchants Trust PLC has, throughout its history, provided shareholders with an opportunity to benefit from investment in a diversified portfolio of leading companies with strong balance sheets and the potential to pay attractive dividends. Merchants aims to provide its investors with an efficient, competitive and cost-effective way to achieve an above average level of income and income growth together with long term capital growth through a policy of investing mainly in higher yielding large UK companies.

The Brunner Investment Trust PLC aims to provide growth in capital and dividends over the long term by seeking out the world's most exciting growth opportunities. We believe that it's the quality of the company that matters, not its location – so through Brunner, investors can access a spread of high-quality growth companies operating in different sectors and countries in a single portfolio. The Trust favours large, well-financed businesses with global reach, pricing power and brand strength.

Allianz Technology Trust invests in a diversified, but focused portfolio of companies that use technology in an innovative way to gain a competitive advantage. Particular emphasis is placed on companies that are addressing major growth trends with innovation that replaces existing technology or radically changes products and services and the way in which they are supplied to customers. The Manager aims to invest in the most attractive technology shares globally, seeking to identify the leading companies in emerging technology growth sub-sectors.

Actual Investors

Independent Global Investment Managers

Baillie Gifford is privately and wholly owned by its partners. This is the crucial underpinning of our approach: we have no short-term commercial imperatives and no outside shareholders to distract us. We can simply do what's right for clients, and that's what has sustained our business since 1908.

We are the largest manager of investment trusts in the UK with a range of thirteen trusts. We have an extensive range of OEIC sub-funds and manage investments globally for pension funds, institutions and charities.

Some see the collective failure of active management as an argument to embrace passive. We see it as an opportunity to redefine our original purpose of deploying clients' capital into tangible, returns-generating activities. And we believe that redefinition is 'actual investment'.

Actual investment is not easy in our world of 24-hour news, where complexity and noise is confused with rational judgement. It requires the resolve to focus only on what really matters, to think independently and to maintain a long-term perspective. It requires a willingness to be different, to accept uncertainty and the possibility of being wrong. Most of all, it requires a rejection of the now conventional wisdom that has led our industry astray: investment management is not about processing power, trading and speed. It is about imagination and creativity, and working constructively on behalf of our clients with inspiring individuals and companies who have greater ideas than our own.

The best investment ideas spring from thinking about future possibilities, not short-term probabilities. Our research covers the globe and we set no barriers to the imagination of our investors, encouraging fresh perspectives and the use of diverse sources of information.

We believe our approach to investing not only best delivers good outcomes for clients, but it also helps to develop great companies that provide for the needs and wants of people, thereby benefiting society as a whole. Investing responsibly for the long term is not counter to outperforming for clients, it's intrinsic to it.

The value of a stock market investment and any income from it can fall as well as rise and investors may not get back the amount invested. Your capital is at risk. Baillie Gifford & Co Limited is authorised and regulated by the Financial Conduct Authority.

Building better financial futures together

Fidelity International provides world-class investment solutions and retirement expertise to institutions, individuals and their advisers – to help our clients build better futures for themselves and generations to come.

As a private company we think generationally and invest for the long term. Helping clients to save for retirement and other long term investing objectives has been at the core of our business for over 50 years.

Today, we are trusted to manage client assets of £441.1 billion* on behalf of 2.5 million investors in the UK, Continental Europe, the Middle East, Asia Pacific and South America.

Truly global and award-winning

Investing requires a continuous research commitment to build a deep understanding of what is driving industries and individual businesses around the world.

With 369 investment professionals across the globe, we believe this gives us stronger insights across the markets in which we invest. This is key in helping each trust identify local trends and invest with the conviction needed to generate long-term outperformance.

Our award-winning approach to investing has resulted in a number of industry accolades, including Global Group of the Year 2020 at the Investment Week Fund Manager of the Year Awards.

Our UK Investment Trust Business

Fidelity has thirty years' experience managing investment companies, and manages over £5.9 billion in assets across six Investment Trusts. These are all focused on equity growth strategies.

Fidelity's range of investment trusts:

- Fidelity Asian Values PLC
- Fidelity China Special Situations PLC
- Fidelity Emerging Markets Limited
- Fidelity European Trust PLC
- Fidelity Japan Trust PLC
- Fidelity Special Values PLC

 To find out more, scan the QR code, visit fidelity.co.uk/its or speak to your adviser.

Past performance is not a reliable indicator of future returns. The value of investments can go down as well as up and you may not get back the amount you invested. Overseas investments are subject to currency fluctuations. The shares in the investment trusts are listed on the London Stock Exchange and their price is affected by supply and demand. The investment trusts can gain additional exposure to the market, known as gearing, potentially increasing volatility. Some of the trusts invest more heavily than others in smaller companies, which can carry a higher risk because their share prices may be more volatile than those of larger companies and their securities are often less liquid. If you are unsure about the suitability of an investment you should speak to an authorised financial adviser.

The latest annual reports and factsheets can be obtained from our website at www.fidelity.co.uk/its or by calling 0800 41 41 10. The full prospectus may also be obtained from Fidelity. The Alternative Investment Fund Manager (AIFM) of Fidelity Investment Trusts is FIL Investment Services (UK) Limited. Issued by Financial Administration Services Limited, authorised and regulated by the Financial Conduct Authority. Fidelity, Fidelity International, the Fidelity International logo and F symbol are trademarks of FIL Limited. Investment professionals include both analysts and associates. Source: Fidelity International, 30 June 2021 and includes assets under management and under administration. Data is unaudited.

UKM1021/36654/ISSCSO00030/0422

J.P.Morgan
Asset Management

About J.P. Morgan Asset Management

J.P. Morgan Asset Management, with assets under management of USD 2.6 trillion (as of 30 June 2021), is a global leader in investment management. J.P. Morgan Asset Management's clients include institutions, retail investors and high net worth individuals in every major market throughout the world. J.P. Morgan Asset Management offers global investment management in equities, fixed income, real estate, hedge funds, private equity and liquidity.

J.P. Morgan Asset Management Investment Trusts

With more than 150 years of investment experience, J.P. Morgan Asset Management is one of the UK's leading investment trust providers. The company combines global investment resources with local expertise to offer more than 20 investment trusts – each designed to help investors build stronger portfolios.

Thanks to its worldwide network of experienced investment professionals, J.P. Morgan Asset Management has the scale and expertise to invest successfully across all major asset classes and regions, and through multiple market cycles.

Investment trusts are a well-established part of J.P. Morgan Asset Management's comprehensive range of investment solutions, with some of its key trusts offering a track record stretching back more than a century – a testament to the company's long-term view and ongoing commitment to its clients.

About Polar Capital

Polar Capital is a specialist, investment-led, active fund management company offering investors a range of predominantly long-only and long/short equity funds including three thematic investment trusts.

The company's open-ended, closed-ended and alternative investment strategies are all based on long-term investment themes, specialist sectors and global, regional or single country geographies. They have a fundamental, research-driven approach, where capacity is rigorously managed to enhance and protect performance.

The investment trusts are in the specialist sectors of technology, healthcare and financials with Polar Capital Global Healthcare Trust (PCGH) being launched in June 2010. Since outset, it has been an opportunity to have exposure to the long-term growth appeal of the healthcare sector, investing in the best opportunities globally, across all healthcare subsectors.

The focus for the Trust's high conviction investment approach is for 80% to be in the more defensive, larger companies in any healthcare sector, in any region in the world. The remaining 20% is allocated to small and medium-sized growth companies which offer a higher risk/return profile.

Its long-term driver is an ageing global population accelerating the demand and the need for increased healthcare provision – something for us all to consider as we live longer. From innovative small-cap biotechnology stocks to global pharmaceutical giants, the actively managed portfolio focuses on powerful growth stories that are shaping the world. With its global and sector diversification, which together help mitigate stock-specific risk, the Trust has a conservative investment profile.

The Trust is run by an investment team of eight, including four senior fund managers and four experienced researchers/analysts, looking at healthcare's long-term, secular growth characteristics.

Polar Capital's investment teams are all based in the company's principal location in London, with investment staff in offices in Connecticut, New York, Los Angeles, Edinburgh, Paris, Frankfurt, Madrid, Zurich and Shanghai.

Quoted Data

Free, reliable research for everyone

QuotedData publishes free, reliable educational resources, research and news on carefully selected sectors and companies, some of which is sponsored. In addition, we provide data, including performance charts and statistics, across the full spectrum of pan-European equities. Our team of expert analysts write with a balanced view and our goal is to provide you with all the information you need to make your own investment decisions, or to understand in more detail what your adviser is recommending to you.

Founded in 2013, QuotedData is part of Marten & Co, our financial services business that specialises in the provision of high-quality equity investment research to professional investors, as well as offering corporates expertise in access to capital and investor relations.

Our services

- Daily news digest
- Company research
- Monthly/Quarterly sectoral round-up
- Investor guides
- Glossary of investment terms
- 'Helpful stuff' section – general tips on investing
- Data bank and performance statistics for all pan-European equities
- Investor events near you database